SPARKS
OF
FIRE

Memoirs

SAIDA
SHERIF

© Saida Sherif 2014

ISBN: 978-1-84200-146-2

Published 2014 by
Ta-Ha Publishers Ltd.
Unit 4, The Windsor Centre
Windsor Grove, West Norwood
London, SE27 9NT, UK
www.tahapublishers.com
support@tahapublishers.com

Cover design and typeset by
FastBase Ltd., London

A catalogue record of this book is available from the British Library.

Printed and bound by
IMAK Ofset, Turkey

Contents

Acknowledgements 5

Glossary 7

Preface 9

Chapter 1 – **Coming of Age** 11

Chapter 2 – **Between Two Cultures** 57

Chapter 3 – **My Years in Pakistan** 79

Chapter 4 – **London Life** 95

Chapter 5 – **Contentment and Turbulence** 127

Chapter 6 – **Venturing into the Balkans** 141

Chapter 7 – **Jablanica** 169

Chapter 8 – **Ostrožac and Sarajevo** 199

Chapter 9 – **"One did not know where to begin"** 231

Chapter 10 – **Amongst caring Muslims** 293

Chapter 11 – **Jerusalem** 319

Reflections 333

Index 339

Acknowledgements

My thanks to my daughter Jasmine, who handed me a file of the letters I had written to her during my involvement in relief work. She was the one who encouraged me to write about my experiences and memories. She kindly corrected the manuscript and worked on the index. Acknowledgements are also due to Dr Jamil Sherif for his editorial help and to my granddaughter Jamila, for permission to quote from her blog on experiences during the Pakistan earthquake. I am grateful to Ahmed Versi of *Muslim News* for permission to use two photographs. In fact I have many friends to thank: in England, Babar Beg, Yusuf Islam, Robeena Tahseen, Farrukh Hassan, Aisha Maniar, Dr. Tasneem, Eddie Wright, Danny Bronkhurst, members of the Muslim Women's Association (MWA) and my dentist friends and their wives, Abdullah and Ruqaya Hoosen, Nusrat and Anis Gatrad; in Canada, Asma and my brother Misbah; in Bosnia, Halima Hadziamacović and Harun Imamovic; in Pakistan, Tariq and Zarina Solaija, Muhammad and Ismet Anwer, Mona and Masood Siddiqui, Brigadier Tariq Hassan; in Malaysia, Dr Fatma and her husband Dr Yusuf Asmodi, and Mustafa Hamat. I am also indebted to Afzal Cheema of the UN and his wife Nusrat and many others whom I have met through the journey of my life who had love and affection for humanity and their support, moral and financial, encouraged me immensely. Finally I cannot forget the help from my grandchildren Ayesha, Jamila, Saba and Tayeb during the difficult times.

I hope that God Almighty will overlook my failings.

Glossary

Angeethi – portable coal fire

Apa – sister, but is also used as a mark of respect for an older female

Baaka – grandmother

Baithak – a formal sitting room

Charpai – a bed made from wood and jute rope

Chandni – white sheet covering the floor

Chaperkhet – Four poster bed, layered with silver inlaid with patterns

Devri – entrance hall

Doli – palanquin – a curtained cot attached to bamboo poles, carried by two or four men

Ganjeena – a net-fronted closet for keeping food, also known as nemat khana

Hauz – an open cistern or tank of clean water, sometimes with a fountain at its centre

Halvai – sweet merchant

Haveli – a private mansion with two entrance halls – one for ladies and the other for men

Hujra – a small chamber in a mosque

Ijtima – religious gathering

Jamia – mosque

Jarrah – surgeon

Kacheri – district court that would also disburse state pensions

Khala – aunt

Khus – a scented grass curtain; water is poured over so hot air
    passing through is cooled

Leechi – a type of fruit now referred to as lychee

Lokaat – a type of fruit

Lota – a small water container with a spout

Lungi – sheet wrapped around the waist, also known as *dhoti*

Manjha – kite string coated in glass powder to cut an opponent's
    kite string

Mohalla – locality

Opstina – municipality, town hall

Pec – a wood-burning stove

Qazi – Islamic judge

Samovar – a cylindrical, metal water container with a
    compartment for burning coal and a tap at base

Shikar – big game hunting

Takhallus – a poet's pen name or alias

Talaab – pond

Tasbih – prayer beads or rosary

Tehreek – movement to bring social and political change

Tiffin box – a cylindrical lunch box made of different tiers

Tokra – a large, round-shaped basket made of reeds

Tonga (or *Tanga*) – a horse-drawn carriage

Verandah – a roofed porch with decorative pillars

Preface

Many people have asked me to write an autobiography. My children and grandchildren started to ask me about events and episodes of my life. Through the journey of life I have witnessed a changing society, along with many wars, partitions and natural calamities. This seemed a memory worth preserving.

All such occurrences, whether personal or collective, leave an impact on one's life. There are patches of sunshine and clouds of darkness, that come and go, as one passes through various stages of life. So I picked my pen, well-aware of my limitations, to record what I had experienced and my responses in different situations. The surroundings and also the geography have changed over a period of time. The names of countries and cities have changed. The boundaries have changed. Above all our values have changed, for the better and for the worse.

In this shifting and changing world, glimpses of the past may perhaps be appreciated. Maybe there is solace in thinking that my children, though more educated and better human beings in most respects than I, might enjoy peeping into the past and see bits of my life and of the family's. I earnestly hope that not only my children but many others would perhaps enjoy reading this book.

The reader will come across some brief historical and political references. There have been happenings that have left a deep impact on me and therefore are woven into the way I think and have influenced my psyche. The names of some of the persons encountered have been altered to preserve their anonymity.

I would request my readers not to judge me too severely and overlook my shortcomings. However I must admit that I have always felt the freedom of a bird – never felt myself caged in. I have always tried to obtain freedom from force and freedom from falsehood.

CB *Chapter 1*

Coming of Age

Iloved Delhi and its beautiful green parks and monuments where I spent my childhood. At the same time, its painful memories still linger in my mind, making a deep and lasting impression on my being.

Delhi, my birthplace, was the capital city of Hindustan, now better known as India or Bharat. This city was considered a second Baghdad. Artists, poets, architects, musicians and intellectuals came and fell in love with it and settled there. Delhi was home to Turks, Mongols and Arabs. Its eloquent preachers, mystics and dancing girls, with their beautiful language and mannerisms, allured many.

In the thirteen century Sultan Shamsudin Altamash (Iltutmish) welcomed refugees from the Caucasus and Turkistan. This became a trend and Turks came and settled and inter-married the princes and princesses of India. Altumish's daughter, Razia Sultana, ruled as the Sultan of Delhi for some years. In this city of sunshine and lovely shades and shadows, the famous poet Amir Khusro was born in 1254 in Patiali. Many intellectuals, philosophers and preachers came from Iran and elsewhere at the invitation of Muslim rulers. Men of learning were conferred estates and gold coins and admitted to the flourishing literary societies of that era.

Hindustan was a rich country. The main motto in those days was "share with those who need whatever it pleases the Lord to bestow on thee". The *baitul-mal* helped the poor. Later Muslim kings opened up the royal kitchens, where food was served free to the poor; *sarai* and inns were built at each city gate where travellers could stay and rest their horses overnight. This was Delhi of the past and India was considered the golden bird by the outside world.

Many of its kings followed the example of Hazrat Umar Farooq and the royalty of Baghdad. They would wear old clothes to disguise themselves and observe the poor districts of Delhi by night to find out how the poor people fared. The next day, ample help was provided to those in need. This was how Muslim justice was applied in those days. A story of Emperor Shah Jahan and his dear wife was well known to us from our school history books and also popular films: once a peasant came to the royal court and complained that the Empress had killed one of his deer. Mumtaz Mahal was then summoned and the peasant was asked what punishment or penalty he required of her. In response, the peasant bowed and declared that he was happy to see justice done. He was bestowed with a bag of gold coins and a deer from the royal gardens.

Delhi was also a seat of learning. I remember my father showing me Shish Mahal near Chandni Chowk and explaining that many old colleges of the past were now in ruins and neglect. Mr J.H.Taylor, the then Superintendent of Education in India, had provided funds for the three colleges in Delhi, but mainly for the propagation of Christianity conducted by missionary societies. St. Stephen's College was established in 1881. I was also shown the red-bricked three hundred-year old Anglo-Arabic School, later renamed Delhi College, with its lush green lawns and red brick Mughal-style building. The English enrolled to learn Persian and Arabic from the Delhi teachers in order to perform their administrative duties. My father told me that Delhi College had been closed for some years after the 'mutiny' in 1857.

In those days and in the days of my parents, poets such as Hafiz, Faizi, Amir Khusro and Rumi were read, understood and appreciated in our households. The Delhi Urdu *Akhbar*, along with many monthly magazines, were in circulation. My father loved poetry recitals and was himself a poet.

India had its rich language Urdu—a mixture of Arabic, Turkish, Persian and Sanskrit words. Although the British regarded Indians as uncivilized, ignorant and barbaric, many Englishmen became skilled in the language and some even wrote Urdu poetry.

Delhiwalas considered the English uncivilised and uncouth. Men like Theo Metcalfe were hated for killing hundreds of Muslims in the aftermath of the uprising of 1857, yet his statue was erected in the gardens adjacent to Jamia Masjid. I remember people spitting on it as they passed by. He was called *kana matka*–the one-eyed *dajjal*–instead of his proper name. A pigeon or a kite had excreted on one eye of the statue and remained so as it never was cleansed.

The independence movement of 1857 was labelled as 'mutiny' against the Empire by the British. The Muslims were thoroughly punished so that they would not raise their heads again. Delhi was devastated and the last emperor exiled. The British fired on the white marble palaces and historical monuments with cannons. The shelling was horrific. Red Fort was completely over-run and the British slaughtered nobles and princes. Many hung from the gallows outside Delhi Darwaza. Some of the nobles bearing resemblance to the royal family fled to Hyderabad Deccan for fear of being killed. My paternal aunt's father- in-law was among them. Sanitation broke down and dead bodies and animals lay about on the streets. The resistance was crushed in such a brutal manner that people hid themselves when they saw an Englishman. The fear of the sight of an Englishman stayed with the Delhi people even when I was a child. The military barracks then and later during World War II were always behind barbed wires as some of the soldiers did not know how to behave with women. When they saw one, they went wild.

Delhi, like Baghdad, had been devastated a few times even prior to the British, for example the plunder by Nadir Shah Quli. It had the resilience, though, to survive. The splendour was gone but its character, culture and above all its poetic language still stand as witness of the glory it once possessed. The Delhiwalas called Delhi '*Dilli*', meaning 'my heart'.

My Early Years

I was born in June 1932 in this city of decaying splendour, capital of British India. As an infant I was raised in Khetri in Jaipur state, about 190 kilometres from Delhi. It was a hilly and green area and there was a large *talab* outside our house where I was told a family of tigers would come and drink water and relax in the moonlight. I vaguely remember that there were a lot of monkeys that used to raid our house.

I was told that I started to walk in Khetri when I was nine months old and headed for the pond. For that reason my father had a wooden barrier built on the marble steps so I would not go in the water. One day the guards washing the marble steps removed the barriers and seeing the opportunity, I ran past the steps right into the water. One of the marble steps hit the corner of my eye. I was brought in the house with a bleeding face. Luckily my eye remained intact. I was told that for days my poor mother sat me in her arms, till my wound under the eye healed. In those days there was no penicillin. The scar under my eye is still faintly visible.

My earlier memories take me to a well-built house in Delhi. It was a two-story building with a terrace and courtyard, and a *maulsari* tree giving us small, scented flowers. I well remember gazing at these little flowers falling on the ground, carpeting the courtyard. There were bushes of *motia* and *chambeli*. At the end of the courtyard was a *baitakh*, with one door opening to an outside terrace which led to the street, and the other inside the courtyard. I remember collecting leaves and cooking meals as a child in the outside terrace of the house. The house was situated in Tiraha Bairam Khan, named after Bairam Khan, a statesman in the time of the Mughal Emperor Humayun.

Tiraha means 'three ways' and at this intersection there was an ancient *peepal* tree with three roads branching off, leaving the tree in the centre of a triangle. One road led to Turkman Gate, the other to Lady Irwin Hospital and the third to Kashmiri Gate. Initially there were some thirteen gates in the *faseel* or wall that protected the old city, said to have been built by the Emperor Sher Shah Suri. There was a small temple and a large mosque in the centre. There were also two water taps, called *sabeel*, placed under the huge *peepal* tree–one for the Muslims and the other for Hindus. Delhi of my childhood was full of green lawns and gardens. We lived peacefully and one could easily notice that Hindus were fewer in number than Muslims.

My Father and his family

My father Shams ul Haq was born around 1875, the only son of the *Qazi ul Quzzat* of Saharanpur, Maulvi Muhammad Sadiq and Mumtaz Begum. He was educated at Aligarh in the mid-1890s at the Muslim Anglo-Oriental College founded by Sir Syed, which later became the Aligarh Muslim University. My father belonged to the generation that was taught by Shibli Naumani, Hali, Arnold, Morrison and Beck.

He was well versed in English, Persian and Arabic. His collection of poems, *Tajalliat e Shams*, was published after his death by my eldest brother. My father was an art lover and fond of music. He played the harmonium. One of my father's sisters, Akhtar, was also a poetess and played the harmonium. She wrote a poem for the Nizam of Hyderabad and sent it to him. In return, he invited her to Hyderabad, conferring on her a *khilat*, a gold-thread embroidered cape and a pension of Rs.15 per month gifted for life. Such was the generosity of the Nizam of Hyderabad! My father had an

My father Shams ul Haq in Khetri, with sons Inam (left) and Islam (right) –
1930.

elder sister who died quite young in Saharanpur. Her name was Bismillah Begum.

My father was first married in 1900 in Saharanpur to Amtul Shakoor, and then to my mother around 1920. His first wife was the sister of Muhammad Mujeeb Ahmad Tammanai, a well-known Persian and Urdu scholar who had migrated from Saharanpur to Hyderabad Deccan in 1920. However my father lived mostly in Delhi and away from Saharanpur where she lived. Though I never saw her, I believe she had a hunched back and suffered from poor health.

My father married my mother Razia Begum when he was around forty-five years old and she was twenty. The marriage took place because my mother's father, Maulvi Saeed, loved his nephew and knew that he was not happy in his first marriage. My mother did not want any pomp or show at her wedding and wore no make-up to take account of the feelings of my father's first wife, who was still alive. She treated her step-children like her own and presented her jewelry and expensive carpets to them.

My father worked in government service, serving for a while as superintendent in the deputy commissioner's office in Rohtak, East Punjab. He was then employed in Jaipur and later Kernal and Khetri. I absorbed many things about our family from my paternal grandmother Mumtaz Begum, who was born around 1850. I remember as a child hearing from her what she had witnessed during the events of 1857. She and her sister took all the books and some jewelry and fled from Delhi in a buffalo cart to Saharanpur leaving behind all other possessions and property. They later returned to Delhi. Mumtaz Begum's *haveli* was in the locality known as Chatta Mongaran.

We were the descendants of Shah Waliullah from our mother's side, who had come from Mashad to India on the invitation of a Mughal emperor. The old king was a very pious man and not happy with the pleasure-loving and lazy life style of the elite. He called on Shah

Waliullah to educate and provide some enlightenment, not only to the notables but the masses. I was told by my grandmother that the royalty would keep their elephant behind ours, as a mark of respect for teachers. My father told me that his ancestors had come from Bilad-us-Shaam, the region of the Levant. There was no Iraq, no Syria, and no Lebanon then. It was said of our family that even the household mice were well-read! Later on my ancestors also taught Urdu, Persian and Arabic to British officials. We were among the well-respected families of Delhi.

Circumstances changed for my family in the aftermath of 1857. The British had supplanted the Muslim Mughals and taken the throne. All the best posts were therefore conferred on Hindus, and Muslims were deliberately kept behind. The land reforms promulgated under the British rule and enforced by Hindus wrecked our family. Land which was gifted to us by the last Mughal emperor for educating royalty and the elite was confiscated. My father went to the *ketcherry* court many times and tried to save our ancestor's land, the two villages near Saharanpur, where my grandfather had been *Qazi ul Quzzat*. Later he lost the will to fight for his land. He was hurt that his right to the land was confiscated and only small portions were left for him. He took retirement from government service at the age of forty-nine or fifty and we used to get by on his pension and the sale of the remaining agricultural lands, as long as they lasted.

My mother and her family

My mother was one of nine sisters and two brothers born to Maulvi Syed Saeed Ahmed and Maseeti Begum. They lived in Sui Wallan near Jama Masjid, Delhi. My mother was very fair with dark brown eyes and dark brown and reddish hair. She was a tall woman. Her father was a court clerk in Delhi and her grandfather a renowned maulana. In our family accounts it is said that the maulana spent much of his time in meditation in a mosque's *hujra* and that before

My mother Razia Begum – 1960s.

entering his house he would knock at the door and ask if there was any money in the household. If there was, he would ask for it to be distributed to the poor and only then would he enter.

One day an old and sick man came to the mosque and requested the maulana to marry his daughter as he was dying. It then so happened that he died while still in the mosque. The girl was sent in a *doli* to my great grandmother, who took her in her house, made her take a bath and put on her own wedding dress for the *nikah* to be performed. Such was the sacrifice of those women for their husbands. The maulana had a son from this wedlock but the mother soon passed away. The son was fair with corn coloured hair, whom we used to call Nana Bhutta after the Urdu word for 'corn'. He had an eventful life.

One day the maulana was caught by a crowd in front of a *halvai*, who insisted that he showed them something extraordinary. Tears rolled down his eyes and he began praying while standing on the street. This took place near a large, hot basin full of milk on the boil, next to a *tanir* of *imerti* sweets. It is said that two snakes came to the shop and drank all the milk, at which point many Hindus fell to the ground and proclaimed that they had become Muslims. However my great grandfather fled to his *hujra*, weeping that he was disgraced. He shut himself in the *hujra* where he died within ten days of this incident. Large numbers, both Hindus and Muslims, gathered to attend his funeral. The whole street of Sui

Wallan till Chitli Qabar was filled and one could only see the heads of the people from the first floor family house. There is no written record of this incident but this was related to me by my mother and my *khala* Kulsum.

My maternal grandmother Maseeti Begum was the daughter of Hafiz Ghiasuddin of Delhi and a lady we only knew as 'Ladli Begum'. My *nani amma* was widowed in 1922 or 1923 and continued to live in Sui Wallan, bringing up a large family of nine daughters and two sons, Syed Safdar Ali and Syed Asghar Ali, on a meagre income. She had a lady helper called Amma Afzal (greater mother) about whom my mother spoke with fondness. The astute Maseeti Begum rented out the ground floor of her property to shops and lived on the first floor with her youngest daughter, Rahat Begum, and youngest son, Syed Asghar Ali. My *nana abba* lived long enough to see the birth of my eldest brother Inam, to whom on his first birthday he presented a velvet cap embroided with two crescents of gold.

My earliest memories take me to a dark staircase that led to the upper floor at Sui Wallan. We used to see a big *chapherkhet* on one side of her bedroom. The floor was covered with a white *chandni* and round cushions were placed by the sides of the walls. I remember Maseeti Begum's disapproving gaze on finding me and my cousins, the children of Syed Safdar Ali, bouncing on the *chapherkhet*.

My mother's sister Qaisar Jahan had red hair and was considered a beauty in her time. I believe that some ladies came to Maseeti Begum and asked for Qaiser Jahan's hand for the famous Punjabi poet, Muhammad Iqbal, but she refused. My aunt unfortunately ended up marrying a *nawab* who was quite ugly and had strange ways of living. My aunt was very unhappy in her marriage and returned back to Sui Wallan with a small son of two years old. Muhammad Iqbal in the meantime became Sir Muhammad Iqbal, the philosopher and a poet famous throughout the world. What a loss to our family! My poor aunt remained single and looked after her son Masood Tabish, a writer and poet well-respected in literary circles. He started his career as a sub-editor of the Urdu magazine *Aj kal* and was also a veteran news broadcaster in Radio Pakistan for nearly thirty years. Many of his poetry books were published in Pakistan, where he died in 2004.

I also recall quite clearly the marriage of my mother's youngest sister, Rahat Begum, to my cousin Syed Bashir Hasan. It was the accepted custom in India in those days to marry within one's family or circle. It was convenient as the family traditions, language and backgrounds were similar. There was an element of snobbery as well, as a man from Punjab or Madras was not considered good enough for marriage to a Delhi girl. It is said that a *tangawala* once picked a customer from the railway station to drop him at Ghanta Ghar. On arrival at his destination, the visitor started to argue over the fare and used foul language. The *tangawala* replied courteously, 'Sir, don't give me any money but please desist from bad language as this is my lady horse (my mare)'.

Maseeti Begum was a determined lady with strong will-power and managed her affairs well and lived with dignity. She loved cats and kept many. I remember her in tight-fitting pajamas and a small *kurti*, which my mother did not approve of but did not dare say anything. Of course my grandmother always wore a large white *dupatta* covering her well.

My Step family

My father's eldest son from his first marriage was Riaz ul Haq. He studied in Delhi till matriculation and continued further studies in Hyderabad, later joining the principality's Police in its Intelligence Department. His wife Ahmedi Begum was a poetess with the *takhallus* 'Wafa'. She was the daughter of Muhammad Mujeeb Ahmed Tammanai. Riaz ul Haq, or Aka bhai as we knew him, was a keen cricketer and a tennis player. They had no children.

My elder step-sister Shaukat Ara also settled in Hyderabad and was married to Mahmood ul Haq Siddiqui, the Post Master General of Hyderabad. They had two daughters, Ismat and Hamda, and a son Saud, who was about my age. Ismet later qualified as a doctor while Hamda passed her BSc in Chemistry and worked in Lederly's Laboratories. Saud graduated from Osmania University, Hyderabad. I met the family for the first time in 1956 when they arrived in Karachi after the Indian Army invaded and occupied the vast and prosperous state of Hyderabad Deccan. My other step-sister Husnara, whom we affectionately called *Apa* Misya, was married in Saharanpur to my father's relative, Mustehsan. He was a *tehsildar* or assistant to the Commissioner and they lived in Kerana and other places where he was posted. Their first child was Azra. My first contact with Apa Misya was in 1942 when she came to our house in Delhi because she wanted to be with my mother for her second delivery. The newborn was a baby boy who was named Aslam. All the step-children loved my mother and respected her and we never stopped loving them. Later I was invited to Kerana for my summer holidays and delighted in the orchards and fruits of that town. My brother-in-law Mustehsan was a handsome man who looked like an Englishman in his khaki shirt and trousers. Azra was then six years old, almost the same age as my own younger sister Asifa. Mustehsen died very young leaving a small baby, Afzal, who had developed a fever in Kerana and became invalid. Apa Misya then went to live with her in-laws in Saharanpur and later moved to Pakistan in 1959.

Childhood memories

My father worked and lived in Kernal, while my mother taught in Delhi for a while after her marriage. This was the same school where she herself had been a student. Their early married life was spent in Jaipur, Rohtak and Khetri. My mother often used to come and spend time in Delhi at the *haveli* of my paternal grandmother in Chatta Mongaran. My brothers told me that the *haveli* was huge and they used to have a lot of fun whenever they came to stay there. They all loved Delhi and its lavish way of life, good food, ice cream soda and picnics in the resplendent green gardens. My elder brothers used to often go to Edward Park or to Jama Masjid of Delhi in the evenings.

Khetri on the other hand was dull and had a large population of Hindus. It had only two plain gardens around the *mandirs* where the cows and buffalos could graze freely. There were a few *talaab* but Muslims could not swim in them. I vaguely remember the monkeys in a big house on the first floor. The Hindu Raja of Khetri used to take my father for *shikar*. The power rested with the British commissioner, Mr G.A.Carrol, who would not tolerate anyone donning a Gandhi cap or wearing clothes made of *khaddar* material, that had become a symbol of the non-cooperation movement. However, Mr Carrol respected my father and they often went hunting together. My father always wore western clothes.

My brothers used to play with the Raja's youngest son, who had an English governess, Miss Russell. She often visited my mother. The Rani of Khetri would invite my mother to the palace. My mother found her sad and unhappy, because it was believed that the Raja had a relationship with his deceased son's widow.

My mother was worried about the children's education as she did not think much of the schools in Khetri. She had decided to coach her sons herself at home. When visiting Delhi she would be perturbed by the lavish life style of my paternal grandmother and her daughter Akhtar, because she could see the family capital disappearing. *Tokras* of mangoes, *lokaat* and *leechis* and stacks of sugarcane would arrive from our lands. Unfortunately no one cared for those lands and property and they were either sold off, or later confiscated under the land reforms in the United Provinces.

She was upset at my father's early retirement. Their third son Misbah was only a few months old at the time and quite ill. She had seen a dream that all the family's wealth had slipped away, and it came true. Her own health was affected and she too fell ill. A home help at Tiraha Bairam Khan, whom we called *Chammi ki Amma* (Chammi's mother), took care of my mother and also cooked. I noticed my mother's gradual recovery. *Chammi ki Amma* used to return to her home and would come back in the afternoons with her neatly-combed hair tied back, wearing spotlessly white starched clothes, to serve us again.

My mother taught arithmetic to my brother Nayar, even when she was ill in her bed. My father taught English to my elder brothers. I loved playing and was closer to my father in those days.

Sometimes my father used to tell me stories. We used to sleep on the top floor in the open during the summer nights. I remember asking him about the shining stars in the moonlit nights and who was their maker. He used to tell me that God had made all the stars and the lovely moon. I would fall asleep in my father's arms while he sang *loris* or lullabies, till I fell into deep sleep.

I remember my father always bought the newspapers and asked my mother to read the Delhi Urdu *Akhbar* and the English *Statesman* aloud to him. He gave preference to the English educational system for his children, unlike most Muslims at that time who did not approve of this. The Bible was taught as a compulsory subject in the missionary institutions.

My father always brought me new toys when he returned from his *kacheri* after collecting the pension. Once, when I was around three and a half or four years old, he bought me some lovely, red wooden pots and pans. My friend from the neighbourhood and I decided to cook a meal for my doll. I went to the kitchen and quietly took the matchbox. We went outside the *baithak*, on to the front terrace, where we found three little stones to make a stove, on which we placed the new red wooden pot and lit the fire. I was wearing a new frock of frills and lace which my mother had stitched. My friend placed the fresh leaves into the pot to cook and I lit the fire with some papers taken out of the *baithak's* dustbin. Suddenly my dress caught fire. I ran inside the *baithak*, rolled myself over the woollen carpet, since I had heard from my elder brothers that one could save oneself and put out a fire by doing this. I was too frightened to go inside the house so I hid myself under a chair. My mother came looking for me and found me under the chair. She picked me up. I was trembling, not because of the pain, but because I had taken the forbidden matches from the kitchen and the shame that I had burnt the new dress.

I remember even now the subsequent days when I stayed in my mother's arms and slept in her lap for days. She would cover me with her *dupatta* so the flies did not disturb me. I could smell the lovely scent of jasmin and mulseri flowers mother always wore in her earrings. Evenings were a nightmare as a *jarrah* would come to dress my bandages. My left leg was burnt and the bandages had to be changed daily. I can still vaguely remember my mother looked pale but beautiful in those days and the comfort I felt being in her arms was inexplicable. My uncle Feroz would came to see me and while I lay in mother's lap, he joked with her and made her laugh. My mother was a shy person and I noticed her cheeks turning red.

I had a baby sister when I was five. Her name was Asifa. The baby slept most of the time and was very tiny, so I could not really play with her. My wound had healed and I was out playing most of the time, usually with the neighbour's son, but never with the matches again.

I noticed how the English midwife sat next to mother, chatting in English as she knitted a sweater. When she saw me observing her keenly, she taught me to knit. The next day she arrived with a pair of needles and some wool for me. Both my brother Nayar and I started to knit. I soon lost interest, but Nayar continued and knitted a long scarf.

Inam, my eldest brother, used to take me out in the early mornings to Kotla Feroz Shah, which was quite close to Tiraha Bairam Khan. He always had a book in his hands, which he would read while strolling on the green lawns. I would disappear in the ruins and would imagine I was a princess and lived in that huge castle or *qila*. I was a dreamer right from childhood and loved roaming around the old ruined palaces and tombs. There were horses and chariots in my imagination and the horsemen all wore white and red uniforms with gold braids, riding in *risalas* or uniform lines. I pretended that they still lived and rode on the curved and clean stone roads. I was never scared, as I could see my brother strolling while reading his book on the lush green lawns.

The grounds of Kotla Feroz Shah had a dark stone circular building, hidden under the ivy where nobody ever ventured. Upon my insistence my mother took me once inside. It had three floors connected by a circular staircase, with rooms and arches of white marble covering the carved patterns of flowers with thick green moss. Mother explained to me that these were the baths of the royal family and were so designed to keep cool in the summer heat. Each floor was reserved for a family and their children. The Urdu word for that building was *bawli*.

I remember an old tower, Qutub Minar. No one knew from where that *minar* had come. Some said King Ashoka had built it many years before. Qutb-ud-din Aibak initiated its construction in the twelfth century in the gardens of Kotla Feroz Shah and the monument was completed by Sultan Iltutmish. There were some inscriptions on it but no one could decipher or read them at that time. It also had some beautifully carved inscriptions in Arabic.

My brother Inam went to the Aligarh University. He was a cricketer and had won many cups. Every time a letter arrived from Aligarh, my mother beamed with happiness and my father also felt very proud of their son. I recall as a child that there were separate *cheshmas* or water taps in the streets of Delhi specifically for use of Hindus or Muslims. Nevertheless there was no unpleasantness between Hindus and Muslims and a fair amount of tolerance prevailed. My brothers Misbah and Nayar were particularly favoured by the Hindu teachers of Ramjas High School, as they were intelligent and well behaved.

I once visited a Sufi gathering of Syed Jamaat Ali Shah with my aunt Qaisar Jahan, who used to attend on Thursdays evenings. I came to know that the group was called Naqshbandis. They remained awake most of the night and prayed in hushed silence. The women were totally separate from men's quarters. I remember everybody wore white clothes and most men wore a turban. Incense and an aroma of perfume along with fresh flowers filled the night air and I used to doze off on the white sheets that covered the praying area. In the early hours of morning my *khala* Qaiser would take me home. I later found out that Qaiser Jahan had also taken my mother there when she was a young lady of sixteen. Syed Jamaat Ali Shah had told her to pray *tahajud* and from then on she was constant in this nocturnal worship.

One day I noticed that my mother was weeping quietly while packing all the crystal bowls and plates. I knew something was wrong. It dawned on me that we had to sell our house in Tiraha Bairam Khan in order to pay for Inam Bhai's college fees. I came to know that this was our last property in Delhi.

Sadly we packed our belongings and moved to Maseeti Begum's house in Sui Walan. She gave her house rather reluctantly to us and asked my father to be kind to her cats. For the first time I saw that one of the cats had kittens. One kitten was not well and I was surprised to see it was consumed by the mother cat. I remembered this incident for days and perhaps as a result I could never become an animal lover. My father really looked after them. When my grandmother came back to her house, we vacated and moved to a rented accommodation in Karol Bagh, a suburb of Delhi.

My parents quarrelled quite a lot in those days. There was no income coming in and we were seven children living on my father's pension of 115 Rupees per month. My eldest brother was still studying in Aligarh University. Perhaps the best that I retain of my childhood at Karol Bagh are the memories of my early schooling in that area.

Years at Jamia Millia and Karol Bagh

Jamia Millia's Karol Bagh school was founded in 1930 many years before the main red brick building in Okhla was completed. I was admitted there at the age of five in 1937. It was a primary school at that time and its teachers were trained in a missionary establishment in Moga, Punjab, run by the British.

The young students were aware of the suppression and dreamt of gaining independence from the Imperial Raj. The Independence movement had emerged and initially both Hindus and Muslims worked together. Our founder, Dr Zakir Hussain, along with Muhammad Ali Jauhar and Shaukat Ali joined Mr Gandhi and Motilal Nehru in the Congress Party. We were politically aware and keen to obtain freedom for India. One of the supporters of the Jamia Millia School was Hakim Ajmal Khan, also the founder of the nearby Tibbia College. I often went from the school to the Tibbia College gardens. Delhi was a safe place and a child could wander about freely. One day, in one of my wanderings, I saw some people there, sitting on the ground in a circle. They were the Khaksars and their emblem was a spade or *bailcha*. I wanted to know what they discussed, so I sat with them but could not understand much of what was said. I came home and asked my brothers. They told me that it was a socialist group.

Jamia Millia was influenced by the spirit of Hindu-Muslim cooperation. The independence *tehreek* at the time stressed the adoption of home grown cotton and I asked my mother not to purchase foreign-made cloth. Jamia was to make a lasting impression on me. One coordinator of the school, Hafiz Fayaz, was imprisoned for four months for participation in the *tehreek*'s activities. The school's main hall built in 1932 was named after him. In 1933 the school at Karol Bagh started four classes. It was a boys school, but Dr Zakir Hussain's daughter Safia and I were the two girls among some two hundred boys. No wonder I was quite boyish. Among the many things I learnt in that school, at a very early age, was that religion and politics cannot be separated.

We often went for outings in our school bus, sometimes to the new premises being built in Okhla eight miles away. Once I got very tired from walking in the forest and my teacher picked me up and carried me in his arms a long distance. I remembered our teachers were extremely kind and loving towards us. As children, we were fascinated to see an ox going round in a circle in the grounds of the Okhla Jamia, drawing water from the ground well, which flowed through channels to various fields.

I learnt to address the audience in the huge school hall and was quite confident in using the microphone. At a very young age we were taught how to participate in debates and discussions. We always discussed current affairs. We knew a lot of Urdu poets and listened to their poetry. I was given a few silver *tamghas* for good performances, including a special one which was in praise of Prophet Muhammed, peace be upon him. I brought it home proudly and showed it to my mother, who had great love for our Prophet.

The Jamia School was growing bigger every day. We had four projects which I remember very well. We would make soap and cut them into small cakes with a thin wire. We would also re-use old paper to make new paper. I was nine years old then. We then packed soap in the paper that we had made. The soap was later used for washing our hands in school and was also sold in our kiosk.

Each class had its own vegetable patch. We were given seeds and each child grew potatoes, turnips and carrots. We sold the vegetables and learnt to write the accounts in our own exercise books. We memorised the sayings of our holy Prophet and learnt to love his personality. We decorated our huge hall with Qur'anic *ayats* cut and pasted on hardboards in artistic calligraphy. We acted in dramas about our Prophet's love for children at *Miladun Nabi* functions.

We were told about Tipu Sultan and his wars against the British in Mysore in South India and enacted a play based on his life. We also felt pride in reading the life story of Jamaluddin Afghani and wondered how he travelled to Paris, Russia, Iran and finally died in Istanbul in Turkey in 1897. We knew that he wanted Muslims to unite and reform themselves. We also knew of our close relationship with the Turks. The Nizam of Hyderabad had married both of his sons to Ottoman princesses. Bilad-ush-Sham, from where my father's ancestors originated, had been an Ottoman province. This explained to me the differences of Indian Muslims in terms of features, foods and customs compared to the rest of Indians. My father would take out an old atlas to show me those places on the map.

As a child, while learning geography, I started to dream that I was sitting on a ship, traversing great oceans, with huge waves of blue waters and that I was travelling far, far away. Little did I know that this day-dreaming in the class would become an actuality one day.

We ran a tuck shop in the *jamia*. A school master taught us how to keep the account for each day's sale in a note book. We had heard that Dr Zakir Hussain had gone to the rich Nizam of Hyderabad to collect funds for the new school at Okhla. The Nizam of Hyderabad gave Rs.50, 000 and also a monthly sum of a thousand rupees. We also collected some money and opened a bank on the premises that was run by senior boys.

We had a library, so after school, our activity was to run it and keep records of the new books, by entering them in the library register. We charged one paisa for a book lent for reading. This was also recorded on the register.

Our school was growing bigger every day. By that time news of the war kept coming in. I noticed that my mother was suffering from arthritis and was again unwell and at times unhappy.

Moving from Karol Bagh to New Delhi

Soon we could not afford the rented flat in Karol Bagh. World War II had started and with it the food prices went up. We moved to New Delhi to live with my uncle Syed Safdar Ali. His bungalow was in Barakhumba Road. He had four very naughty sons at the time, Akbar, Akhtar, Afsar and Parvez. I loved to be with them. The eldest son, Akbar, was my age. He later became a well-established doctor in Karachi. We played cricket and in the process many of my clothes were torn. This was because it was my task to go into the bushes to retrieve the ball; otherwise I was not given the chance to bat.

My mother by now had given up on me. She started to call me Said ul Haq, a boy's name. I wore Akbar's white shorts and boy's shirts and canvas boots. My uncle, with his family, used to be posted to Shimla Hills in summer and the house was left to us.

I stopped going to Jamia Millia as my parents did not have the money to pay for the bus fare. The memory of that loss always came back as I lay awake in bed at night. I could not tell anyone how sad I felt for not going to my dear Jamia Millia. That school had given me everything: loving care and confidence at such an early age that I was ready even to conquer the world. The thought that Akbar would supersede me in studies made me weep quietly.

We did many naughty things while living in Barakhamba Road. We used to go to the railway line, which was at the back of the bungalow, and placed stones on the track to see how the big wheels crushed them while we hid in the bushes, thinking that possibly the train might fall. We also tried to put common pins to see if they could be turned into little swords, but that did not materialise.

The gymkhana and the riding club was quite close to our bungalow. We would climb up the gymkhana's boundary wall and see the British riding on beautiful horses and also could hear the music. We were not allowed in as it was exclusively for the British. That used to make us sad and jealous.

Every morning a sergeant walked in front of our bungalow. One of my naughty cousins Afsar and I decided to take our revenge for not being allowed into the polo ground of gymkhana. Afsar climbed a tree that leant over the footpath waiting for my signal. I hid in the bushes and when he saw my raised hand, he peed directly over the fat tummy of the sergeant. The sergeant turned and in anger declared: "Oh, no, not the bloody monsoon again."

We loved to walk around Connaught Circus that was built by the British. It comprised neat shops and surrounding gardens where the band played every Saturday evening.

My paternal aunt also sold her big *haveli* in Chatta Mongaran and moved to New Delhi. Her only son Bashir Hasan worked in the radio station as a Russian translator. He introduced me to Miss Ahuja and Baji. After an audition they hired me for the children's programme. My sister and I would go every Sunday morning. I wrote stories and jokes, and Asifa, who had a lovely voice, used to sing. Our program was a success and became quite popular under the guidance of Baji and Miss Ahuja. There was also Naseem Mirza who portrayed a parrot, *Mithoo mian*. Many years later I met him in London. He married a distant cousin, Parveen. He was posted as a diplomat to Britain and later on joined the UN.

One of my brothers would bring me home from the All-India Radio station on their cycle and I used to sit on the carrier. I used to get tired out from a five mile journey and would fall asleep as soon as I came home. My eldest brother Inam would buy me a hot mug of milk served in the earthen ware and would make me drink it. He would get upset with my parents that for the sake of five rupees, I had to go so far away. My weekly trips to All India Radio's children's programs lasted for nearly three and a half years. I was actually pleased to go on the radio and earn five rupees per program for broadcasting stories and jokes. Public speaking and debates in Jamia Millia Islamia School had given me enough confidence to broadcast live on radio. Besides, I loved it.

After some time we moved back to our old *mohalla*, Tiraha Bairam Khan, but this time in Tehri Haveli. The *haveli* was owned by the people who had bought our house.

In the hot summer days, we slept in the open courtyard on our *charpai*s. There was a *hauz* in the centre of the courtyard. The toilets did not have a flush system, so every time we went to the toilet we had to carry hot ashes from the clay stove to cover the excretion. It was compulsory for us to take a *lota* or water container to the toilet and wash ourselves. The *hauz* was empty most of the time and the fountain was out of work, but a turtle lived there and there were always a couple of pots of *chambeli* or *motia* placed around the *hauz*. The *hauz* was close to the kitchen. The mingled smell of cooking and the scent of *motia* and *chambeli* still haunt me some times. Water containers were kept with soap to wash our hands at the edges of the *hauz*. We all performed *wudu* by the *hauz*.

There was electricity, but water was brought over by the *bahishti* or *siqa* in his lamb's *mashkize*. Running water made its way in 1942, rather late in the old *haveli*.

Tehri Haveli was a double storied building with a courtyard on one side. There were many rooms and store houses. It had a stable and a trough in the *devri* for the horses to drink water from. But we had no horses! The second *devri* was also quite large, which opened to the courtyard and had a separate staircase. The *devri* had a large wooden cupboard as well, which probably was used to store the saddles or hay and such items. The narrow lanes of old Delhi could not be used for *tongas* and probably people moved around on horseback or in *dolis*.

We had a hand-drawn fan in the central hall of the main building made of long frills of cloth that hung from the ceilings. Outside the halls was a long veranda. In summers, we would take turns to tug the fan's cord, sometimes by our feet rather than hands, and roll on the white *chandni* for the afternoon siesta. I also recall the lovely scented *khus* curtains in the veranda when the hot winds blew in Delhi. Water was poured on the *khus* and the cooled and scented breeze blew in.

In the afternoon, thermos were filled with ice cubes broken from big slabs of ice. My mother made fresh lemon or *falsa* (a kind of blackcurrant) drinks. Sometimes wheat was boiled, dried, roasted and then milled and ice and sugar added to it for a drink called *sattu*. Food was kept in a net cupboard, called *ganjeena* or *na'emat khana*, probably for protection from flies. In the summer season, mangoes were bought and placed in the steel bath tub filled with slabs of ice. We could eat as many as we liked.

We waited desperately for rains so Delhi could be a cooler place. During the monsoon season everything looked bright and green. My paternal grandmother, Mumtaz Begum, whom I had never seen walk, sometimes came to stay with us. She was bed-ridden. She liked music and often called musicians at home to play for her, while she sat behind the *chilman*, thin wood-stick curtains. She also played the harmonium and knew a lot of Persian and Arabic poetry. Unfortunately, she did not know how to manage her affairs well after her husband's death. The *dallals* – touts or money lenders from whom she borrowed money took her property away when she could not return the loan. My mother noticed all those unpleasant things but could not stop them from happening.

Our old lady helper came back to us when she knew of our return. My mother was happy to see her, since she had the extra work to look after my grandmother. She passed away when I was ten years old, but my sister Asifa and I missed her funeral as we were sent to the house of our eldest maternal aunt.

A group of children with Sultan Jahan Begum at her daughter Farida's
bismillah ceremony; my sister Asifa is in the front row, left-most;
I am right-most in the back row – early 1940s.

My mother took me one day to visit the grave of my *dadi amma*,
Mumtaz Begum. She was buried in the back of Kotla Feroz Shah,
on the high grounds near a fig tree. My mother sat by the grave
and recited Qur'an while I ate the figs from the trees, and as usual,
roamed about in the forest not far from her. She told me, as we
sat by the grave on the high grounds, viewing the city below, that
all the land backing Lal Qila or Red Fort's wall was given to us by
royalty, but had been confiscated due to the so-called land reforms.
It remained locked and no one was allowed in.

My eldest maternal aunt Sarwar Jahan used to live in Chitli Qabar.
She was married to Dr Inayatullah Khan who was an Afghan. I
recall that whenever any of us brothers or sisters fell ill, we were
placed in a *doli* and sent to her house. She took great care of us.
She felt that she was a *sayyid* and perhaps was dismayed at being
betrothed to a Pathan. Dr Inayatullah Khan respected and loved

her. His first wife had died and my aunt was his second wife. My uncle would come in the evening from his *matab* or clinic and checked us patiently. Once I had a septic thumb and was sent to my uncle's house for a week. Dr Inayatullah Khan gently dressed my thumb after he returned from his clinic. He always dressed in white trousers and white coat. He had won the sword of honour for his services in France in the British Army during World War I and it hung on their drawing room wall above the fireplace.

Dr Inayatullah's eldest son was Hameedullah Khan, who studied in Lucknow. His second son was Samiullah Khan, married to Sultan Jahan Begum whom we affectionately called 'Mughal Begum'. She had a formidable sense of humour and a heart of gold. When she celebrated her daughter Farida's *bismillah* ceremony, she encouraged Akbar, my cousin Nasima and myself, to keep our first fast.

A feast was prepared for the four families at her house. Farida recited the *Iqra* verses from the Qur'an as was the custom. After the ceremony, when the time came to break our fast at *Maghrib*, we were all given presents by our elder relatives.

My cousin Samiullah was very fond of watching films of actress Naseem. Once, his wife strung all the cinema tickets in a safety pin and attached it to their newborn baby's garment. She then took the baby to Uncle Dr Inayatullah. When he saw all those cinema tickets clipped on to the baby's outfit he was very angry: "What is this. Let Sami come home this evening, I will reprimand him. How come he leaves his wife and baby alone and dares to go and see a film every night."

I became very close to my cousin's wife and their family. Years later, in 1965, when I went to London, she housed us in her flat near Finchley Road and was very kind to us.

St. Francis School

I was admitted to St. Francis School, a girls' missionary school in Darya Ganj where my mother and her sisters had been educated. The girls spoke very shyly, keeping their *dupatta* next to their mouths and giggled endlessly. All this was strange to me, so I was the odd one out. I was admitted in the fifth class and did not know much English. I tried to make sure that I spoke just like Miss McDonald, the principal. I copied her high pitched English accent and pored over my books, day and night. We had to speak in English in our school, otherwise we were fined or had to stand in the sun for an hour. All our teachers were very affectionate and caring. Most of them did not marry and devoted their life to education. The school assembly consisted of the recitation of hymns and prayers from the Bible and at the end, when the school principal would say 'Jesus the Lord God', we Muslim girls used to quietly say under our breath, 'Jesus the prophet of Allah'. Announcements were made at the end of the prayers and on one such occasion, our principal spoke about Israel and asked for the prayers to be made in its support. I was sad as I knew that Palestine belonged to Muslims from the time of *Khalifa* Omar when he entered Jerusalem in 637.

Sometimes we were taken to Purdah Bagh for sports. It was a ladies' park and had bigger grounds than our school. The boys went out to play football and cricket in the evenings to Kotla Feroz Shah or outside Turkman Gate near Irwin College. It was also called Ram Leela Ground, where every year the Hindus enacted Ram and Seeta's story, describing how the monkeys made a bridge so Ram could rescue Sita. An effigy of the character Rawen was brought out as the bogey and burnt.

On our return from the school, my sister and I used to go to a lady's house to learn Qur'an. The lady who taught us was known to our family and lived near *Phool ki Mandi*, the Covent Garden of Delhi. The whole street had flower shops, selling roses and *motia* and garlands. It was a custom in Delhi that men returning from their mosques would buy flowers for their wives. Some romantically-inclined husbands even used to have a waist coat made out of scented flowers for their wives. Once a year, a cortege consisting a huge mounted fan made of fresh flowers used to emerge from *Phool ki Mandi*. The whole road would waft with the fragrance of flowers. I was told that this fan and the cortege would go to the grave of Nizamuddin Aulia, revered by both Hindus and Muslims as a saint. I longed to go along but was only allowed to see it from the gate of Tiraha Bairam Khan.

Our school hours were from nine to four in the afternoon. We took our lunch in a *tiffin box* and had it at lunch break. There was no dining hall. We used to eat in the open grounds under the shades of the trees in the school's big courtyard. There were only one or two Hindu girls in the whole school.

While pressing my father's aching legs, I recited poetry to him or, book in hand, would read aloud while he corrected me and explained the meanings of difficult words. I knew the only way I could succeed in my class was to be good in my studies. It was not difficult to concentrate as there was no television or radio at that time. Our mother never allowed us to go to cinema. There was no telephone either. Some homes did have a record player with a huge metal loudspeaker and a handle to turn round to make it work. One had to buy small needles and replace them quite so often. We did not even possess that. The only item of entertainment in our house was a harmonium.

My father was a good teacher, played chess with us and cheated playfully during games of *carrum*. At home our studies were given prime importance. We did not have to be told to study, we just turned to our books whenever it was possible. My father and mother discussed politics. I heard my father say one day that it was wrong for Germany to invade Russia. We would look up the places on my elder brother's globe.

Stalin, Roosevelt and Churchill were always discussed at dinner times by the elders, and by listening to their conversation we would try and grasp the war situation. I remember my father explaining to my mother that the Tehran Conference held in 1943 would bring peace and stop World War II. I would often wonder why my father, so intelligent, handsome and well informed about everything, was not earning any money.

My brothers studied in a side room. There was one red table and a few chairs. It used to be the boys' den. I remember their Bunsen burner, on which they practiced their chemistry experiments. Occasionally I was also accepted in their company. I was not good in mathematics, so I had to beg my brothers to help me. In return I had to wash their dirty football socks. I loathed doing it, but since I did not want to be considered a laggard at school, I agreed each time. Nevertheless, they loved me and my sister, Asifa.

I heard my brothers discussing various novels and books and tried to read these with the help of a dictionary. I was maturing quickly in those war years.

We had some of my brothers' classmates during the summer holidays from Aligarh University. The boys loved to spend their summer holidays in our house. They studied together and went in the evenings to play football or cricket, via Turkman gate. In the long winter nights we would all play *carrum* or chess. Brother Islam could score all points and bag the queen disc in one go.

My father was strict with the boys and they had to return home at *Maghrib*. Once when the boys were late one evening, he took out his belt and lashed it out on their back. I was quite upset.

Summer evenings after dinner were spent on the top floor of Tehri Haveli as it was cooler there. A *dari* was spread, and on moonlit nights, my father played the harmonium and my mother sang. He encouraged us children to sing and told us about the various *raags* and melodies. My mother liked to sing the last Mughal King Shah

Zafar's poetry, in particular a sad verse written while he was in Burma in exile:

lugta naheen hai jee mera is ujrey deyaar main

I am ill at ease in this desolate abode

Delhi winters were very cold. My mother made thick cotton curtains, filled with fibre from the kapok tree, for the long halls and *verandahs*. The curtains had wooden bamboo poles at both ends. As soon as evenings came, the curtains were drawn and were tied with one another closing all gaps. The coal fire of *atishdan*, fireplace, would warm the big halls and the rooms.

My mother also organised the baths. We had a water tank made of marble slabs in which water was stored. My mother placed the *samawar* in the bathroom. The *samawar* had a tap and a long pipe in the centre which was filled and lit with coal fire to heat the water for the baths. Those were the days of charcoal, iron fireplaces and *samawar*.

We often visited two sisters, the last of the Mughals, who were my mother's friends. Their pet names were Pacho Begum and her sister, Mumdo Begum. Pacho Begum had moved from Shish Mahal to live in Darya Ganj, but her sister lived in Panipat. She was married to the Panipat *sajada nasheen*. My mother and Pacho Begum studied at the same school. They had met after a long time. We used to hold dramas and plays in their house. All the elders were invited and tickets were sold. The grown ups comprised the audience. My friend was Jahangir, who was also twelve years old. My brother Islam was fond of his sister Ismat. I found out their secret when I saw a pencil sketch of two robins, beak to beak, perched on a tree. Each robin had an 'I' written on it, very discreetly. No one else in the family knew about their secret liking for one another except me.

My brothers studied hard and always stood first in order to obtain scholarships. My eldest brother had passed his Masters in English. He was then nineteen and a half years old. He was very fair, had blond hair and blue eyes. Lord Mountbatten came to Aligarh University and gave prizes to the first division boys. When he saw Inam, he asked, "What are you doing here, my boy?" Inam bhai smiled and said, "Sir, I live here." "Oh, so you are local!" was Mountbatten's reply as they shook hands. My brothers gave tuitions while they themselves were students. Inam taught the BA class at Aligarh while he was doing his Masters; Misbah, studying engineering at the same university, also taught junior students. Nayar, while still in Matric, taught boys for two rupees a month. My second brother Islam was an artist and studying for his BA. He had a lovely voice. He was a very handsome man. Islam had made a huge scenery with a rail track between hills and tunnels on one courtyard wall of Terhi Haveli. Little did we know that he would be the first to leave Delhi and migrate to Pakistan and would also soon leave this world.

One day, as I got up from my bed, I heard that Burma had been attacked by the Japanese. My maternal uncle, Syed Asghar Ali, had joined the army and later served in the Royal Navy, one of the 274,000 Muslims from the Indian subcontinent who fought for Britain in World War II. Many Pathans and the Punjabi youths were recruited in the Royal armed forces. The fields were therefore left unattended and food shortages occurred. Strict rationing started in India and even sugar and eggs were scarce. Trenches were dug in Delhi

My uncle Asghar Ali obtained supplies of corn flakes, powdered milk and powdered eggs from his army shop for us. He also brought navy blue woollen material, called serge, which my mother used to make trouser suits for my brothers. Mother saw to it that we always looked well groomed and neatly dressed in spite of our economic difficulties. All the property was now sold and my mother borrowed money to run the household. My eldest brother Inam taught at Arabic College, Delhi, and also gave tuitions in the evenings. He played cricket and was very dashing. He participated in the plays at Hindu College's *Shanti Nuketen* in Darya Ganj. I was invited to see a play called *Buth Tarash* (sculptor). My third brother, Misbah, had red hair, blue eyes and was very slim so he was given the part of a young lady–a statuette!

Inam was twenty one years old and wished to get married. He was initially engaged to my cousin Shamima, who was graduating from Indra Prahasta College. Her brother had gone to England to study. Shamima's father, Feroz Hasan Zaidi was a wealthy government servant and Shamima's grandmother, who lived with them, was a vain lady from a *nawab* family. When my mother went to ask for Shamima's hand, she reproached her saying: "Razia, what have you to offer my granddaughter?" Mother had no answer and came back feeling sad and humiliated.

My uncle Feroz had a car with a balloon-like horn. He would park his car outside on the Tiraha, because the street leading to our house from the main gates was small. The visit caused much excitement amongst the children and we would go and touch the car. My father would just frown quietly and mutter under his breath "the Britishers' stooge" – I found this bizarre because he himself had English friends like Mr Carrol in Khetri. In any case my father would welcome Uncle Feroz.

One of my aunts, Hafeez Begum, was widowed and came to stay in Tehri Haveli. She was young and beautiful. Her husband was a trolley driver who checked the railway lines and someone had shot him while he was on duty. She had a young daughter Swaleha and a son, Saleem. She knew Persian and read Hafiz and Saadi with my father's help. Later her brother Mushtaq also came to stay. He was very quiet and walked with difficulty, which I found strange. I overheard the adults talking about him in low voices. He had apparently been shot in the stomach by the Police at a burial procession that had taken place in defiance of orders. The procession was for the man who had murdered Ram Lal, the author of a book slandering Prophet Muhammad, peace be upon him. The Muslim responsible had been apprehended and killed by the Police. The British Government banned the *janaza* procession so his coffin was secretly taken out at night from Lahore and brought to Jama Masjid Delhi for Friday prayers. The Police came to know about it and opened fire on the burial procession to disperse the crowd. Mushtaq was hit in the stomach but could not go to the hospital as the Police would have caught him and thrown him into prison for disobedience to the Crown. Uncle Mushtaq walked with his hand on his wounds for months. He kept a pair of pigeons in his *verandah* and shared the living quarters of the left wing of Tehri Haveli with his sister Hafeez Begum and her two children. Swaleha was going to Queen Mary's School and Saleem went to the local school nearby. He was fond of flying kites and I enjoyed going to the roof top with him to help him hold the *manjha*.

I managed to buy wool and gold satin for a dress from the money earned at the radio station and knitted a golden sweater to match the golden suit my mother stitched for me to wear at my brother's wedding. My mother had made flowers from silver ribbon and had stitched those on to the *garara* and on the shirt's cuffs. I was delighted with the beautiful outfit. My cousin Nasima was quite a lady and under her influence I transformed from a tomboy to a young girl.

My brother Inam married in 1945. His bride Salima Begum was the daughter of Hakim Shams ul Islam of Bombay. She had finished high school. I remember my brother's wedding very well. Salima Begum came as a young bride to our *haveli* and brought with her a *chaperkhet* with red chiffon curtains and little stars stitched on them. She dressed elegantly. She occasionally asked me to help her with the makeup. My brother had a happy marriage.

The war came to an end in 1945. Hitler was said to have committed suicide. Germany had surrendered. Clement Attlee became the Prime Minister of England. Everyone was talking of independence from the British. My father told us that his nephew in Saharanpur was imprisoned because he spoke of freedom from the colonial rule in a speech.

My step-brother Riaz ul Haq came from Hyderabad Deccan to Delhi. It was the first time I had seen him. He took me to Saharanpur where some of his mother's relatives lived and we stayed in *Mohalla Qazi*, which was named after my paternal grandfather, the judge. He also took me to the Mussoorie Hill station. The Mussoorie Hills and its coniferous trees captured my heart.

I had become quite close to my mother. Many of our conversations took place while she sat in front of her sewing machine and I learnt how to make button holes on my brother's shirts. We had a charcoal iron which mother used on every seam she sewed. She spent many hours on her Singer sewing machine.

I remember mother always washed her face with Pears soap and kept a bottle of Snow White cream in her steel trunk. She wore high-heel court shoes when she went out. Our clothes were kept in separate trunks but always ironed before wearing. The summer clothes would be packed away in winter in steel trunks and all the warm clothing came out. At the end of summer all the warm woolen clothes were washed and packed in the trunks with moth balls or lavender leaves. I started to help my mother in house work. I embroidered a tray cloth and learnt how to sew. I had stopped going to the radio station as my studies were more demanding.

We used a lot of natural herbs and berries in cooking and otherwise. My mother used *reehta* to wash the woollies. The washing soap was made at home but was not used for woollen clothes. We had homemade tooth powder. My mother prepared it by burning the branch of a *neem* tree, which was then powdered finely along with rock salt, mixed with oil and filled in empty jars. This was applied to the teeth with our forefinger, which massaged the gums too. My brothers used *miswak* to clean their teeth, which was made out of a fresh *neem* branch. It was bitter but effective. My grandmother had all her teeth till the age of eighty-eight and she could chew fresh sugarcane. When my uncle Syed Safdar Ali came to England in the 1980s for an operation, and was cared for by his son Dr Akhtar and daughter-in-law Muriel, the nurses in the hospital kept insisting that he should take off his dentures. Much to their surprise and to his amusement, he informed them that the teeth were his own notwithstanding his age! Those early techniques must have worked! Ladies' hair was washed with an herb called *sika kai* and *amla*. Leaves from the *neem* tree were used as medication for small pox or chicken pox.

My brother Islam had a friend called Matloob who was a captain in the Royal Army. He once brought a huge parachute for us. It was circular and was made of cream and green silk. We undid it and my mother made dresses and long flowing skirts from the material. We saved its silken thread and my mother crocheted a lace for her petticoat. She was quite creative for her time. Alas we did not see Matloob again and my brother told me that he was killed in the war.

My sister Asifa was still sucking her thumb when no one was looking and at the same time holding on to the satin ribbon that was tied to her hair. I used to make her hair every day. One evening while we were all sitting down and having our meals I could see the beautiful silhouette of her face on the wall and I drew it with a pencil. She had the most beautiful eyes with very long eye lashes.

Soon there were more relatives staying at Tehri Haveli. My paternal aunt moved to the top floor and my mother's sister Kulsum came to stay with her four children. Her eldest son Syed Athar Ali was a noble young man of seventeen then. Terhi Haveli had a capacity to accommodate many people. My aunt Kulsum was often sad as she had a difficult life: her first husband, a professor in Arabic College, was a lot older than her and had died. She re-married again but was unhappy in her second marriage too. *Khala* Kulsum had a daughter from this marriage whom my uncle Syed Asghar brought back to Delhi. She moved in with us. She had an excellent command of English and was the first lady in our family who went out to work in an office. She would come home tired and then cook for her children. I would often go to her room to tidy up before her return.

Many years later her son Tahir and I became good friends. He worked as a journalist and published a book of poetry. He later migrated to the United States and worked with the "Voice of America". My *khala* spent her last seven years in London at her son Athar's house in Wood Green. He was assistant director of Eastern Services in BBC. Both he and his English wife Lynne were exceptionally kind people. Athar was a great help to me when I arrived in London in 1965.

One day my mother's uncle Nana Bhutta came to see us. He had travelled to America in 1932, but on his third or fourth day there, was robbed at gunpoint outside a bank and left penniless. He did not even have money to book his return ticket. We did not know all the details but had heard that he was hired as a hand on a cargo ship to India to pay for the passage. It took him three or four months to return. He was very loving and all the children would gather around him to listen to his experiences. He also possessed the skill of reading palms and told my mother that I would be travelling a lot to faraway places, though this seemed farfetched then. While my palm was being read, my younger sister Asifa was sitting next to me and she also eagerly offered her little hand. He told my mother to take care of her as she was not going to live very long. We all laughed it off and no one took it seriously. My sister died when she was hardly thirteen.

Begum Salima's mother came from Bombay to stay with us. She sat by the sewing machine and sewed baby clothes. She told me that my brother and his wife would soon have a little baby. In those days baby clothes were stitched at home. Soon Salam, my little nephew, was born. My mother was overjoyed.

Once Inam invited a friend from Aligarh to Tehri Haveli. He wore a khaki army uniform and he told us that he was posted in Shah Jahanpur in the procurement department. We knew him by his pet name Qadir Pasha but his actual name was Ansaruddin Sherif.

That summer, independence was announced. We were free in India and no one could dominate us anymore.

Partition of India, 1947

In August, parades were held and the band played at India Gate. Girl Guides from our school also participated in the ceremony. One day uncle Safdar came with news that a massacre was planned and armed Sikhs and Hindus were coming in truck loads to Delhi. Nobody could believe this. Muslims had lived peacefully with Hindus in Delhi for six hundred years. The Hindu girls used to throw colours of holi on to the Muslims in the Tiraha and sing *parh key kheloongi main holi bismillah*–the Muslims did not like the colours thrown on them but tolerated it. However, the Brahmans did not allow us to drink water from their glass or from their containers; we had to drink water by having water poured into our cupped hands. There was strict caste system in India among Hindus. Nevertheless, we lived happily with one another without interfering in each other's lives or customs.

One evening everyone gathered at the Ram Leela Ground outside Turkman Darwaza. My brother Islam and Asifa were asked to sing on the microphone. There seemed to be at least 10,000 people outside the *faseel* (city walls) and the crowds extended till Lady Irwin College. It was a pleasant evening. When my brother Islam sang an old song sung by Saigal, the famous Hindu singer, there was hushed silence. He then introduced my little sister Asifa and she sang. Her voice was like magic. When she finished, people lifted her in their arms and on their shoulders. That was our last good evening in Delhi.

Slowly people from our neighbourhood started leaving. One night we woke up to the sounds of firing and screaming. The next day there was a curfew. We could hear women screaming and smoke of burnt houses filled the air. When we sat for our evening meal we were thankful that we were together.

My brother Islam was selected to work in the Pakistan secretariat. He left for Karachi. My grandmother's huge mahogany Burmese wooden trunk, packed with a few *fermans*, handwritten in gold by royalty, and land papers along with a few valuables, were shipped to Karachi by Islam before leaving. A few days later all flights and rail journeys stopped.

Misbah was away in Hyderabad Deccan and had gone to London from there but we had no news of him. Nayar was in Nowakhali in Bengal. Mother was worried for him but his Hindu friend Kawal came to see us with news of his safety. We heard the shootings night and day. Then there was a hush. There was no food left in the house and the shops were looted or burnt. My little nephew Salam who was one and a half, and baby niece Nafisa just five months old, had to go without milk.

Misbah's friend Irshad was stranded in our house. When he saw the baby crying for milk, he took a little brass bucket in his hand and went over the roof tops. The shooting had started again and everyone was worried for him. He managed to get some milk for the hungry baby. Alas, the songs of happiness evaporated in smoke and dark clouds of sadness and sad memories refuse to be blotted out from my memory even after sixty years.

When the curfew lifted my brother Ameen went to take his matriculation examination. The day passed and he did not come back. My mother was frantic with worry for him. Three men wearing *lungi* or *dhoti* came inside our house and told my father, "You are old and we do not mean disrespect to you but you must now go to your land Pakistan, as we have come to live here". My father responded with a shocked voice that he was old and did not intend to leave this *haveli*. That did not help. A woman came forward, grabbed the pram of my nephew Salam and threw him on the floor saying, "this is mine now". We were all frightened. We had fifteen minutes to leave. A few clothes were taken along with some blankets. I noticed how difficult it was for my father to climb on to the *tanga* due to severe rheumatism and gout. I could see tears in my mother's eyes as we rode towards the refugee camp.

Humayun's white marble tomb, normally a tourists' venue, was turned into a refugee camp. The Old Fort and Humayun's Tomb were the most scenic and beautiful spots of Delhi. People visited those places for picnics and outings. We were shocked to see tents pitched on the grounds and hundreds of people in the camps. I noticed some people did not even have a tent. They were perched on their metal trunks. The evenings were now getting cold and frosty.

My eldest brother was not at home when we left Terhi Haveli. He later took a *tanga* and rode to the refugee camp, with a Sikh following him with a sword. He was frightened but the *tangawala* prompted the horse to run fast. After searching the refugee camp for a few hours he managed to find us at night. There were thousands of people everywhere, uprooted from their homes. The camp stretched from Palam airport to the Old Fort and Humayun's Tomb.

As the day broke, I tried to find some familiar faces in the camp and was worried about my best friend Azra. All I could see were strange and blank faces. We did not know anyone and my parents did not move from the tent we were occupying, in case someone else took our place. Most times we slept on our suitcases or sat on them.

I am an optimist. I thought the camp was exciting. It reminded me of the camping times when I was in Jamia Millia and St.Francis School. We discovered a well and someone brought a rope and a bucket and we started to pull water from it. I liked going to the well and brought drinking water to our tent. Bathing in the camp to me was fun. We had to borrow two *charpoys* and drape them with a sheet. Then we had to fetch water in empty Dalda *ghee* cans. We did not even have a bucket. I bathed under the open sky for the first time and felt exhilarated. I saw that both my parents remained very quiet. There was no more poetry in their conversation and no newspapers to read. There was no food and no cooking either.

Finally someone told us that there was tea available for the refugees. I was sent out for it, since mother and my sister-in-law observed *purdah*. I used to wear a long coat but never liked to wear the cape which was supposed to be tied to the head and descend down to cover the shoulders and chest. I saw a long line of people queuing for a cup of tea. It was ages before my turn came. I was given a cup of tea with sweet and salt mixed. I took one sip and took it quietly to my mother.

We had a visitor in the camp. It was exciting to see *Chammi ki Amman*. She had risked her life and somehow came to the refugee camp, just to bring us some food. She brought lots of *parahtay* for us. She kissed my little sister Asifa and said that she missed her. We all ate half a *parata* each and saved the remaining for the next day.

People were leaving by train from Palam station for Lahore. We tried to board the train twice but failed as there was only one and hundreds of people. It is just as well that we could not board that train. We heard later that three trains never reached Lahore or Bhawani Junction. These were looted and burnt. Some 20,000 women disappeared during those days. The third train also left Palam station from Delhi, full of refugees. It met a similar fate.

I still feel a chill after so many years when I see a Sikh gentleman. Later in life, when I worked in the Bank of England, I became very fond of a Sikh girl and we became best of friends, but somehow I still could not bring myself to talk to a Sikh gentleman easily.

Chammi ki Amman came just once more to the refugee camp and brought us food.

Life in the tents was pretty grim. My eldest brother contacted Jamia Millia School at Okhla as it was a relatively safe place. Dr Zakir Hussain, a future President of India, called us and we stayed at one of the teachers' residence. The Jamia Millia staff insisted that everything would be fine in a few months. We knew that Delhi would not be the same again

We stayed for a month in Okhla. There was no news of my three brothers, Nayar, Ameen and Misbah. Brother Islam had opted for Pakistan. We hoped that Misbah was safe in Hyderabad Deccan. The Nizam of Hyderabad was said to be one of the richest men in the world and there was no trouble there as yet.

Once the curfew lifted, Salima Begum's father, Hakim Shams ul Islam, sent his eldest son Qamar to bring us to Bombay. After two nights in their small flat we boarded a cargo ship for Karachi. We stayed on the deck. We got the news that the Matriculation Examination Hall was burnt down in Delhi. My mother wept and prayed for Ameen.

That was my first trip across the sea. A rich Bombay diamond merchant asked my mother for my hand in marriage. My mother brushed him off saying that I was very young. It took us three days to arrive at Karachi port. My brother Islam found us. It was a very gloomy homecoming. We saw sand and dust everywhere. We missed the lovely green lawns and parks of Delhi. Finally we arrived in Jacob Lines. These were two-room barracks built by the British for soldiers.

We still had no news of Ameen and prayed. We came to know that Maulana Ihtesham ul Haq's sixteen year old nephew was burnt alive in that hall. We were lucky to have the barrack quarters. Many people were living around us in huts. A Sindhi friend of my brother Islam came to see us. He was very kind and had brought us some blankets and beddings. He had a Chinese Muslim wife.

My parents and Aunt Akhtar Jahan often discussed the logic in the creation of Pakistan and were bitter about the unfairness in the way the boundaries of Pakistan were made. Pakistan had five frontiers, India, China, Afghanistan, Iran and Kashmir. East Pakistan was another morsel of land, a thousand miles away in Bengal. One did not see any logic in accepting such an unfair partition of a country. Delhi was the seat of Muslim culture and the capital city of the Tughlaqs, the Khiljis and the Mughals. It was a city with a majority of Muslim population for centuries, yet it was handed to the Hindus by rigging the population count.

The Pakistan state treasury was empty. There was not even paper to print the currency. There was no Secretariat, no government blocks and no municipal buildings. My brother Islam and other government employees worked from their desks in the open sun and dust. Lord Mountbatten's remarks to Jinnah came to light after 30 years that "his moth-eaten Pakistan will not last more than 25 years". Pakistan, though by the Grace of God, is still very much on the map.

The resilient and determined Pakistani people worked hard and built the country by their toil and continued enthusiasm. My brother Misbah came back from Britain after his engineering training and started to work in a sugar factory as a manager. The factory was in Landhi, a suburb of Karachi. It was owned by Laiq Ali Khan, a Hyderabadi industrialist who had interviewed Misbah in London. Misbah later built and managed two more cement factories in Pakistan. My eldest brother Inam had joined Pakistan Air Force (PAF). Another brother Nayar had become a locomotive engineer in the railway service and was in Chicago for training.

We got news of Ameen through my aunt in Lahore. He had escaped the inferno and managed to reach Lahore. My mother prayed *nawafil* to thank Allah for his safe arrival. Ameen had also passed all his examinations. He worked during the day at State Bank of Pakistan and studied at nights. He later went to London to train as an actuary.

I was reconciled to the new school and took part in plays and debates. On one occasion Ms Fatima Jinnah came to attend the ceremony. She was tall, frail and very fair with sharp features and addressed us in English. I passed my exams after attending school for four months.

In those days many people lived in tin quarters near Gora Qabristan, a Christian cemetery, and in mud huts along Lyari River. Relatives came and stayed with brother Islam in our two rooms at Jacob Lines. It was always packed with refugees. Islam welcomed every one of the relatives with an open heart and accommodated them.

After a while my elder brother Inam's friend, Ansaruddin Sherif, who had known us in Terhi Haveli, offered us his quarters on Lawrence Road. He was a bachelor with relatives still in Madras. My parents accepted the offer and we shifted to Lawrence Road. These were barracks too, but better. Meanwhile Inam was posted to Hyderabad. He wanted me to come with him and his family, but Hyderabad seemed to me a remote place in Sindh of which I knew nothing about, so I declined.

Marriage

While we lived in his house, Ansaruddin Sherif started to teach me English. I was very shy and did not feel comfortable in men's company. Though my mother was quite conservative, she did not mind my learning English with him. He had passed his Masters and also his law examinations, LLB. He sometimes would come to pick us up from our school or college. One day he took me from my college to Gymkhana Club. I was very bashful. The sight of all those men in their neckties and suits and fashionable ladies dressed up in *saris*, shaking hands with Englishmen was all new to me. Ansaruddin Sherif swept me off my feet completely and bewitched me with his compliments. He was going to join the United Nations International Labour Organisation in Switzerland and asked my mother for my hand in marriage. My parents were happy that he was fond of me and loved me. Even though he was almost twice my age, I married him without any fuss. We were married within two days in a hurry in 1948, without any pomp or show, with a few relatives present. I was sitting at Karachi Airport lounge, quite bewildered and missing my younger sister Asifa, on the third day of my marriage.

My husband introduced me to Begum Shaista Ikramullah at Karachi airport, who was also leaving for London to attend a labour conference. I did not feel any warmth towards her. She was busy talking to her two daughters who had come to say goodbye. I was missing my family as none had come to bid farewell. My parents had returned to Jacob Lines because the Lawrence Road quarters had to be returned back to the government. My husband did not show the same warmth to my parents when we went to say goodbye to them in Jacob Lines. Maybe he expected a lot of presents or money from them, which they did not have. I was feeling very awkward wearing a fur coat that he had bought before leaving Karachi. I did not like it, but wore it nevertheless to please him. The plane journeys in those days were long. It was my first flight. I was sick in the plane and did not move from my seat even once.

We arrived in London after a fourteen hours flight. There was only one airport in London then. We came to the city by coach. There were no underground connections to or from the airport. We stayed in Pall Mall Hotel near Piccadilly Circus. This was a new world for me. I was fascinated by it all. I did not move out of my hotel and watched the huge horse-driven carts, through the window. In India we had never seen such big and strong horses. In the evenings people gathered around Piccadilly Circus and sang songs. I saw many soldiers in uniforms, cars and big red buses. Looking out from the hotel window was my favourite past time.

I did not like the food served and went hungry a lot. I did not know how to use a knife and fork. I was used to eating by hand, chapatti dipped in the *shorba* of *aloo gosht*. The hotel food tasted bland. I was also aware of my husband's scrutinising gaze as I held the fork and knife, rather awkwardly. I wondered if he didn't like me. I felt lonely in this strange world, where everyone spoke English in high pitched voices. I was not used to so many men looking at me. I had been brought up in a protected world and was easy only with my family and a close circle of friends.

This was a different world. Dinner time was the most torturous for me as I did not like to face so many people in the dining hall. At times my husband would get irritated when he would order some strange dish like roast beef and boiled potatoes and I would not taste it fearing I might drop the piece of meat from the fork. He was well aware of the club manners of gymkhana and I was the young child bride who did not know anything.

The other thing which bothered me most was that in the hotel bathrooms there were no washing facilities like bidets or *lotas*. Instead there was a packet of thin transparent, non-absorbent paper. Most houses in those days cut the newspapers up and placed them in their toilets. It seemed very unhygienic to me. On the other hand I noticed that newspapers and a bowl were left on the pavement on an old sheet for sale and people would make their purchase and leave the money quite honestly. No one dared to steal it.

I was afraid to go out alone on the streets and spent time looking at the outside world through the hotel windows, with a full view of Piccadilly Circus. I could view and hear the soldiers and some ladies sitting around the fountain and singing old, famous songs. It was a happy time as the soldiers were all returning to their homes after the war. I would only venture outside the hotel with my husband. We walked hand in hand in the Marble Arch area and Connaught Place and witnessed the bombed and half destroyed buildings. The houses were being sold for as little as nine hundred pounds as they were war damaged. My husband told me that many Jewish people who had fled Poland and Germany were buying property.

Sherif Sahib was busy arranging visa formalities for Switzerland and received instructions from Geneva office about his arrival. We arrived in Switzerland in a small plane. The flight was short and lovely. I was fascinated by the mountains and the lakes covered with grey blue clouds which I could notice through the window pane of this little airplane.

Between Two Cultures

My new life in Geneva started in August 1948. The plane glided through the beautiful snow covered hills. On landing, I felt elated in the fresh air of pine trees. The sight of the lofty peaks wrapped up in powdered snow, looking so pure and majestic, made me feel strong and happy. Mountains give me inner strength and courage. The plane stopped near a wooden cabin by the runway as Geneva did not have an airport building. We were taken by coach to the city and arrived at the Hotel Balmoral. Though three languages were spoken in Switzerland, English was not one of them. I was happy that we stayed in a hotel and I did not have to cook.

I noticed that women in the hotel spoke to my husband quite freely and in fact it seemed to me that they liked him. Of course he was very handsome and knew how to dress up and wore lovely silk neck scarves, but I felt awkward when they spoke to him and laughed with him so easily. An Iranian lady came to my room and told me what lovely legs I had! I was surprised at that comment as in Delhi we only commented on horses' legs.

The next evening we went for a stroll on the Lake Leman. I was wearing a *garara* and a shirt with a beautiful *dupata*. I felt good in the beautiful August evening. The tall fountain of Lake Leman jetted out its plumes on to the lake. As we strolled along, many people turned and some came close to touch my hair. They had never seen anyone dressed like me with such long brown curly hair.

It became embarrassing for us and we decided to go back to the hotel room.

The next day, my husband said at breakfast table that he could not take me out the way I was, so I must have my hair cut like the other ladies. I loved my long hair. My mother had taken a lot of trouble over it, by applying all kinds of herbal oils and special herbs. I did not go to the hairdresser and stayed indoors. Evening came and again my husband rather strictly told me that I should go with the hotel manageress the next day and get my hair cut just like hers. After seeing her hair well set, I agreed to go to the hairdresser with her.

The Balmoral Hotel manageress took me to Chez Charlie, a chic salon on the quay of Place de Longemalle. It was the first time I had stepped into a hair dressing salon and the strange smells of bleaches and ammonia reminded me of my brothers' laboratory in their den of Terhi Haveli. There were women of all ages sitting there, but when the hairdresser saw my long beautiful hair, he took them in his hands and kissed my locks longingly and said, "Oh no! *Madame, je ne peau pas couper ces beaux cheveaux*". Madam, I cannot cut such beautiful hair. He was nearly in tears and asked if he could use my hair for making a wig, to which I agreed.

My next transformation started with a change of dress. My dear husband wanted me to look like the other young French and Swiss ladies and not a *junglee,* as he called me one day. He took me to the big store of Geneva, *Le Grand Passage,* and selected European outfits for me. So I agreed to step into this new Saida which he wanted me to be. It is said an Asian woman's first and maybe last love is her husband and she lives to please him.

We stayed in the hotel for nearly a month and then shifted to a flat in the centre of Geneva in Place de Longemalle. It was close to the lake and near all the shops. The flat was beautifully decorated. We were happy to be there, but I had not cooked before and I was worried about cooking meals.

None of us then spoke French and it was difficult to do any shopping. We both started French lessons at home. I later joined Ecole Berlitz where I finished a course in French and also learnt shorthand. I used to love reading novels and short stories. When the time for lunch came, I would quickly get up and place an egg and a potato on to boil. At times I would go back to reading and on one occasion realised that both the egg and the potato were burnt and the kitchen full of smoke. I then quickly tried to prepare an alternative, but the only things I knew was egg and potato curry or an onion omelette. I must admit my husband was very patient and never grumbled. Instead he would always commend my efforts and describe them as delicious.

We began to meet my husband's colleagues socially. One particular French couple had a villa by the lake and we were quite often invited there. I made mental notes of all the details of the decor of the table and the way food was presented. Everything that we ate at Madame Plainmaison was delicious. Previously I had found French food bland and even difficult to swallow, but I soon developed a taste for it. When our turn came to invite them, I was flabbergasted. Luckily I had made friends with my next door neighbour. She was a middle aged kindly lady and worked as a couturier. She showed me how to prepare various salad dressings and deserts. I learnt to whip cream with vanilla essence and other recipes. After all I had to compete with the high class UN dinner parties.

Soon I was able to converse with my neighbour in French quite easily. She had a rather sad look on her face. I used to notice a gentleman coming in and out of the flat rather discreetly. I asked her if it was her husband. She told me that she was not married to him but they were living together. She explained to me that divorce was not permitted in Catholicism so they lived in sin and she felt guilty about it. Catholics followed their religion strictly in 1948. Church attendance was regular and during the forty days of Lent many would only eat a dish of polenta once a day.

Almost every weekend we would drive to France for lunch. French cuisine was famous in those days. The restaurateurs really knew how to look after their customers and lunch was prepared while the guests sipped red or white wine. The hors d'ouvre was served in style. Some people ate a snail in sauce which was served in a tall, stemmed silver dish. The main dish of fish or meat would be brought in front of us, with wine poured on the grilling beef steak. The whole meal lasted for at least an hour and a half.

I found Swiss cooking not as imaginative as the French. The main Swiss speciality was fondu, freshly melted cheese soaked in white wine, into which one would dip pieces of bread or potato. Italian cooking consisted mainly of pastas and different types of macaroni. Nona, my Italian neighbour in the flat downstairs once showed me how she preferred to make her own fine spaghetti at home. I had started to cook a mixed type of cuisine at home. My husband liked the way I prepared *pilau* and would always praise my cooking.

Once coming back home I was sick in a friend's car. I was very embarrassed but my husband knew immediately that I was expecting. The pregnancy did not last and I aborted at two months. My mother wrote me a letter from Karachi that she had seen me in a dream and was worried. She always saw events in her dreams when something had to happen. My husband realised my age and wanted me to go to the Geneva Lycée but I was still then quite shy and did not like the free atmosphere of the mixed university. So I didn't bother, but continued my Berlitz course.

We came to know that most of our UN friends were buying or renting flats in the well-cared for locality of Chemin Creek, near a skating rink and the large Parc Bertrand. We too booked a flat there. I wanted to buy luxurious and modern furniture for the flat and decorate it beautifully. We had a few arguments as my husband went ahead without consulting me and bought Louis XIV replica furniture with burgundy red velvet coverings. We started to argue on little things. I would frequently visit Nona. She lived with her only son, who had married a peasant girl. In fact she was a plain looking girl who did all the errands. Nona used to dress most immaculately and thought the world of me for no reason and I learnt most of my Italian from her.

I gradually lost my shyness in male company and became more confident. I spoke perfect French by then and was asked to translate at a United Nations conference when Sir Zafarullah Khan had come to give a speech on the Kashmir issue. Both my husband and I were shocked to see that he did not really say much and just kept on repeating that a fair plebiscite was required. His speech did not last more than two minutes. I remember getting red in the face and could not help giving him a hard stare and wondering if it was incompetence or deliberate.

One day my husband brought a big Alsatian to the new flat. It was stronger than I. In those days I only weighed about 90 pounds. When leaving for work he asked me to take the dog out for a walk during the day. I attempted to do so, but it so happened that instead of me taking him for a walk it was the other way round. The dog refused to go and instead spoilt the brand new parquet floors of our new flat with its urination and excretion. This drama took place for three days and I got tired of cleaning the dog's mess on our brand new floors, which I kept polished. At times I vomited. One day when my husband came home, I had to tearfully inform him that either the dog stayed or me. He became very quiet and took the dog away but for the next two days he did not eat or speak to me.

The flat above us was occupied by an American couple. The husband, Woody Palmer, always criticised the Arabs, called them lazy and no good, and said how glad he was that Palestine had been taken by the Israelis. I loathed him for his judgment but his wife Ruth, a German, was more understanding and perhaps more intelligent. I swallowed most of her husband's unkind comments but because of Ruth, our friendship continued. I wanted to ask Woody what would have happened if the Palestinians had not hosted all the refugees who fled from Germany during the war when Hitler was on the killing rampage. But I was so angry that the words just stuck in my throat and I would just leave them.

I was now expecting again. My husband desperately wanted a baby and took good care of me. We went for walks in the evenings after he got back from work, but the vomiting did not stop. I could not keep anything down. The sickness continued till the last month when I literally lived on Coca Cola, apples and peppermint. On one of our lunch outings in Evian in France we met the old Agha Khan and his French wife. My husband told me that the Aga Khan was one of the richest men in the world and was weighed in gold by his followers, the Ismailis, on his birthdays. He was particularly favoured by the British. We exchanged greetings and spoke for a while but he did not impress me. His wife used to take him in the wheel chair by the lakeside. On weekends we would sometimes drive to Aix-les-Bains or Annecy in France for lunch. I was surprised to see hundreds of Algerians building roads and highways in France. My husband explained to me that Algeria was a French colony and hence Algerians provided cheap labour.

I got news from Karachi that my sister Asifa had developed a brain tumour and was very ill. My parents were refugees with little money. Brother Misbah was in London and helped as much as he could. My eldest brother with his wife and two young children in Hyderabad Sind. The responsibility for the treatment fell on my brother Islam. In each letter I was told that Asifa was missing me very much and wanted to see me. I pleaded with my husband to let me go but he did not allow me to fly for two reasons: we only qualified for a free passage once in two years, and he did not think that the long flight from Europe to Karachi was advisable in late pregnancy. Asifa died in September 1949 and I was heartbroken that I did not see her. I missed my family very much.

The winter months in our new flat were quite bearable as we had the *chauffage* keeping the flat quite warm and comfortable.

Central heating and the bidet became public first in Europe and reached Britain much later.

Motherhood

On 8th January 1950 I felt a little sleepy and tired with a slight back ache. It was a week end. The next day I awoke at 5.30 in the morning with severe pain. I had been checked regularly by Dr Rene Melon and was booked in the Bois Gentil clinic for delivery. My husband put a dressing gown on me and was ready to take me to the clinic. My neighbour Ruth had made my husband promise that I should call her when I was ready to leave, but I did not want anyone to see me having a baby. I did not like the idea of Ruth seeing me lying exposed in delivery room, but my husband took her. I was in extreme pain and could not argue at the time. As soon as I reached the hospital, I fell asleep or perhaps they gave me an injection. I did not recall anything afterwards. I was woken by the nurse at about nine a.m. and found myself lying in between the white sheets of the hospital bed. She woke me gently, and congratulated me saying that I had a lovely baby boy. I opened my eyes and through the window I could see the grounds and the trees all covered with snow. Everything looked white and pure and fascinating as I witnessed my first snowfall. My gaze returned from the window as I quickly put my hands on the tummy and realised that it had squeezed back to its normal small shape. Just then the gentle nurse brought me my son wrapped in white blankets, sleeping peacefully. The staff congratulated me as it was their first baby boy born in the new year of 1950. Not only I, but everybody thought he was a beautiful baby. My husband was absolutely on top of the world with happiness.

I missed my mother and Asifa very much that day. I had asked my husband to send a telegram to my mother to inform my family of the arrival of the baby, but he never did, though he told me he had. These were some of his lunacies which I disliked. He bought me an expensive gift of an electric Singer sewing machine, that has travelled with me ever since. The little sewing machine surprisingly is still working after serving me for over sixty years. My husband was quite patriotic and out of admiration for the founder of Pakistan, Muhammad Ali Jinnah, named our son after him. I did not approve of the name and neither did my family accept it. My mother was particular about her *syed* ancestry and felt that adoption of another surname was far-fetched.

I returned to my flat in Chemin Creek with my little bundle. The Swiss used to wrap their babies in a shawl and I learnt to do the same. All the necessary items, like a cot, a push chair and the baby's furniture were bought and we had a nurse-cum-maid to help me. Everybody was surprised to see that my figure was back to normal after childbirth. Unfortunately I could not breastfeed my son. Once while my husband was away on a trip, the baby did not stop crying. I became anxious and took him to the doctor who examined and laughed. There was nothing wrong and the baby just needed more food.

I recall an incident that left me feeling silly. I was busy buying things in the Grand Passage department store and had left my baby in a designated area by the entrance, under the supervision of a sales supervisor. After making some purchases and checking out a few things in the sales, I looked at the time and realised that Sherif Sahab would have come home and I had not cooked any food. I rushed to catch a bus and when I arrived at Chemin Creek I realised that I had left my poor child in the store! My heart stopped. I ran back to find my baby sitting alone in the store in his pram, looking very calm and an attendant was speaking to him. I picked him up and kissed him and ran back home with my baby. My husband was not angry but quite amused at what I had done.

I met a young girl, Sylvia, in Chemin Creek. She once invited me to her flat for a get-together. I met Karim Aga Khan there. We were almost the same age. I learnt to dance in her flat and enjoyed it as we met in the afternoon for tea. My husband was a good ballroom dancer. I wanted to show him that I could also dance. Those were the days when United Nations held balls at the Palais des Nations. The ladies came in their long flowing dresses. My husband also bought me long gloves and a cigarette holder. I was smoking by then. I was out to prove to my husband that I was as good as the other European girls in every possible way. He admired the European ladies and, I felt, compared me to them. He might have felt sorry as to why he married me, when he could easily have had a European wife. Luckily he usually kept his thoughts hidden.

In late 1950 it was time to visit Pakistan. We travelled to London and stayed at the Savoy. Food was still rationed and there was not much choice. We met Frank Sinatra in the Savoy salon. He kissed my little boy and held him in his arms and asked for his name. Before I could say anything my husband said, "his nickname is Jimmy". The name then stuck. We sailed from Southampton in a luxury liner of the P&O Company. I remember a stopover at Gibraltar–the latinised name of *Jabl-at-Tariq*. It was once a Muslim stronghold. My husband told me that a lot of arms and ammunition remained stored from the war times underneath this rocky city. Back on board, my husband told some passengers that I could read palms and a whole lot of people gathered around me. I had to read dozens of hands. On reaching Karachi I was full of joy seeing my family but missed my sister. My mother fell in love with my baby. When we asked his name he would say "Bimmy".

Soon after returning to Geneva in 1951, circumstances led me to visit my brother Misbah, who was pursuing further engineering training in London. I took up a course in Journalism in Regents College and also worked in Selfridges in the Bought Ledger department. One day I decided to wear Pakistani dress to work. To my amazement, I was sent back home without explanation. I gathered that if I wore Asian clothes I would not be accepted, even though I was not in sales but in the top floor office. However I was treated with a lot of respect and my pay was more than the other girls who worked on the Burroughs machines. I worked late in

My visit to London, June 1951.

With Jimmy, March 1951.

the office voluntarily. This was also necessary because my evening classes started late. My weekly salary was £5 and ten shillings which was considered a good pay. On the pay packet my name was written 'Sandra' rather than Saida, and it remained so even though I pointed out the error several times. The BBC studios were then in Piccadilly and I used to participate in plays. I was once given a part in *Othello*. I could also easily translate English programs and broadcast live from English to Urdu, as well as translate scripts from French to English. I used to get five guineas per program for that work. I lived with my brother Misbah in Landsdown Crescent in Holland Park, quite a posh area. The landlord was Greek and lived in the basement. His wife was quite friendly and told me that they purchased the house for nine hundred pounds and were still spending money to repair parts of it.

Working at the BBC, 1951.

My brother Misbah was very fond of me and looked after me well. At weekends we met friends at the Lyons tea house in Marble Arch where we could eat sardines on toast, or fried egg on toast with baked beans and a cup of tea, all for a penny and a half.

Later we would see Rita Hayworth films in the Odeon cinema next door. Rita Hayworth was married to Prince Ali Khan, the son of Aga Khan the senior. Rationing of sugar and eggs still continued in those days. Meat was expensive and not always available.

I missed my son so in the Christmas holidays I returned to Geneva. He was under the care of two maids. One nurse maid, Elaine, had knitted him a striped horse which he carried everywhere for a long time. We were both very happy to see each other. This exposure matured me and I learnt a lot during my stay in London.

Back home to Geneva

Jimmy at a children's party in Geneva –1954.

Life was pleasant in Switzerland. We had a black Vauxhall car and would go driving around the snowcapped mountains or explore the picturesque lakes. We would watch movies quite often and Betty Davis starred in many. I remember seeing a Russian movie about the Cossacks and I learnt for the first time that there were many Muslims living in Russia. Our history books did not reveal such facts. I had found a good friend in Kay, whose husband also worked in ILO and we lived in the same neighbourhood. Her daughter Shirley was the same age as Jimmy and they played almost every afternoon while we used to have our afternoon walks in Parc Bertrand and later tea together. Kay had a stroke of polio but recovered in six months.

My husband brought a little kitten in a small basket. It had white paws and a white neck with shiny fur. I was happy that it was not another Alsatian. One day, I had a ladies' tea party at home and as the guests arrived, I placed their fur coats in the bedroom. I became engrossed in serving and speaking to my guests, not realising that the bedroom door was left open. Unfortunately things did not proceed smoothly. When the time for the ladies to leave came, I went to the bedroom to get their fur coats and saw that the kitten meanwhile had entered the bedroom and entangled its paws in the fringes of the silk bedcover. White foam was coming out of its mouth. Panic stricken, I froze and could not move. I called out to my friend Teresa who was waiting for her coat. I was too frightened to touch the little kitten alone so we both managed to somehow release it and called the vet. He arrived at the same time as my husband but it died within the hour. The little basket lay empty and my poor husband again felt very sad and sorry. A few days later we acquired a pair of gold fish in an aquarium. This time I was determined to take good care and would give them regular feed. My husband was very good at handling the fish and always changed the water of the aquarium. We had a net to scoop the fishes from our kitchen sink to place them back in the aquarium. Things went fine till my husband had to go on a trip for a few days. I have always been a very clean person and was a proud housewife. I wanted the house to look immaculately clean and tidy all the time. I decided to change the water of the aquarium. I emptied the aquarium in the kitchen sink and washed and shone the glass aquarium thoroughly and placed all the pebbles together with the flora back. When I scooped out the fish from the kitchen sink to place them back into the aquarium, one jumped out of the net and landed right into the sink outlet. I really felt bad. The other fish remained for a few days more but it also soon said good bye to us. My husband said that the fish died because it was lonely.

After these three incidents with the pets, my husband did not try any more. I felt bad that I could not really look after pets, even though I did try. There are some people who prefer to be animal-friendly rather than human-friendly. Many years later, while working in the Bank of England, I noticed that my friend Pat used to buy a two pound of lamb for her dog and only buy a pound of mince meat for her husband. I was surprised and laughed when she said that her dog was more faithful than her husband, so she fed the dog better.

My husband was very much into politics and explained to me things I did not know. From one of his Egyptian colleagues, a Mr Zawad who was married to a French lady, we heard of the Brotherhood movement in Egypt and of the unsuccessful attempts of Egypt's new leaders, Muhammad Naguib and Gamal Nasser, to seek help from the United States against Israel. According to Mr Zawad, Nasser later turned to the Soviet Union and started to eliminate the religious people from the country to please the communists. We came to know of the circumstances of Hasan Al-Banna's assassination. We also hosted delegates from Pakistan to UN events on many occasions. These included Mr A.K. Brohi, a senior Sindhi lawyer, who came with my husband to our house for lunch one day. It was delightful meeting him. He was a plain looking man but full of knowledge and spoke eloquently on a variety of subjects. He recited Shakespeare and paid me a lot of compliments. He and my husband became good friends as they shared a legal background. He told us about his daughter Masuma who was studying at the American College in Beirut.

Our next trip to Pakistan in 1952 was aboard the luxury liner *Batory* that we boarded in Italy. The sea voyages lasted for ten to twelve days. Travelling was fun as we always managed to get the top cabins in the luxury class for our voyage. I had never seen anything like the *Batory*'s velvet draped cabins before, not even in films. There were shops and hairdressing salons, along with tennis courts and a swimming pool, and a huge ballroom for a live orchestra at mealtimes. We often dined at the captain's table. The luxury class passengers had cabins on the top deck, while the lower ones were for the economy class. Unfortunately during the journey I lost many items of jewelry because of pilferage by the stewardesses. I remember when we crossed the Mediterranean and arrived at Port Said in Egypt, the authorities at Suez Canal who checked our passports were all Egyptians in smart uniforms. Some

British passengers though were fretting and feeling quite gloomy, but I was happy and marveled at the way the Egyptians conducted themselves and handled the passport control so smoothly and efficiently. In Aden I noticed how the second class passengers from the lower decks threw fruits and coins to children diving in the ocean. The great liner took us to Bombay from where we boarded another ship headed for Karachi. I always wanted to spend a longer time with my family and often returned to Geneva alone.

Travelling taught me a lot, in particular to adapt and be accepted in most situations. I found that meeting people removed ignorance and promoted tolerance It is a blessing of Allah that people have always been friendly and very kind towards me.

Les Diablerets

I had another miscarriage and my husband decided to send me, on our doctor's advice, to a Swiss hill station called Les Diablerets. We travelled in a little train of two bogies from Geneva to Lausanne and Montreux. We changed trains at Montreux and passed Leysin and then finally stopped at Les Diablerets. The fresh air of pine and coniferous trees was exhilarating. The three snow-covered hilltops of Les Diablerets standing side by side looked majestic. Below was a glacier that changed into a spring and reached the plains where the cows and sheep grazed.

This was a train journey that Jimmy and I would take many a time. During the winter he went on his sledge and I would ski in the hot sun. It was a lovely feeling to be able to ski. The hill resort was less famous than Zermat, but it was known for its good climate and sick people came here to recuperate. On our first visit we stayed in a hotel *pension* called 'Les Lilas'. Its proprietor was a lovely, kind lady, called Mademoiselle Moillen, who was not married. Her younger family members used to help her in the hotel and called her 'Tantine' or aunt. We later rented a chalet from her brother, Mr Moillen, next door to 'Les Lilas'.

Mr Moillen took Jimmy trout fishing in the summer holidays. He had no sons, only three daughters and the family loved having a little boy around. Les Diablarets turned lush green when the snow melted and disappeared. The valleys had scented flowers covering the hills, and seeing my son running after the butterflies was a delightful sight. At night he clutched Elaine's woollen horse. I met the wife of Max Conrad, a pioneering pilot among the first to fly across the Pacific and the Atlantic in a

With Jimmy at Les Diablerets –1954.

twin engine plane. She had come with her ten children to spend holidays in Les Diablerets while I was living in 'Les Lilas'. It was my first close contact with an American, other than the Palmers of Chemin Creek. I noticed that she was very intelligent and understanding, but found her children arrogant. They were crazily patriotic and considered America the biggest, the richest and best! I hired one of her young girls for babysitting and for helping me when I moved in to the chalet.

Tantine showed much love towards me and my son. Whenever the Pension was full, I would help her out by taking one of her guests in the chalet. She was very grateful for this favour and would immediately invite us for supper in the restaurant.

Tantine's sister and nephew André were the proprietors of a restaurant called 'Après Ski Café'. I used to go there after skiing and at times serve tea to the skiers who were waiting for their hot coffee and cakes. I knew most of them as they had helped me ski to the higher slopes. I left Jimmy in the Après Ski café as the higher slopes were dangerous and I was afraid that he might get hurt. Later, when it was less busy, André would serve us hot chocolate and lovely patisserie which both of us enjoyed immensely in the cold weather.

There was a 'salle commune' at Les Diablerets where various fêtes such as the ripening of the grapes would be celebrated. Someone played the accordion and people danced a simple step dance. Everybody danced, so I did not feel that there was anything wrong in it. I did not have snow boots at the time and had to walk back in grounds covered with knee-high snow. My feet were ice cold by the time we returned to the Pension. My Tantine and her sister both rubbed and massaged my feet and legs with warm oil. I cannot forget their affection to this day. Tantine could never pronounce Pakistan and would always say 'Padistan', which made me laugh.

We went on sledges in the moonlit nights, as by now I had become almost a member of the Moillen family and was asked to join in with them on all occasions. Ten or twelve sledges would be tied together and many of us would slide on the snow, singing while the full moon in all its glory shone above the glistening snow-covered grounds. The experience was most exhilarating while in my heart I wondered at the beauty God Almighty created.

With my son Jimmy and Mademoiselle Moillen, her sister and sister-in-law in Les Diablerets – 1954.

I remember one day in March Jimmy was going up and down the nursery slopes with his sledge sliding on the snow. It was noon time and there was not a soul around us. Everything was covered with white powdery snow and the sun was shining. I was wearing a thick green sweater and was able to go on higher pistes. I took off my sweater and skied under the glistening sun with just a bra on. I did such daring things but then I was the only one there except my son.

We rented the chalet on an annual basis from then on as I spent a lot of time there. We were often invited by Tantine for dinner and at parties at the pension. On one such occasion I met John Wayne, the famous American cowboy actor. He was fascinated by me and we danced the whole evening. During one such dance he lifted me on his palm and the hall echoed with clapping. He was a six foot giant and I was small and frail looking. Mrs Conrad later told me that men went crazy about my eyes and smile, but I did not believe her. He wanted my address in Geneva but I did not encourage him. I was maturing. I was changing. I had become modernized. I acted just like a western lady. Yet the deeply-grounded faith in my Allah never left me. I always prayed if not five times at least four times a day and so did my husband. He kept all his fasts and read Qur'an during Ramadan. There were no mosques in Geneva then.

It is amazing how one can feel so close to God when one witnesses beautiful natural surroundings. I always loved the heights, the mountains and the lakes and felt at peace with myself. More than once I could feel the immense presence of Almighty God, the Ruler of this world and the universe and felt awe when alone in such places.

My brothers Misbah and Nayar visited me in Switzerland. Misbah came often from London to Switzerland and started hydroelectric plants. Both the brothers stayed in the hotels and not with me. Somehow they could not relate to my husband. Nayar also visited Les Diablerets on his way back from Baltimore to Pakistan. He was welcomed with a lot of affection by the Moillens. It was from Nayar that I heard for the first time the situation of the black population in the United States and how badly they were treated. There were separate schools in Baltimore for whites and blacks. The Mexicans, the Indians and the Blacks could not board the same bus that carried whites. According to the Americans, the black slaves had no soul. Nayar was very fair and blue-eyed so he did not meet any intolerance and was quite liked by his fellow Americans. My cousin Dr Manzoor Zaidi, the cancer research specialist, also came to Geneva and visited me. We had tea at the Jardin Anglais in the afternoon and he took many photographs of Jimmy.

I realized that not only I, but my whole family, could easily mix and mingle with people and could speak their languages flawlessly. We traveled and made friends with Europeans and other foreigners, easily. I personally could adapt to different ways of life without trouble, though at times I wondered if I had a personality of my own at all. Having spent so many years of my life in Switzerland, I became a mixture of East and West and took to the best from both.

Final years in Geneva

Jasmine was born on 24 June 1954 at Bois Gentil, the same lovely little clinic situated in the forest where my son was born. I felt terrible birth pains and it was not an easy delivery like the first time. I received a dozen lovely red roses from my husband. He named her Jasmine after Rita Hayworth's daughter and hastened to add Fatima, which was his mother's name. My husband loved his mother and had told me that she was a pious lady who had passed away in *sajda* during her *fajr* prayers.

Jasmine's room at Chemin Creek was fitted out with pine furniture. This time I was more experienced and confident and wanted to be a perfect mother. I tried desperately to breast feed Jasmine but developed milk fever and was down with very high temperature. Jasmine developed a rare skin condition for which I had to bathe her in starch water. She was fed on special milk called 'Guigot' that was a combination of milk mixed with carrots. The bottle's nipples had to be enlarged and she was to be fed slowly. As time went by, Jasmine became the favorite child of my husband, though of course he loved both his children dearly. She too was much attached to her father and would be upset when he had to return to work after coming home for lunch.

We bought our first brand new Grundig radiogram, the latest in those days as it had a record player, a tape recorder and a radio, all enclosed in a highly polished veneer. Everyone in Chemin Creek admired our radiogram. I remember taping a speech by Winston Churchill as I considered him a good orator.

By the time my son turned four and a half he was enrolled at École Bertrand, situated near the Park and quite close to Chemin Creek. I picked up Italian from our maid Gabriella as well as from Nona who lived below. Later I had an Austrian girl as a helper, who came with me to Les Diablerets too. She became very fond of my brother and managed to knit a beautiful pullover for him in five days. She learnt to cook Indian-Pakistani food. She was very loving. I was sorry to let her go. My Hindu friend and good neighbour Kishen was married to Prince Mohan Kaul, who represented India at the World Health Organisation and was related to Indira Gandhi. Kishen was a good neighbour and her fifth child, a daughter, was born at the same time as my daughter Jasmine, for whom she made a beautiful pink smock dress.

I began to notice that Sherif Sahib was not entirely happy at work, which perhaps explained his depression. His superiors included a Qadiani, Mr Choudhury Nasiruddin, and a Hindu Brahmin, Mr Rao, who, though also from Madras, harboured a grudge against Pakistan and Pakistanis. Moreover the director general of ILO, David Morse, was an ardent supporter of Israel. My husband could not mix and make friends easily with a lot of people. He was also quite open about his patriotic feelings for Pakistan and perhaps that did not go down well with his bosses. Things started to look grim.

Our trip to Pakistan in the autumn of 1954 was again on one of the luxury liners. I was not very happy on that voyage. The deep sea was frightening at times as the huge waves hit the sides of the vessel. I pondered over the fluctuating moods of my husband, but was unable to find an answer. In Karachi, arrangements were made by my sister-in-law Nusrat's father, Raisuddin Sahib, for us to stay at Baluch Mess near his residence. It was clean with large gardens. My daughter slept most comfortably in her white pram in the open lawns. I had adopted European clothes and spoke in French with my two children. Nobody in Baluch Mess thought that I could speak fluent Urdu or English and that I was not French.

In those days it was customary for a mother or a sister to look for a suitable bride for their sons and brothers. At times though, the brother would tell the sister of his choice and then the family would proceed to make contacts with the girl's family. Nayar was dashingly handsome and very popular. As we waited at Karachi airport for my return flight to Geneva I suggested that he consider our cousin Muhammadi as a bride. They were to wed the following year.

Sherif Sahib's contract at the ILO was terminated in 1956 and he was upset. He had purchased new furniture and flooded the house with silverware and crockery. I looked at the beautiful furniture and felt sad that all those things I ever wanted were there but now there was no job and no security. We would have to move to Pakistan or to some other place, not knowing what lay in store for us. Before leaving Geneva, Sherif Sahib showed me a few small houses to purchase there, but without a job, I did not feel it was the right decision. Both of us thought it best to save funds and move back to Pakistan as there could be better job prospects for him.

Our bags were packed. I took most of our clothing, but the rest of the luggage and all furniture had to be crated and shipped. Geneva was a cosmopolitan and elegant city with lovely gardens on the banks of Lake Leman. After many happy and memorable years, leaving it all behind was sad.

My husband drove us via Nice to Genoa to board the ocean liner and then returned to Geneva to fight his case for compensation. The Italian authorities did not believe that my Jimmy was six and

Jasmine two years old, because they appeared bigger and well-behaved for their age. I had to show their passports and birth certificates again before boarding the ship.

Once, during the voyage, Jasmine's finger got trapped in the heavy cabin door. Her screams brought my next door American neighbours Mr and Mrs Nicols running. They were also going to Karachi as Mr Nicols was assigned to work in an American oil company. He was very kind and lifted my daughter in his arms, while the wife brought some ice to be placed on Jasmine's fingers. We became good friends and dined together. I remember participating in a fancy dress party arranged by the Captain. I had a green *sari* which I wore as a skirt and took a brass flower pot from the salon and held it on my head as an Indian water carrier. I was awarded second prize with a lot of applause.

The good times on board soon came to an end. I had mixed feelings on the return journey. I quite enjoyed being away from my husband and was happy at the prospect of spending time with my family and friends. Although I was much concerned and worried for him too. He stayed behind a whole year and managed to get what he wanted, but never confided his inner feelings to me.

My Years in Pakistan

My brother Nayar picked me from Karachi port where the ship had docked and brought me home to his spacious Railway Officer's bungalow on Victoria Road near Frere Hall. There were tall coconut trees on the driveway and gardens with guava and plum trees. My mother, my aunts and cousins were very happy to see me and my two children. My old friend Irshad came regularly to see us and we spent hours together. He had put on weight and was in the Air Force, but had the same smile and jolly disposition. My eldest brother Inam had also come to Karachi and was serving as a flight lieutenant in the education section of the Air Force, based in Mauripur. Misbah was working as a factory manager in Landhi, where he lived with his wife Nusrat and first-born son, Imad. Islam continued his dedicated work in government service, also organising public health film shows in his small backyard in the evenings in Jacob Lines. My youngest brother Ameen was employed at the State Bank. I was happy to see my brothers' progress.

I soon received the Bill of Lading and the containers of our furniture and an Opel car arrived at the Kemari docks. Nayar and I spent a whole day at the docks to get the items released. We had to pay duty on the car even though it was slightly used but not on the other goods, which included several hundred packets of sugar cubes. My container was laden on to a cart pulled by a camel, which made its way to Victoria Road. Sugar was rationed in those days in Karachi and I was able to offer some to many relatives. Nayar's house filled

My brother Misbah –1950s.   My brother Nayar –1960s.

up with my radiogram, refrigerator, freezer and all the furniture. Everyone was happy. I received lovely cards for Jasmine from my husband. She missed her father too.

My first step was to find a good school for Jimmy and I made an appointment with Reverend Glazebrook, the principal of Karachi Grammar School. He scowled at my son's Swiss-style tunic trousers but admitted him under the name Jimmy Sherif. My son initially had difficulty as he was fluent in French and knew very little English, but he got on with his studies and was happy to be reunited with his desk and chair from Geneva. He was patient and calm in the circumstances. On one *shab-e-qadr* my mother took him to the Jacob Lines mosque where they offered prayers the whole night. The imam was Maulana Ihtishamul Haq Thanvi, famous for his *duas* and supplications. My brother Nayar took him to school daily in his old Citroen. Jimmy would be punctual and waiting on the *verandah* steps so that my brother did not even have to call him. These were some of his characteristics from childhood.

If I left Jasmine for a minute alone she would run to the servants' quarters to play with the sweeper's daughter, a chubby girl of the same age, and share her toys. Jasmine fell ill with whooping cough. I was worried and stayed up nights with her. It

Jimmy and Jasmine in Karachi, 1957.

lasted two months. One day the Railway Health Authority came to vaccinate the children for small pox. Jasmine had already been vaccinated in Switzerland. It so happened that she got vaccinated too while in the servants' quarters. I was very upset but nothing could be done. Jasmine became ill with vaccinaria and her whole body was covered with spots because of the double dose of vaccination. Thank Allah that children have a remarkable resilience and she recovered. I tried to provide my children the same standard in Karachi as their Swiss lifestyle. I used to take them for walks to Frere Hall in the afternoons and kept their timings for meals and sleep. Jimmy would be taken for horse riding in the plain open ground opposite Frere Hall, which later became the site of the US embassy. Sometimes he would go and play with his friend, the Chief Commissioner's son, who lived next to Frere Hall. He managed to learn English. I waited anxiously for my husband to return.

Working life

I needed to find work quickly to pay for Jasmine's special canned food, her special diet, Jimmy's school fees and the daily expenses.

One day, I went for a walk and noticed an Air France office outside the PIDC building, next to the Palace Hotel. I went in and enquired if they needed someone who spoke faultless French. The Air France manager was a Frenchman and I was hired on the spot.

I started to work at Karachi airport as a ground hostess. I had to go at odd hours and leave the children asleep, so at my request I was shifted to the head office.

Islam came to stay with his wife at Nayar's house. He had a minor heart attack and needed rest. He liked my radiogram and loved to listen to music. Nayar's wife Muhammadi was very lively. Nayar's colleague Mr Puri often came to visit us. We went for picnics in Puri's smashing Chevrolet that he had brought back from the US after his training. Soon we were joined at Victoria Road by my step-sister Shaukat, her husband and three children who migrated from Hyderabad Deccan as India invaded the Nizam's kingdom. My nephew Baba, Saud ul Haq, shared the bedroom with me and my two children. He had graduated from Hyderabad as an engineer.

One day Irshad's mother visited me and asked me to either stop seeing her son or get married to him. I hugged her and promised to distance myself. I was never physically attracted to him though I admired his wit and amazing memory. Next time Irshad visited us at Victoria Road, I went in front of him with Mr Puri in his Chevrolet. Irshad never came again. After a few months he married a lady named Surayya and was promoted squadron leader.

Inam was posted to the air force base in Risalpur. My mother visited him and took Jasmine with her. One day mother phoned to say that Jasmine had high fever and was very ill. I was frantic with worry and kept on praying for her health. I flew to Chaklala and brought her back. The flight encountered a storm and engine trouble, but Allah saved us. I feel that I have never thanked my Allah enough for He had been so merciful and kind to me in spite of all my failings.

All good times come to an end. Nayar's transfer orders to Rawalpindi had arrived and although he wished me to accompany him, I decided to stay back. I decided to sell things as my husband had suggested. He wanted me to sell everything and buy a house. I rented a place and postponed buying a house till he joined us, as I respected his judgment. Unfortunately that did not happen. I continued to work in Air France and rented a flat near *Lal Kothi* on Drigh Road, with an English couple, the Parkers, as neighbours. Jack Parker worked for British Petroleum.

Finally, after a year my husband arrived by ship. I went to pick him up with his brother Mr Tajuddin, who was a State Bank employee. He was very happy to see the children. I made him promise that he would not leave us again for such long periods. I wanted a child to strengthen our marriage ties and became pregnant. Neither my husband nor Air France wished me to leave my job. I was translating IATA rules from French into English. I decided not to continue. I was hoping that my husband would find employment but matters turned out differently. We were well-settled in our flat and my husband also became friends with Jack Parker. His daughter Linda was at Karachi Grammar School and he would drop Jimmy and her in the mornings on the way to work.

Throughout my pregnancy I was worried, as I had left my job and my husband was out of work. Bad times follow good times. These are the tests of endurance and it is amazing how one can cope. My husband wanted my mother to come and stay with us. I was happy to note that his attitude had changed towards her and he showed respect. The obstetrician Dr Zubeda Subhani told me that I had only fifty-fifty chance of a normal delivery as I was quite unwell. My mother kept praying for me all the time and was by me. My third child, a son, was a normal delivery. We named him Ajmal after the name of my childhood hero, Hakim Ajmal Khan of Delhi. I was lucky that I could breastfeed Ajmal and he grew into a healthy, cuddly baby. He had pink cheeks and curly hair. We had a Pathan from Parachinar near Hangu in the high mountains of NWFP

Ajmal with his elder brother, Karachi 1958.

(North West Frontier Province), who would come to clean our car and would take Ajmal in the pram to the park. His name was Khayal Akber. Each time Khayal Akber would return from his home in the mountains, he would bring us pure honey and walnuts from his land in Hangu. Pathans are well known for their hospitality and are fond of giving gifts, no matter how poor they may be.

My brother Islam adored Jimmy and presented him with an expensive air gun on his birthday. My son played 'cowboys and Indians' wearing a red hat and matching red leather frilled jacket. Later when his father returned to Pakistan, he too got Jimmy an air gun, so now he had two. One day Naima, a friend of mine, came with her son. Seeing the boy cry for a gun of his own, Jimmy gave away the one received as a gift from my brother. It was typical of my son to be generous even as a child. When my mother came to know of this she told me that Islam had purchased the gun on monthly installments as he was short of money. Such was the love of my brothers.

Once my mother awoke early and wanted to visit my brother Islam in Jacob Lines. She told me of the bad dream she had about him. She dreamt that she was in her mother's house in Delhi. The autumn leaves had covered the *verandah*; my brother Islam was lying in bed covered with a white sheet and the sheet itself was laden with autumn leaves. She dreamt moving Islam's bed in the corridor. I tried to reassure her, but she left that morning to go and see Islam. A month or so later, she left for Rawalpindi to visit Nayar.

After a few months, Islam's wife Fatima Sultan visited me and told me that Islam was in the hospital and was not very well. I went to see him in the hospital. He was very pale. I spoke to Akbar, who had recently passed his Medicine and worked at Jinnah Hospital. I was worried sick as none of my brothers were in Karachi. My dear brother Islam was in a general hospital and I did not have enough money to get a private specialist for him. The doctors told me that he had an enlarged heart. The hospital was ill-equipped, with hardly any medications and Islam was neglected.

Sherif Sahib had still not found a job. My mother arrived but Islam's condition deteriorated. My husband visited him at the hospital. He noticed that my brother was feeling cold so he covered him with his coat. He came home and said that after Islam it will be his turn to go. True enough after ten years later he also left this world. Islam passed away in February 1959. My mother spent the last day in the hospital with him. He kept on speaking to the angels and welcomed them in the ward, but would quietly tell mother that the doctor had not allowed so many people entry. In actual fact there was only mother and him in the hospital room. Did it imply that the angels had come to receive him? He passed away completely conscious.

I went to Jacob Lines and spent the night in agony. The house was full of relatives and well-wishers. I could not pray or read the Qur'an; I just sat in anguish. In the morning my mother came to me. She kissed me and told me to go home and have a bath and read Surah al-Baqara. I marveled at my mother's calm behaviour, her patience, her acceptance and her absolute trust in Allah the Almighty. My mother was a true *Muslima*. It is so hard to accept the loss of a young and handsome son but she faced it humbly. I was haughty and complained to my Allah. We human beings are so ungrateful that we forget that we all belong to Him and we are His property. He bestows and He alone can take it all away whenever He wishes. I have learnt so much from my mother at every step but even today I have not attained the qualities she possessed.

I recited Surah al-Baqara almost every night. I loved my brother and was angry with my other brothers, who did not or could not come early enough. I was angry with the doctors and I was angry with myself. Why did I not sell my jewelry and give the money for his treatment? Such regrets do not really help anyone. Gradually Surah al-Baqara helped and I managed to find peace within myself after six months. I started to take interest in life again, but even today I cannot blot out the painful memories of the loss of my handsome dear brother, always smiling, with a sparkle in his blue green eyes, always gentle and loving. I pray to Allah not to put me through such tests ever, *Ameen*.

My mother left for Hajj with my eldest brother and aunt. Nayar Bhai came back to Karachi and I went to stay with him for a few days as I was suffering from dysentery. I was given some tablets at the Seventh Day Adventist Hospital. This was a missionary hospital and Christians did not have to pay for treatment. My brother Nayar threw away the cortisone tablets I was given and I was fed on sago pudding and yoghurt. I recovered and returned home.

One night, thieves entered our flat through the balcony. We remained in a deep sleep, but at some point I woke up to see things scattered about. I tried to scream but my voice froze in the throat and I could not even call out to wake my husband. Both my husband and I felt quite scared and decided to move. Sherif Sahib met a Sindhi gentleman who offered us accommodation for rent in Sindhi Muslim Housing Society. He and his family occupied one of the flats and the rest were let out. The landlord, Mr Sittai, edited a Sindhi newspaper *Hurriat* and always wore a *shervani*. We were soon happily settled in a three-bedroom modern flat with a garden and a car porch. Sherif Sahib started to revisit Gymkhana Club and Sindh Club and would read the law books there or go to the Courts. He would also drop and pick Jimmy and Jasmine from school.

Ajmal fell ill with rheumatic fever when he was two and a half. We kept on giving him quinine, thinking it was malaria as Sherif Sahib did not want to go to a doctor. I was worried as Ajmal complained of pain in his left leg. Our neighbours were a caring and distinguished family from Allahabad and they sent for a doctor who was their relative. Ajmal's fever was diagnosed as rheumatic fever and I was told that he must have complete bed rest.

My husband was averse to meeting relatives. He did not even attend the wedding ceremony of his younger brother Ghaus Pasha and instead went to visit some American friends. We had started socialising with the Americans based in the Embassy in Karachi. The Americans had come to Pakistan under the AID programme's projects. An American lady began taking lessons in French from me and in 1962 offered me her job to teach the language in the American School in her place. The pay was good and I made a lot of American friends. One of my students, Steve, was a spoilt young boy. He used to write funny letters to me while pretending to sleep in class. His mother Barbara visited my home one day. She was worried the boy took drugs and requested me to give him private coaching. I did not mention his behaviour in my class as she was already distressed. When Steve discovered that I was a mother of three children with responsibilities, he improved tremendously in his studies and secured high marks in his French examination. His mother was very grateful. The American textbooks introduced me to the new teaching methodology and the importance of lesson plans. Material was well presented and could be easily understood by the students, and above all the teacher's guides that accompanied each book made teaching a lot easier and more interesting. These books were very different from the books used by the English system that had stayed unchanged for forty years.

We were now moving with the colonels and once the American Ambassador's wife also visited us. We were particularly close to Jean Thompson and her husband, who had been a marine. Thanks to them we benefited from the products available at the Embassy's commissariat stores. Jean and I became good friends and she started to wear *shalwar qamees*. She told me that it was her second marriage. Her first husband drank a lot and once broke her front teeth. Her second husband was a good and kind man, but was strict with his five year old son, Edward John. We used to go to Bunder Road's *Sarrafa Bazaar* to buy antique silver jewelry.

 Our landlord Mr Sittai did not like us to meet Americans. My husband needed to meet influential people in the hope of getting a job. He only obtained an assignment with the USAID for a two month period. Unfortunately he could not find a job of his choice.

As a family we often went for walks on Clifton beach. Once Jimmy fell ill with hepatitis. My husband said that there was no cure. In despair I phoned my cousin Ehsan, who was a homoeopath doctor. He came every day to treat him. The illness lasted several weeks and left Jimmy very weak. I did not have enough money to give him fruit juices. Our house had all the latest gadgets and furniture and friends thought that we had a lot of money. They did not know the truth. The litany of illnesses continued.

When Jimmy recovered, Ajmal and Jasmine succumbed to double pneumonia and measles. Our kindly neighbour's doctor again helped out, but this time he was very angry that I had not called him earlier. How could I tell him that we had no money and I was embarrassed to seek his help without payment? I could not bring myself to tell the doctor that my husband again insisted that it was just measles and there was no cure for it. The children were given antibiotics and luckily treated in time but both retained a weak chest even later on in life. Allah saved them. I accepted life as it came. I accepted every challenge and tried to conquer it. The will to be successful made me stronger and as my brother put it, I became a fighter.

In Karachi I had to contend with not only the children's sicknesses, but there was an ongoing fight too against cockroaches, mosquitoes and bed bugs, even in the well-to-do and clean locality of Sindhi Muslim Society. I used to go round closing all the sinks holes and placing phenol balls every night, but in spite of all the hygiene and care, cockroaches would be found everywhere. My cook was very clean. He was happy to work for us, as we had given him a nice living quarter and a table and chair so he could eat his food in comfort. He was happy to wear a white apron. We had learned to respect the labour class after seeing how the servants were treated in Switzerland and England.

Misbah was now the general manager of the Rohri Cement Works, the first non-Englishman to fill the post. My father was happy under the care of Misbah and his wife in Rohri. My brother often invited the children to spend their summer holidays in Rohri. I would sometimes join the children and my father was happy to see us. He liked to live in comfort, with servants hovering around him. He would dress up after the afternoon siesta in his suit and read the English press in the garden, occasionally testing the children's knowledge of difficult words. The spacious grounds had a swimming pool and numerous fruit orchards. My children's health improved there. Jimmy collected rare pieces of flint and stones. Misbah had opened a small hospital-cum-clinic for the factory employees and remained extremely busy. My sister-in-law Nusrat was an enterprising person. She initiated a ladies' club and other social welfare activities for the wives of the factory employees. The mayor of the nearby town of Sukkar invited her to advise on the establishment of a women's college. Our children were good friends. Nayar, the brilliant railway engineer, cared for my mother

Ameen and his wife Peggy – 1963.

and he and his wife Muhammadi also welcomed my children during their holidays in the various towns that they were posted in.

My youngest brother Ameen had completed his accountancy studies in England and was working in Goa. When Misbah visited Bombay on company business he was surprised to see Ameen's German visitor, Mechthild. They clearly liked each other and the marriage was solemnised in his presence.

My sister-in-law became better known to us as Peggy and she later visited Pakistan for the first time around 1963. Muhammadi and I fetched her from Karachi Port and took her shopping. We bought her some gold jewelry, according to our family custom of presenting such a gift to a new bride. She left by ship to Germany the same night. She had asthma and found it difficult to breathe in Karachi.

My husband asked me to accept the post of vice principal in Islamia School in Karachi, an educational establishment run by one Mr

Qureshi. My cousin Siraj ul Islam had studied and taught there too. I took up the job. My husband liked Mr Qureshi and trusted him. I resigned from American School and took charge of some three hundred students in Islamia Primary School. My teaching experience at the American School allowed me to introduce changes and soon the strength of the school grew to five hundred and I was given a free hand in the running of the school budget and management. I also maintained a good relationship with the American School. When they received their new course they let me have their old books. Islamia school teachers particularly loved the science books. My daughter, however, continued to attend the American School.

I was now thirty and realized that I had a complex personality. On the one hand I hated the strict *purdah* system of Delhi where the ladies covered their whole body and the face and then sat in a *doli* or *tonga*, that itself was enclosed within curtains all around with no air to breathe. On the other hand I also disliked seeing improperly dressed people in public places and did not really like to participate in dancing and drinking. Hence I developed into a rather confused person. I did not know whether I belonged to the East or to the West. At that time all I knew was that I was modern like other European ladies, yet at the same time a deeply grounded faith or *iman* and fear of Allah was always present in my heart.

We had to vacate the flat in Sindhi Muslim Society and found another one in Muhammad Ali Society. I hated the new flat because it absorbed the heat from a bakery's huge oven that was located underneath. I fell ill and lost a lot of weight as I could not tolerate the heat.

Faced with disappointments in Pakistan in establishing himself as a lawyer or obtaining other employment, Sherif Sahib was sure that if he went to America or to Canada his friends would help him get a job in the United Nations again. How mistaken he was! He also had the idea that Jimmy should be given a British public school education. Father and son both left for London in 1964, Jimmy having obtained a place at Wellington College near Reading, thanks to the recommendations of our friend in British Petroleum and my husband's former career in the British Indian army. Jimmy packed his prayer mat along with his collection of fossils and flint stones he had uncovered in the hills behind the Rohri cement works. When he left there seemed a void in my heart.

My husband did not want to sell the car before he left because he just could not face public transport or travel in a rickshaw. I learnt to cope alone as usual with two small children. I worked at various places and sold the car and the household goods to repay loans. Before leaving, my husband presented our favourite Swiss clock to Qureshi of Islamia College and made me promise to sell other items to him. My heart sank as I delivered all my nice bone china and many dinner sets to his house for a very meagre sum. I was not very wise in doing business or in haggling for the price. I learnt the value of money later on in life. I kept missing my son and the economic situation seemed dire. Sherif Sahib settled Jimmy at Wellington and found an English couple, Mr and Mrs Maidman to be his guardians. After staying in London for about six months, Sherif Sahib proceeded to the United States but kept drifting about.

I waited a whole year, finally disclosing my difficulties to my cousin Syed Athar Ali, who worked in BBC in London and was visiting Karachi. It was quite difficult for a young single mother to work and live respectably. Athar promised to help me and advised that I should leave immediately for the UK.

I borrowed money from Nayar to purchase air tickets. I packed my suitcases, along with my Singer sewing machine, and booked a KLM flight to London via Frankfurt, with my two younger children. Ameen's mother-in-law, Muti, had invited us to Germany, so I broke my journey in Frankfurt and she came to meet us at the airport and took us to her house. It was an hour's drive from the airport to her house in Ernsthausen, some 90 km away. Muti ran a small guest house and it was set amongst woods and fields. Her husband was a former army soldier who had been a prisoner of war during World War II. He raised chickens on their large plot of land and apart from Peggy, had two young and friendly girls, Ingrid and Juta. We became friendly very soon seeing their warm-heartedness and hospitality. Ingrid prepared a basket full of fruits and sandwiches for us to take to Frankfurt in case the plane got delayed. We happily and warmly said our good byes and boarded the plane for London on 29 May 1965.

It was my youngest son's birthday and the hostess made us celebrate the birthday, by bringing a cake and toys for Ajmal. In those days airlines took great care of their customers. The airport was brand new and London looked prosperous. I recalled what Heathrow was like in 1948 and the propeller planes. What a contrast!

London Life

When we arrived at Heathrow the passport officer subjected me to a grilling. He wished to know exactly what my plans were and how long I would stay in London. I could not provide any satisfying answers, except that my son was studying in a college and I also presented the bank account statement belonging to my husband that had been sent in to Immigration by the Maidmans. I was expecting to see my son's guardians Mr and Mrs. Maidman. Finally we came out and I was glad to see their smiling faces. They had been waiting patiently and drove me and the two children to their home in the countryside in Berkhamsted. They had a four-year old daughter called Marieatta. Luckily I had brought along with me silver spoons as drink mixers which I offered to them as a gift. Inga Maidman and I made flower arrangements together. I was much relieved that they made us welcome in their home as I did not have money to stay in a hotel. The next day I went to see Jimmy after school hours and was horrified to see his tiny dormitory room with a hard wooden desk. He did not say much and did not complain about anything either. Later on I came to know the students were not provided dinner but only tea in the evenings. The public school fees were high but the comforts appeared nil.

Help from relatives

I contacted my cousin Samiullah Khan and was invited to stay in their house. He arranged for another cousin, Mr Munzir Ahmed to collect us at Paddington station and escort us to their flat in Greencroft Gardens, Finchley Road, with all our bags and baggage. I thanked Allah that I was now among relatives. They gave me both comfort and hope. This mutual help and support are remarkable features of a Muslim family. I started my search for a job immediately as I only had one five pound note in my pocket. My cousin had informed me that there was a vacancy in the shipping department of the Pakistan Army Technical Liaison Office (PATLO) in Kensington. I applied and started to work straight away.

I attended the Speech Day at Wellington College in July 1965 with the Maidmans when Jimmy was awarded a form prize. I was introduced to the headmaster, Mr Stainforth, who praised my son and noted his love of the library. After his 'O' levels, Jimmy continued into the sixth form at Wellington. He did not disclose much to me but I came to know later that he spent a lonely time there. I noticed his hands full of chilblains. Maybe the dormitories were not heated but Jimmy never complained either of hunger or of cold.

My cousin Samiullah was expecting some friends from Germany so I felt I had to move out. Cousin Athar's friend, David Stride, who was the head of BBC Eastern Services, invited me to stay in his house as he had spare rooms in his house, perhaps as a result of a recent divorce. Ealing was a quiet suburb and we stayed with him for three weeks. Such was the cordiality and civility in those days.

Amongst my first tasks was to have Ajmal referred to the Great Ormond Street Children's Hospital in Holborn. He was kept under observation for a week and the doctors confirmed that his heart murmur was no longer present and all his other reports were also clear. It meant that he could run around and participate in swimming and other sports. I brought him home happily. My nephew Salam Ansari was selected for training at Sandhurst by the Pakistan Army, and he also came to visit me in Ealing. After a while I moved back to my cousin Samiullah Khan's flat as I was uncomfortable drawing on David Stride's kindness too long. I lived with my cousin, his wife and with his children for six weeks. Their house was always full of guests and relatives. People loved to come to their flat due to Bhabi's warm and jolly nature. They were very kind to me and asked me not to leave in a hurry but again I was embarrassed drawing on their hospitality. My cousin and his wife did not let me spend any money on food, nor did they accept even a small contribution towards expenses.

I had postponed finding schools for Ajmal and Jasmine, as my priority was to find a place to live. After six weeks in London, I had saved enough money from my job at PATLO and thanks to Cousin Athar Ali's help, assignments at the BBC Urdu service. I rented a flat in Mountfield Road in Golders Green. It was a top floor flat without any central heating.

I had made many friends at PATLO and lunched at Barkers on High Street Kensington with my Jamaican friend Marjorie Brown. An East Pakistani gentleman, Mr Choudhry, often invited me to tea during the breaks but there was another Bengali colleague who kept a distance. He was deeply influenced by communism and one day I found him secretly photocopying material on the office photocopier for a separatist movement.

Later on, a young family friend, Mubin, and his newly wedded wife shared the flat with us. Golders Green was a good locality with decent schools, but I decided to move to another flat on Essendine Road in Maida Vale that was more central. It looked sensible and warm and easier to commute to work, particularly since my workplace had shifted from Kensington to Lloyds Avenue in the city after PATLO's merger with another shipping organisation. Initially we shared the flat with an Indian gentleman but he moved out and we had the place to ourselves.

I received three letters from my father from Rohri. He was much concerned for me. I read his letters but did not reply, waiting for the moment when I could write from my own house address. He passed away on 16 December 1965. While I was in Air France in Karachi he had often expressed to me his wish to board an airplane, but unfortunately I was too preoccupied in those days to meet this request. He died with this wish unfulfilled. My mother wrote a long letter to me describing his last peaceful moments. She was with him in Rohri reciting *Surah Yasin*, with his head in her lap. He was a loving father who suffered deeply his children's deaths. After Asifa had gone he never again played the harmonium. I often feel remorse at the thought that I did not reply to his letters while he was still alive.

I hoped that Jasmine would be admitted to an all-girls' school next door, but the principal did not accept my daughter even though she had good recommendations. Later on I realized that this school was mainly run for Jewish girls. She started at a school off Harrow Road. Ajmal too was admitted in a nearby school. I was not at all satisfied with either of their schools.

We had our first winter in London. Jasmine and Ajmal lacked proper winter clothes. Our flat was heated by Paraffin heaters and we took the cans down to the street to be filled up by an Esso Blue tanker. My husband had stopped writing letters. This was a difficult period for my two younger children as the change of accommodation and schools had been stressful. However the Essendine Road flat was warm and often filled with visiting friends and relatives. These included my nephew Salam and his friends who were pilots in the Pakistan Air Force under training at Cranfield. Misbah's brother-in-law Nazir had come to study Chartered Accountancy and I invited him to come and stay in our flat. At weekends we used to go to Hampstead Heath and Jasmine and Ajmal loved to roll on green hills of the Heath on sunny days. We attended a parents' evening at Jasmine's school where she sang the Spanish song *Guajira Guantanamera*. I also had two Jewish friends in the neighbourhood, Sylvie Gellman, whose husband Derek drove a black cab, and Catherine Israel, who had a son Ajmal's age and they were friends.

Ajmal went to the same Jewish school as Catherine's son. Unfortunately the school did nothing for him. He obtained 33 merits but I did not see any improvement. He was unhappy and I did not realize it. He developed a habit of fidgeting his neck and was quite a nervous child. Unfortunately, I could not teach him though I realized that he needed help in studies.

After PATLO's offices at Lloyds Avenue closed I sought work in Olympic Airways and then Air Lebon. My duty was four nights at Heathrow and three days at the head office. Both the jobs were short-lived. I did not like brewing black coffee with cardamoms for the director and his guests.

I had heard about the introduction of computers and looked for opportunities to work in this field. I applied to the Bank of England and after a delay of nearly four months I was offered a post in early 1967. My immediate boss was Miss Kay, a very kind and gentle lady from Scotland. The work initially was easy as we checked the printed cheques and postals for the gilt shareholders.

June 1967 was a sad month as Israel launched a six day war and East Jerusalem was conquered by General Moshe Dayan. Many Palestinian homes were bulldozed and new settlements initiated for Jewish 'settlers'. One day I met two Palestinian ladies, Zahra and Laila, at the Regent's Lodge mosque at Baker Street, who told me about their bulldozed houses. The orange groves and farms of Jaffa oranges were taken away from Palestinians. They were thrown out and now seeking refuge in London. After the encounter with these two ladies I kept watching the news on TV of Israeli expansion and aggression.

By the summer of 1967, Jimmy had finished his studies at Wellington and was with me in London. He accompanied Jasmine for her interview at the all-girls Sarah Siddons School on Edgware Road. He later started work in the research laboratory of Ever Ready Batteries and decided to study Industrial Chemistry at university. My mother soon made her first journey to London and stayed with us for six months. My daughter Jasmine was greatly influenced by her puritanical nature and refused to wear the short skirts prescribed in the school uniform. The considerate headmistress allowed her to wear matching school colour trousers under her skirt, which I sewed at home, and a matching small scarf to cover her hair. Jasmine would ask me to write letters of sickness on swimming lesson days because she told me that the pool was shared with a boys' school and she did not feel comfortable due to the bad behaviour. She had difficulties focusing on the blackboard and was prescribed spectacles, though the NHS frames were not to her liking. I also organized orthodontic treatment to straighten her teeth that took several months and was uncomfortable for her. I insisted that Ajmal too had a similar treatment for his crooked teeth. Their initial treatment was with the Polish dentist at the corner of Elgin Avenue near Maida Vale tube station. I was often unable to take them for the appointments and my caring cousin Munzir bhai would help me out. The dental practice was later taken over by Dr Abdullah Hoosen, a young dental surgeon from South Africa. He and his wife Ruqaya were to be my life-long friends.

One day, a lady who had been visiting Sarah Siddons School accompanied Jasmine home. This was Rabia Naseef from Jeddah, who was planning to open girls' schools in Saudi Arabia. After spotting Jasmine in a headscarf, she wished to know more about her and her family. She told me that I should be proud of my daughter. In later years I was to meet her and her distinguished son again.

An opportunity arose for me to travel to the United States on a special friendship flight that was organised for staff at the Bank of England. It was on a chartered flight and the fare was low, and I was also desperate to find out my husband's situation in Canada. I flew to New York in September 1967 with my British colleagues. Everybody was invited to the cabin crew by the American steward but he turned to me arrogantly and said, "You don't come to the cockpit since you are not one of us". I was upset by this discrimination. Even my friend Jean Brown, who sat next to me, was equally shocked at that rude behaviour. This was the first time I realized that if I wore a different dress I could be segregated and discriminated, but as long as I wore European dress and looked and behaved like them, I was accepted.

On arrival I went to the Grand Central Station. It was nighttime and to avoid incurring hotel expenses I decided to keep awake inside this huge station. Luckily all the shops and restaurants stayed open. I found it unusual to find a place still bustling at all hours of the night. At six in the morning I went to the Greyhound Coach station. The hall was huge and the counters for coaches were open. As I stepped into the big hall, I noticed that the two Mounties picked up a black gentleman and threw him along the floor of the polished hall. The man was small and well groomed. I came to the counter and asked for a ticket to Montreal. I put the money and ticket in my purse and saw the same gentleman give a twenty dollar bill to the two Mounties and then he came to purchase his ticket. I was taken aback seeing the helplessness and the plight of black people. The man was humiliated yet he paid a bribe to purchase the ticket for wherever he was going. The thought flashed through my mind that this was still the same America which my brother Nayar had described to me a decade earlier.

I bought milk at Grand Central station and drank it only to realize that it had gone stale. I was sick for a day. On reaching Montreal I changed the bus for Patawawa, where my late brother Islam's brother-in-law worked at a nuclear plant. I spent a night there with him and his young family. They wanted to drop me at Kingston where my husband was living at the time, having found a job in Kingston Penitentiary. I refused their kind offer as I was not sure of my husband's response. I had the address of his house and was carrying a brief case labeled 'Bank of England'. This was a good advertisement, as wherever I went in Canada, it prompted smiles. At the time Canadians did not seem to disapprove of Asian dress styles such as the *sari*.

I had yet to reach my destination when an English girl greeted me with a 'hello'. I was happy to see her. She was very friendly and told me to walk along with her as she lived in the same neighbourhood as my husband. We became good friends very soon. She told me that she had left her four children and husband after falling in love with a Canadian man. She missed her children and her ex-husband did not agree to give her their custody. She was from a prosperous background and her children were looked after by a nanny. Her present husband was a learned professor of Canadian history and anthropology, conducting research on native Indians. Later we were invited to their home. He told us about the indigenous people and their enslavement by the English and French settlers to build roads and highways and that many were drowned in Patawawa Lake when the work was completed. I was horrified to hear these tales of cruelty. He also showed us some pieces of native Indian pottery and jewelry recovered from the Lake. He was sure that there were many other sites like this and was determined to carry out his research.

I liked the little town of Kingston, surrounded by the hills of Quebec. My husband bought some clothes and bow ties for Ajmal, while I kept thinking of the pros and cons of settling down in Canada. I could not really live with three children in the little uncomfortable flat. I had a good and stable job at the Bank of England, whereas my husband was still struggling to get decent employment. I kept these feelings to myself as I did not wish to discourage him. I did not think he enjoyed working with the criminals in the Kingston Penitentiary. I suggested to him to come to England and stay with the family, since I had a job, a flat in Maida Vale and the children were settled in their schools. He did not commit.

My husband wanted me to visit Niagara Falls before I left for the United States. He wished to accompany me but could not as he had to go to work. My English friend volunteered immediately to drive me to Niagara Falls. On the way I promised her that I would definitely see her children in England, but unfortunately I found that they had moved from the address I was given. Once in

New York I had a day to spare before the return flight. Catherine Israel had given me a friend's phone and I decided to contact the gentleman. A small man with an arm in a muslin sling came to fetch me from the Greyhound coach station and showed me the sights: the UN building, the huge skyscrapers, the boat ride to Manhattan Island, witnessing the shining Statue of Liberty in the golden sunlight. In the evening we went to a kosher restaurant where many bearded people eyed me with curiosity. It was hot in New York and the ceiling fans were churning away while we ate our meal which tasted different. I spent the night in his flat and headed the next day to the airport to catch the flight back. My friend Jean Brown handed me two large whisky bottles to take through Customs for her as she already had purchased her share of duty-free liquor.

I was happy working at the Bank of England even though my job was not stimulating at all. I waited for the day when I could be trained in computers, but the call never came.

My brother Ameen and his wife Peggy came from Goa. Later they settled in Kuwait but travelled to London and Germany regularly. My brother Misbah was now an international cement consultant based in Jeddah and often came to Switzerland on business. He always made it a point to stop in London. The children loved the Swiss chocolates and confectionary. My cousin Muzaffar Zaidi's wife Nasreen stayed with us while attending a floral course organized by Moyses Stevens. She became an expert in Ikebana flower arrangements and an excellent piano player. My Uncle Syed Asghar Ali's daughter Naheed was an air hostess and often stayed with us. She later settled in the United States and married an American professor. My cousins Dr Akbar and his wife Qudsia, whom we all called 'Baigma', were frequent visitors from Pakistan. Baigma became a renowned figure and won many international prizes in floral displays. Among other visitors was my dear cousin Syed Mazhar Ali, Baigma's brother, who was a leading civil engineer in Karachi. I was happy with lots of friends and family around me.

In the park near our flat in Maida Vale – 1967.

There were Indian and Pakistani films screened on the weekend in a hall in Haymarket in Piccadilly, to which we went occasionally. Sometimes we walked from Marble Arch to Maida Vale after missing the bus at midnight. There was not much street crime in those days and one could even walk in Hampstead Heath at night without any fear. There were trips to the Serpentine and the Heath.

From around January 1968 I began to meet more of Jimmy's friends involved in Muslim student activities, such as the publication of *The Muslim* magazine. One particular friend with a charismatic personality was Tariq Solaija, on a scholarship from Pakistan to work on his doctorate. He was extremely intelligent and religious and had a warm and loving nature. Tariq kindled the dormant faith within my soul. Among other friends in this circle of young Muslims was AbdulWahid Hamid from Trinidad, Ebrahimsa Muhammad from Penang, Hanifa Razik from Ceylon and Mr Hashir Faruqi who conducted entomological research but later left this to launch the *Impact* news magazine. My son was active in organising a study circle at Malaysia Hall in Bryanston Square, and also the Saturday evening meetings of the London Islamic Circle at the Baker Street mosque. I felt happy to be accepted by the students and benefitted from their company.

Ajmal had a love for animals. Once I noticed that we were unexpectedly running short of milk. My daughter then told me that there was an injured dog in the basement being nursed by him! Ajmal's kindliness was also apparent in the way he cared for an elderly neighbour on the ground floor, a Mr Mills who was losing his eyesight. Nine-year old Ajmal would hold his hand and take him out.

Jasmine was a strong-willed girl who practiced her religion resolutely. Her other Muslim friends joked about the way she dressed and that she prayed in the school during her lunch break, but she remained steadfast. In one of her History assignments on the Ottoman Empire she took great care and referred to the books of Thomas Arnold. The teacher responded by crossing out whole pages with red ink and told Jasmine in an angry tone that the Turks were cutthroats and she should only write what was taught in the class room. Jasmine had a tough time in those days but she too, like Jimmy, found good friends within the Islamic circles and gained confidence working on the *Zenith* magazine with Ziauddin Sardar.

One day around May 1968, when I arrived from work, I was surprised to see my husband sitting in the drawing room. He had come suddenly without informing anyone. My younger son called him 'uncle' but then corrected himself after seeing the sad look on his Papa's face. The children had not seen him for four years and they remarked how his hair had turned silvery white. We were all pleased to see him. I had kept all his suits that I had brought from Karachi, but they were all too warm for London at that time.

While Sherif Sahib was in London we visited the mosque at Baker Street together. Begum Daultana invited us for an *Eid* function and there were about twenty ladies present. I met an English Muslim called Peggy, who was married to an Egyptian-Palestinian school teacher, Mr Arafat. My husband and I were invited to their house in Alperton. There I noticed a young Tunisian youth reciting Qur'an in their house. This was Tijani, who later became a learned sheikh and talented teacher in his own right. We were also invited by my friends Sylvie and Derek for tea. I was happy to be with my husband and hoped that this time he would stay in London, meet people and get a job.

My husband brought a *non-zabih* chicken which I cooked but did not eat. He was very angry but his mood soon changed. He bought me a lovely yellow coat and a hat for Jasmine. My husband did not like Paraffin heaters. One night he had a terrible nightmare and shouted 'fire, fire' in his sleep. The next day he asked me to remove all the heaters. The weather was changing for the better so it did not matter. I noticed that after the dream he became rather quiet. I was however happy to see that he had listened to me and

With my husband when he visited London – 1968.

applied for a job as a teacher and was called for an interview on 12
July 1968. Over the week-end he seemed depressed. While I was
cooking a Sunday lunch he came to tell me that he was leaving as
he thought that the children and I were quite happy and content
without him. I could not understand what he meant. He picked up
his suitcase and left. I was still at the cooker wearing an apron so I
asked Jimmy to go and stop him. By that time a taxi had arrived and
Jimmy accompanied him to the Red Sea Hotel on Edgware Road. I
was in a state of shock at his sudden decision. He looked so nice in
the pink shirt and the navy blue suit which we had bought together
for his coming interview. I was angry as I could not understand his

logic. His handsome face still lingers in my memory. That was our last meeting.

Life carried on. I noticed that my friend Rebecca did not want us to meet on Friday evenings. One Friday evening I went to see her. She was sitting in the dark and I asked her the reason. She replied rather hesitantly that the electricity was not working. I offered to mend the fuse or change the bulb but she said that I ought not to worry as her husband David would soon be coming to attend to it. It was only later she told me many things about the Jewish faith and their strict observations during Sabbath, which included not switching on electricity or socializing. She also wore a wig to conform to the Jewish requirement that women should not expose their hair. Many Jewish ladies also wore scarves or hats or adopted the short hair styles of Vidal Sassoon that permitted them to look pretty without being conspicuous. I was happily surprised to notice that the two religions had almost exactly the same divine laws. Rebecca, Catherine and Sylvie were my Jewish friends and I will always remember them with fondness.

One of my daughter's close friends was Shamila Harun, daughter of the chief imam in Cape Town, South Africa. Her father was imprisoned by the South African apartheid government after he delivered a *jumma khutba* declaring that in Islam everyone was equal regardless of colour or race. Imam Harun was tortured and his wife was only able to see him in prison after four months. He managed to smuggle out a note saying, 'If you hear that I have died in prison by accident, you will know that it will not have been an accident'. One evening in July 1969, Shamila arrived in a bad state to our Maida Vale flat and told us with tears flowing that her father was tortured to death in the Cape Town prison. She was only seventeen years of age and frantic with grief. I held her tight in my arms and kept her with me that night. She was awake the whole night, angry and frustrated. I tried to console her and hugged her. Later on the newspapers described the event and a special service was held in St. Paul's Cathedral for Imam Abdullah Harun.

Fatima Bugaighis, a Libyan doctor was another of Jasmine's friends. She adhered to Islam totally. Fatima sometimes stayed with us at weekends. She came one day to say goodbye as she was going to be married and took a flight from London to Libya. That plane unfortunately was shot down by Israel and she perished in the crash. Jasmine and the rest of us were very sad for days.

One day out of the blue I received two letters from my husband asking us to come to Montreal as he had received letters from the Canadian Department of Immigration and Manpower granting me and the children permanent residence status along with the facility to ship our luggage from London. The immigration papers kept staring at me. I tendered my resignation to the Bank of England but later decided against it and withdrew it. I did not have the handy cash at hand to purchase the tickets even if I uprooted my children from their schooling and disrupted Jimmy's plans for university.

I took Jasmine for a ski holiday in January 1969 because I felt that mother and daughter should get closer to each other. After a gap of twelve years I rang the bell of Mademoiselle Moillen's *pension* in Les Diablerets. They were happily surprised to see us at their doorstep. Mademoiselle Moillen had sold her inn and moved to a chalet close to the one we used to rent in the past for our ski holidays. I wanted to rent a room but she insisted that I stay with her. When the time came to say goodbye, I insisted she accept my gold ring that she had admired. Jasmine became more relaxed with me and the gap between us narrowed. We had a good time and enjoyed skiing down the slopes of Les Diablerets. I had an instinct in Geneva to call my husband, while Jasmine and I walked by the lake side. I remembered our early days as a newly wedded couple. I twice went near the telephone booth but my pride kept me away and I did not make the call. Little did I know that I had missed the opportunity for which I would regret the rest of my life. Jasmine and I walked on the quay and I showed her from a distance the United Nations Building where her father had worked.

It was the last day of February 1969. I had taken the photos of our ski holiday to show to colleagues at the Bank. I returned home and to celebrate my homecoming we all went to see the film 'Frozen Submarine'. We did not get the earlier ticket so we waited for the late show. Jimmy had not come with us and when we came home in the late hours he was up and praying quietly in the drawing room. We were all astonished to see him praying at such a late hour and we kept joking. He completed his prayers and broke the news very gently that his Papa had died in a fire and he had received a call from my husband's brother Ghaus Pasha. I then frantically tried my husband's phone but there was no answer. I then phoned Ghaus Pasha who told me more of the circumstances. He himself had not been living with my husband and had heard the news on the radio that a building on Stanley Street near YMCA in downtown Montreal had caught fire, and a man's body found by the firemen had been taken to the mortuary. Pasha went to identify the body and found his brother there. Jimmy had been cautious in breaking the news. For a moment I went hysterical and did not know whether to laugh or cry, but then slowly accepted the fact that he was gone. Pasha told me that Sherif Sahib died from asphyxiation. Only his index finger was burnt. The flat was sealed so my brother-in-law could not examine it. There was a French-Canadian caretaker who perhaps acquired his gold watch which was always on his wrist and whatever cash he had. Nothing else except some old furniture was retrieved.

I was in turmoil. I did not know whether I should leave the children and go to Canada to attend his funeral, but somehow I could not make myself go. Every time I decided to go and went to book my seat my legs gave in and I felt numb. I kept on thinking that it was of no use going now, as the person was gone and I will not be able to see him again. I felt guilty that I had not responded when he called me. I should not have been angry with him for leaving me and the children alone for five and a half years. The thoughts kept coming to me that perhaps I could have saved him if I was with him when the fire broke out as I was a very light sleeper and he always used to have deep and sound sleep the minute he hit the pillow.

The sadness and the turmoil kept me awake many a night and it was only reading the Qur'an that healed the sadness. Sorrow makes one human. With humility, I returned to my God to seek *tauba* and forgiveness. The time once gone does not come back and we all learn from our mistakes, alas sometimes too late. Even now it has been difficult to write about his death although some forty years have passed. When the grief lessened, I tried to get hold of the money which I knew was still held in a Swiss bank. I also knew from the old cheques I received by post that my husband had transferred a sum of £10,000 from the Midland Bank to the Royal Bank of Canada before his departure. I provided an affidavit to the Bank's solicitors Freshfields as a result of which £2,000 was released from his Swiss bank account and distributed among my three children. The remaining assets were not retrieved, including the ten thousand pounds that he had transferred to Canada. I was most dissatisfied with Freshfields, to whom I had paid £200. God only knows where that money went. At that time the loss of my husband mattered more than the money. Ghaus Pasha did not contact me for a long time after my husband's death. Then suddenly he started to phone me and the old relationship was restored. After many years I went to see him in Canada and was able to visit my husband's graveyard in the small town of Farnham, Quebec.

My mother came to London from Karachi to stay with me a few months after my husband's death. She desperately wanted me to become more religious. Once a week we went to Hussein bhai's house near Drummond Street, Euston, for a ladies' Tablighi Jamaat *ijtima*. He kindly used to come and pick us up in his car. My mother would give the talk and we used to pray for peace for the *ummah*. Rashid Ahmad Siddiqui of the UK Islamic Mission would also take my mother to deliver lectures. He was an ardent disciple of Maulana Maududi. My mother became close to his wife Ayesha who visited us quite often. Dr Nazir Ally JP from Guyana also came regularly to take my mother to give talks to ladies in Walthamstow.

I had started to teach French in the evenings at Holborn Polytechnic and also decided to pursue further studies. I had an immense amount of strength and could work at two jobs without getting tired. I sat for a banking exam and passed. I was transferred to a new department at the Bank of England but was not given a chance to work in computing because I had crossed the age of thirty and my grade was that of a 'supplementary'.

Among the friends of that period was Zulekha Bibi who had come from Rangoon. She was an adorable person with green eyes and a sad story behind her. Her first husband left her for an English lady after a son Ameen was born. She married again but the second husband also left her for another woman. The son from the English wife was called Tinker, and he loved Zulekha. Eventually she and Ameen were able to leave Rangoon for London as a result of Tinker's efforts. Muslims were tortured under the military regime in Burma and many people were forced to flee. I used to react adversely to my mother's strong religious beliefs but Zulekha's approach was more practical and it appealed to me. In those days there were not many places where the Muslims burial arrangements could be made and she showed me how to bath and wrap the body.

Alistair Duncan and his wife visited us in Essendine Road. He presented me his book 'The Noble Sanctuary'. They loved Jerusalem and were distressed by the Israeli occupation. They had a premonition that *Baitul Maqdis* with its golden dome and all old Muslim historical buildings would be bulldozed and disappear and hence the importance of a photographic record.

My first supervisors at the Bank, Miss Kay and Mr Caldwell, were kind and never treated me differently. They always passed complimentary remarks whenever I wore a *sari*. The situation changed under Miss Jackson, who ridiculed this mode of dress and referred to them as 'curtains'. She wanted to see me dressed in

European clothes all the time. I was the only Muslim in the bank and called 'coloured'. While serving in the Bank I came to know of an English girl who experienced discrimination because she had married a Cypriot. I was not happy at work. The figures bored me to death and the work was tedious. One worked like a robot and there was no chance to use one's imagination or creativity. I managed to plod along as the Bank provided financial security. There were a few good friends who encouraged me to join the Royal Horticultural Society and to participate in the Bank's annual flower show, in which I managed to win a few prizes. Once I took part in a Bank's function and met Lord Balfour, the Chief Accountant, who later brought some herbal plants for me from his garden. He told me that he and his parents loved India. In the back of my mind I could not help thinking of the Balfour Declaration.

The Bank of England offered employees loans for purchasing houses and this enabled me to move to a semi-detached property near Dollis Hill. Normanby Road was relatively far from the Baker Street mosque and our other favourite places like Hampstead Heath, but then every place has its own charm. We had a lovely little garden in our own little house with exotic shrubs and fruit trees. I had central heating installed by one Mr Spence. He also became a good friend and as soon as I opened the door for him he would say, "Put the kettle on". Owning my own house gave me comfort and happiness. By this time Jimmy had started his Industrial Chemistry training which involved commuting to places like Slough and Egham. Ajmal was now at the Quentin Kynaston School near Swiss Cottage. The summer of 1969 was memorable because we were glued to the TV following Neil Armstrong's moon walk. My family has always been interested in scientific developments and admired technological progress.

My late husband's friend Mr A. K. Brohi always kept in touch with me and each time he came to England he would call on us. He once invited me to the Savoy Hotel where he was staying and I was introduced to Aziz Baluch. This Sindhi gentleman had a doctorate in Music from Munich and was quite well known for his research linking the origins of flamenco to the *kafi* music found in Sindh. I was presented with his book and vinyl record. He played the guitar for us in the hotel. Later on I went to see him a few times. He was living in absolute poverty in a flat in Notting Hill Gate. He had no family and died there alone.

In the summer of 1971 my brother Nayar's youngest daughter was taken ill with a kidney problem. She was brought to London from Dharan for treatment. I was hoping that she would get cured here but alas, the thirteen year old's condition worsened. My cousin Samiullah Khan saw the child at his daughter Farida's house in Dollis Hill and told me that she was very ill. He was a homeopath and practiced it as a hobby after retirement from the Pakistan High Commission. I had to take leave from my work because Uzma could not be left unattended. My department head Miss Jackson hated me for some reason and was quite unsympathetic. Uzma went into a coma. The doctors had given her blood transfusion which her ailing kidneys could not bear. Her parents also arrived and she was transferred to Hammersmith Hospital. While at work, rumour spread that people like me take the advantage of free medical treatment available in London. When I heard this I was furious and told my friend Teresa that my brother has been paying for her daughter's treatment as a private patient. One nurse loved Uzma very much and she cried for her as perhaps she knew the outcome before us. At Uzma's death I realized that she was as dear to me as my own children and the grief I felt for her was immense. I had prayed desperately to Allah to save her but her time was up. Kidney transplants were rare in those days. Dr Nazir Ally and his dear wife Zubeda made all the necessary arrangements for Uzma's burial in Chingford cemetery. They themselves had also lost a girl of five years of age.

Air travel became more affordable and there was greater prosperity. My brothers and their wives travelled via London fairly frequently. I was smoking then and would also get cigarettes from my brothers from duty-free even though none of them smoked themselves. They were broad-minded and never criticized me. We often had visits from brother Ameen's sister-in-laws in Germany, Ingrid and Juta. Ameen had purchased a hotel in Germany in Rhoda and called it 'House Jasmeen' after one of his daughters. Peggy's mother ran the hotel with a good number of staff. We made many German friends. Ingrid was full of fun and life. My niece Habiba from Pakistan also worked for a while at Rhoda and visited me briefly in London

I took my youngest son Ajmal a couple of times by car to Rhoda for his holidays. On one occasion we were driving back in our VW with a load of German juice bottles that were rattling away at the back. While engrossed in map reading, rather than watching the road, our car found its way off the newly built autobahn into a muddy ditch two metres below, stopping with a thud in front of an electric pole. There were no road signs around and no one else in sight. There was no use arguing amongst ourselves so we sat in silence. Then Ajmal spoke up: "Mum, you always recite *salat ul hajat* when you need God's help, so why don't you pray now?" At this timely reminder I quickly said two *nafil* prayers seeking Allah's help. Lo and behold, within a short while four tall and hefty men appeared walking in our direction. They smiled at us and in a jiffy lifted the car up and placed it on the road as if it was a toy. I opened the window and offered them a bar of chocolates in appreciation. They did not say anything but smiled again and disappeared in the wilderness without accepting the chocolates. We tried to spot them while driving along, but there was no sign. To this day I wonder who they were and where they had come from!

Life was thus never boring as we always had a lot of friends and relatives stay with us. Our new friends included Rachid Benaïssa, whom Jimmy had met during his travels in Algeria after graduation in the summer of 1972. We were introduced to Berber dishes and came to know a little about the life in the Kabbyle. We learnt much from him about the Algerian war of independence and the heavy price that had been paid in peoples' lives – fifty-two members of his family alone. He was also bitter at the turn of events in his country after independence and later took up a job in UNESCO based in Paris.

The changes within me continued. I started to teach Qur'an on Sundays above a butcher's shop in Willesden and later at a Sunday school that was established in nearby Pound Lane. The weekend teaching program was launched by Mr Ashraf Ali of Regent's Park mosque. Unfortunately this dynamic gentleman from Trinidad died young. I also attended meetings of the Muslim Women's Association (MWA) at Regent's Park. Among the active members were Begum Jan, an English convert, Nisa Ashraf Ali, Leila El-Droubie and Samina Hassan Farooqi. I was made the head of religious affairs. Samina was Swiss and an artist. Her husband Sultan Farooqi was a fine poet and friend of my brother Ameen. Leila and Samina produced the monthly magazine of MWA containing lectures, recipes, youth articles and reports of activities. Funds were collected by organising bazaars and other events. Mrs. Hassan became our president and her dedication and hard work made the Association grow. Alas, she is no more with us as I am typing my book.

My brother Ameen was always generous and kind. Without any fuss he sent me £4000 so I could pay the mortgage off for the Normanby Road house. I also had the money from Switzerland and so this combination cleared my debts to the Bank. I have been a very lucky sister as all my brothers love me and always try to please me. I cannot thank God Almighty enough for all His bounties He bestowed on me. Strong family ties are a big support and a blessing. I admired some aspects of my culture. Jasmine too made many friends and used to bring home interesting people. One day a blonde young lady, Nazli Aly, accompanied her home. She had come from Helsinki and told us that her grandfather was a minx hunter. He had fled from Communist Russia and walked on foot to Finland. The Finns had given asylum to many Russian Muslims at the time. They raised minx and worked in the fur business. A few years later, inspired by Nazli's life, I wrote a story in Urdu entitled *Firar* or 'Escape' which was published in a London Urdu society's collection.

Jasmine received a couple of marriage proposals. She really did not want to get married. I should have encouraged her to study but I was not sure as Jasmine did not disclose exactly what she wanted. When a proposal came from my nephew Salam, now a Major in the Pakistan army, my mother insisted and Jasmine and I gave in. The trousseau, clothes and silver that I had collected for her were sent to Pakistan through our friend Ahmed Hassan Qadri, who was a pilot in the Pakistan International Airlines. My brother Misbah and Nusrat took care of all the wedding preparations and organization that took place in their luxurious house in Wah. I learnt that ever since my husband had died the two had been saving money separately for Jasmine's wedding. Jasmine and I had come to Pakistan after a gap of eight and a half years. Jasmine did not know Urdu well and spoke perfect English. None of her brothers could come and she was feeling lonely but never disclosed her feelings to me. My brother Nayar and his wife came from Dharan to attend the wedding ceremony.

The entire bungalow in Wah was illuminated for a week. Marquees were erected and the carpets were laid out on the green lawns. Coal fireplaces were placed in between guests' tables and a five course meal was served. Jasmine looked beautiful but could not comprehend the sense of the various rituals, such as the groom's sisters demanding money from their brother. My brother Inam's house in Harley Street in Rawalpindi was also lit up for the wedding. A reception was organised by Salam and his father at Pearl Continental Hotel in Islamabad. The young couple left for Murree Hills to celebrate their honeymoon. I was missing Jasmine so my brother and his wife took me to Murree to give them a surprise visit. The hills were covered with snow and I was happy to see my daughter happy.

Parting from children can be very painful. Salam was posted in Lahore and that is where Jasmine moved to. I felt very lonely wandering in Misbah's huge gardens and seeing the carpets being moved after the marriage ceremony. I flew to Lahore after a week to see how they had settled. She received me at the airport and looked stunning in an apricot dress and holding flowers of the same colour. I stayed with her for a few days to help in the unpacking of their gifts and presents. Seeing that she was happy, I left for London.

I began to face further hostilities at the Bank. The word had spread that I was a Muslim. Even though I was given the responsibilities of an assistant superintendent for a very short period it was not recognized in my job title. I was told that I was a supplementary and should not worry as my pay was not affected. Teaching French at Holborn Polytechnic and working in the BBC's Urdu Section were good outlets for me.

My first grandchild Omar was born in January 1973 at St. Mary's Hospital in Paddington, when I was forty-one years old. Salam was not with Jasmine and she coped alone with the delivery while I was at work. Baby Omar had colitis and used to vomit all the feeds. Doctors had said that an operation could cure the problem, but on the other hand, the baby would get better in four months. I was always wary of operations so both Jasmine and I nursed Omar patiently and waited. Meanwhile Jasmine had developed severe pain in her leg and could not walk properly for nearly two months. Luckily my mother was there to help us.

One Miss Holyman was particularly hostile during my stay in the Bank. She called me to her office one day and told me that I was lying about my children's ages and even doubted me when on another occasion I asked permission to leave the Bank a little earlier to attend the convocation ceremony at which Jimmy was awarded an MSc. That was a big day for me. He introduced me to his tutors, who spoke of him with admiration. I wanted a photograph of him wearing the gown but he characteristically avoided it. However there were other good friends at the Bank like Teresa, Betty and Ruby.

The house in Normanby Road was getting smaller for our needs with my two sons and mother staying with me and also Jasmine and her baby on occasional visits. I started looking for a bigger house. The main advantage of employment at the Bank for me was the opportunity to obtain a mortgage for house purchase at minimum interest. I also had taken out a few saving schemes that were maturing. Jimmy had started work in International Computers Limited and purchased Normanby Road from me. I then began house-hunting and my preference was Willesden Green and the Mapesbury estate, but this could not be touched by a so-called 'coloured person'. The estate agents would simply refuse to show me any houses in good areas. However I managed to purchase a large property on St Gabriels Road in the Mapesbury estate. The previous owner, Mr Glass, owned a fruit shop in Willesden Green, leaving the property unoccupied for some time. There were old mattresses, stinking carpets and litter everywhere. The grass was knee high in the front and in the back. The garden had a war-time broken shed. There were penny boxes for the gas everywhere. There was neither central heating nor electricity. At the time of purchase the house looked like a ghost's dwelling. I had liked its entrance hall with wooden beams and an old antique fireplace. Mr Spence again came to my aid and installed the central heating. I had the house rewired and the bathrooms refitted and soon the house looked habitable. Careful planning, budgeting and looking for bargains became second nature to me. Jimmy with his work and other activities, such as editing a students' Islamic magazine, could not be of much practical help to me.

Soon after we had settled in the new home there was a burglary by the builders who were restoring the kitchen. I lost valuable jewelry, Swiss watches and a gold clock. My mother was not with me and it happened while I was at work. The thieves were able to saw through the doors of the room where all the jewelry was kept locked in a cupboard. The police merely shrugged their shoulders and told me that there was nothing they could do unless they caught the thieves red handed. I was completely disgusted by this attitude. I was upset and could not leave the house. A sympathetic gentleman came from the Bank's insurers to assess damage and I was given some compensation.

My youngest son Ajmal was now able to obtain some private tuition, thanks to Jimmy, and passed his 'A' levels. He was growing into a tall and lovely looking young man. He was practical-minded and with his first student grant purchased iron grills, which he fixed on the windows to prevent further break-ins. He laid the kitchen floor with ceramic tiles of Aztek design, which I simply loved. I was too afraid to have builders in the house after the theft. Ajmal was very good with his hands. He also managed to single-handedly build a toilet and a shower on the third floor of our house risking life and limb.

I introduced a few girls to Jimmy but he proposed to Tayyaba, daughter of my eldest brother Inam, who was studying at the Fatima Medical College for Girls in Lahore. They corresponded and liked each other. Jimmy ordered new, white furniture and I decorated their bed room. He went for *umra* during Ramadan, and then on *Eid* proceeded to Peshawar for his wedding. This took place in the few days off that Tayyaba had between her written finals and the viva. My mother was very happy at the match and made a beautiful red dress for the bride on which she stitched a flower pattern using gold thread. Tayyaba was also given the family heirloom – the gold *gulubund* that my grandmother had given to my mother on her marriage. It was a miracle that this was one item not burgled. Maybe it was providence the family jewelry ended up with its rightful owner. My son returned to his work in London, while Tayyaba's visa papers were being processed. Tayyaba arrived wearing a long coat and *niqab*. Seeing her in *niqab*, I secretly prayed that she would not wear it. I had wished to hold a reception or a welcome dinner for the couple but Jimmy insisted that there was no need as all the ceremonies had taken place in Peshawar. I was disappointed as I did want a reception for them.

One day as I was walking from the tube station towards my house I saw a gentleman mowing his lawn. I thought he was a gardener so I stopped and smiled and he also smiled back. I asked him if he was a gardener and whether he could tend my lawn as I needed somebody urgently. He introduced himself as Bertie and took my address. The next day Saturday afternoon someone rang the bell. To my surprise it was the same gentleman whom I thought was a gardener in a suit and bowler hat and holding a brollie. He said to me, "I have come to do your garden Ma'am!" M. Bertie Kidd and I became good friends. He had been a test pilot during the war and would often come and have tea with us. He kindly gave Tayyaba driving lessons. We came to know that the lady with whom he lived, Betty, was his wife even though he first described her as his housekeeper. He never brought her to our house. My mother, normally strict about *purdah*, also spoke to him face to face as he was an elderly gentleman. We remained friends till his death. We often spoke about religion. He was a Catholic but liked to hear about Islam. Once he came to our house and after our tea and conversation he knelt on his knees and prayed. He started to have pain in his right leg and in his back but even then he would come and build a cupboard with Ajmal's help to house our boiler. I would visit their flat, particularly around Christmas, to deliver presents.

Thirteen years later, I came to know from Betty that Mr Kidd was ill and in hospital. I went to visit him with some flowers decorated in a flower-vase. He was sitting in a chair and stood up upon seeing me. I said a prayer for him, the *Surah Fatiha*, and left the hospital, thinking of all the kindness and help he gave us. After two or three days I enquired about him and Betty told me that he had passed away. She returned my flower holder and told me that Bertie insisted that she gave it back to me. I came back home and when I removed the oasis to wash the flower holder, to my surprise, I found a set of six gold crowns from his teeth hidden inside. He must have pulled

Burg-e-Gul's poets and writers, London – My cousins Professors Nasima Tirmidhi & Quddusi Kazmi (third and sixth from right respectively) with Firoza Jaffer (centre) – late 1970s.

them off before his death. I kept these for some time and did not know what to do with them. Later I took them to my dentist and asked him to use them on some poor patient. I attended his funeral on a cold and frosty Sunday and met Betty's daughter from her first husband and Bertie's nephew John. We had a long chat in the funeral parlour after the burial ceremony. I mentioned to him how fond his uncle had been of him.

I realized that a consequence of living in England was the loss of contact with our mother tongue Urdu. My connections with the BBC Eastern Services came in handy and a few of us banded together and formed a literary club named *Barg-e-Gul*. Shahida Ahmad, Parveen Mirza, Anwar Khalid, Firoza Jaffer, Mohsina

Jilani, Safia Siddiqui and I met at Stanley Street mosque's first floor and read our own short stories and poetry written in Urdu. I met Faiz Ahmed Faiz and Ahmed Faraz, who were good friends of my cousin in the BBC, Athar Ali. A few of us started to write for the *Daily Jung*, an Urdu newspaper.

A couple of Urdu magazines like *Seda* were soon being published, as more people from the subcontinent of India and Pakistan were now settled in England. Urdu was also understood and spoken by some Kenyans, Guyanese and Mauritians. I organised a literary evening at St Gabriels Road that was attended by Parveen Shakir, a young and elegant Pakistani poetess who, alas, was soon to pass away. It so happened that more men were present in that gathering than ladies. The *Daily Jung* the next day reported the event with a photograph, but also with the comment that the male presence was dominant in a lady's home. Newspapers always have to rub it in.

Jimmy did not live in his house in Normanby Road but with me in St Gabriels even after the marriage. He sometimes let friends and students stay there for free. I would be cross with him for I knew that if people did not pay for something they did not respect or appreciate it. Tayyaba gave birth to Jamila in November 1978. This was to be my second grandchild. Little did I know that Jamila would become so close to me. I loved her childhood as she grew up in the big house with me. I rented out some rooms at St Gabriels to a young couple also very dear to me, Kausar and Shabbir Ahmed. They adored Jamila and would look after her for hours. My mother was also very helpful. She brought Jamila's cot to her bedroom so Tayyaba could have time for the medical studies needed to qualify in Britain. Fourteen months later Jimmy and Tayyaba became parents again with the birth of a baby boy, whom they named Tayeb.

Tayyaba obtained a house job in Hairmyres Hospital near Glasgow and went to live there with Jamila and Tayeb. Jimmy meanwhile was working in London and busy preparing his doctorate on databases. He used to visit them at week-ends. Luckily Tayyaba found a good nanny in Glasgow, Amma Ratna. Born in Rangoon, she had cared for many children in her career. Amma Ratna was employed by a German family, the Von Halems, attached to the Goethe-Institut in Karachi. They were good friends with my cousin and his wife, Muzaffar and Nasreen Zaidi. When the Von Halems were transferred to Glasgow, Amma Ratna accompanied them. After some years they had to return to Germany and could not obtain a visa for Amma. Thanks to Nasreen's help, Amma then joined our family.

The Bank of Commerce and Credit International (BCCI) had been launched very successfully in the UK with many branches. It was the first Muslim bank and many of us became its account holders. Agha Hasan Abidi and my cousin Shamima's brother-in-law, Mr Burney, were the pioneers of that Bank. The Bank had decorated its branches with eastern artifacts and Persian carpets. The Bank also opened an *Urdu Markaz* to promote Urdu language, with Iftikhar Arif, a well-read and able poet well known in literary circles, as its organiser. Our literary club meetings were also held there. It became the hub of all the poets from the subcontinent of India and Pakistan. Those were the great days.

Mother always bought her own newspaper and also paid the milk bill. The milkman used to deliver fresh milk bottles daily at the door step and Mother would keep the account and make the payment from her own money. Once an officer from Social Security called on mother and asked her to fill forms as she was a widow and over seventy years of age and thus was entitled to a pension and some benefits. She offered the gentleman tea and explained to him that her sons were well off and she did not want help and that money should be given to some other poor family. The Social Security officer was completely taken aback. He told me that he had never met a lady like her who would refuse to accept the money which is being given to her by the State.

By 1979 Margaret Thatcher was the Prime Minister and Tories were in power. I resigned from the Bank of England in July that year on medical grounds. There was a staff farewell party and I received many presents. I was happy to be at home and concentrate on my teaching assignments. Tayyaba and the babies were also back in London and it was a pleasure to be with them when needed. I think it is natural to love one's grandchildren.

I taught at Hammersmith and North Kensington Community School and also took evening classes at the Aylestone Community School. I started to teach locally English as a second language and tried to help the community in whatever way I could. I realised that many refugees from Uganda and parts of Africa had started to settle in Britain. I must admit that the British were very accommodating to immigrants coming from Africa, partly because they came with capital and were good businessmen. A change was taking place in British society. Vegetarian meals and halal shops opened alongside the many existing kosher shops. English people started to eat curries and samosas. I helped my brother Nayar and Misbah purchase houses in London and was happily involved in their furnishing and decoration. Jasmine also purchased a house in Chesham and I kept an eye on it while she was away in Dhahran, where Salam was now working, after having left the Army. In the winter months in particular it was important for me to visit the empty house in case of burst pipes. I used to drive to Chesham and on one such cold morning, while thinking of my daughter, some images entered my mind and took this form in words:

> The lush green valley has turned cold
> Mist is over hilltops
> Mist is heavy in my heart
> How silent is Chesham
> While passing through the forest
> Snowflakes fool me
> As white virgin flower petals
> Spread everywhere

My heart freezes, thoughts tremble
With cold and fear
The longing is there to see her
I think of her and pray for her
One day, when all of a sudden
The snowflakes will turn into dewdrops
and tall trees will dance in Chesham
And the summer will come
The fragrance of Jasmine will spread
in the green valley of Chesham.

I was soon to exchange such scenes of the gentle hills of Chesham for life in Jeddah and some experiences of both contentment and crises in the immediate years to follow.

Contentment and Turbulence

In 1981 I was interviewed at the Holiday Inn in Swiss Cottage by Dr Tawfiq Al-Shawi, founder of Manarat International School projects in Jeddah. I was offered a teaching post on a two-year contract. I was asked to teach Islam in English to thirteen and sixteen year olds in the all-girls school, which provided me a double opportunity: firstly with my brother Misbah working in Jeddah and my daughter in Dhahran, I was happy to be in Saudi Arabia; secondly, it would permit me to learn more about Islam than merely follow the rituals.

A couple of students of 9th and 10th grade were more aware of Islamic teachings than I. It was necessary to undertake some research and I had the chance to devote time for the study of the Qur'an and take help from other books. Somehow the students were happy with me as I related to them stories from the Qur'an of previous prophets and civilizations and tried to show how Qur'anic rules can be accepted and implemented in our present-day life. Luckily I had the access to Abdullah Yusuf Ali s translation and commentary. I told them of his travels to the various historical places mentioned in the Qur'an.

Our school was considered very prestigious. The students were very well-behaved and their parents mostly belonged to the elites, holding important posts in Saudi government and in private lucrative businesses. There were sixteen British teaching staff with an Egyptian lady as head. I was one of the four Muslim teachers employed. On occasions Dr Al-Shawi would visit and extend his hospitality to all the staff. Dr Shawi's German wife took a greater interest in the running of the school. The expatriate teachers from Britain were happy as they were accommodated in comfortable apartments, received good salaries without tax and avoided the student rudeness found in British schools. All teachers were bused from their flats, which were newly built with all amenities. Teachers gladly donned black *abayas* in the school while I marvelled at their compliance to the cultural norms – was it the money? I did not wear the black *abaya* but luckily no one objected. My brother Misbah did not want me to stay alone in the apartment allocated by the school and brought me to his own luxurious flat in the posh Salmya area, where I had the access to his car as well.

My brother was very popular in Jeddah and had many friends. He frequently organised dinners, poetry recitals and *ghazal* evenings and he himself possessed a good knowledge of Urdu and Persian poetry and a fine singing voice. It was on one of these occasions I met the famous *ghazal* singer Mehdi Hassan. I was happy to be accepted by all his friends and never missed a party.

The remarkable hospitality in Arab culture and the way guests were welcomed overwhelmed me. The shops were flooded with quality foods and merchandise and I noticed that the shopkeepers tipped the scale in favour of the customer. They also removed any rotten or damaged fruit which they would not sell to a customer. It is only in Saudi Arabia that I noticed this type of honesty. The gold markets and *souks* glittered with the abundance of gold. It was remarkable that the gold shops remained opened while the Saudis went to the mosque for their prayers. Nobody dared to steal anything as everyone respected the Islamic law. I found the heat difficult to bear, being a mountain girl myself. I did not like to venture to Jeddah's beaches even in December.

One day in July 1981 I found our Palestinian neighbour very sad. She and her family had been up the previous night watching TV reports of the Israeli bombardment of Lebanon. She told me that in Sidon alone some thirty five thousand people were killed by Israeli air raids. They were in a state of shock as they desperately tried to phone their relatives in Sidon, but in vain. I was sad and felt sorry for my neighbours and took some flowers on my return from the School. When I talked of the Sabra and Sidon's bombings to an English friend at the school the response I received was: "I don't watch Arab news on TV – it is all propaganda!" I remained silent but realized the extent to which we in Britain had succumbed to one way of thinking on matters relating to the Middle East.

The loss of Muslims and their killings always made me very sad indeed and I wondered why so many innocent people were killed by the Israelis in spite of the kindness that had been offered to Jewish refugees fleeing Europe for Palestine during the World War II. It was two months later that the horror of the massacres in the Palestinian refugee camps of Sabra and Chatila became known to the world.

I was in contact with *khala* Rabia Naseef and her daughter Fatima and my rebellious thinking transformed to a more accepting approach. My brother Misbah also introduced me to Professor Zain al-Abidin, with whom our families had ties from Delhi. He edited the *Journal of Muslim Minorities*, and his wife was Fatima's colleague at the university. On a trip to Dhahran I met many of my daughter's friends, including the Islamic scholar Dr Zafar Ansari and the professor of geology, Dr Zaghloul Najjar, who had studied verses in the Qur'an relating to his subject.

Umra and Hajj

I read the Qur'an daily and soon felt ready to perform *Umra* and Hajj. I went with the School's Muslim staff to perform *Umra* during our mid-term holidays. I loved the drive towards Mecca, wearing a white robe and singing the praises and names of Allah. We performed the *tawaf* at night and I felt awe each time I glanced at the magnificent Kaaba. We later boarded a bus to go to Medina. It was a four hour drive through a desert landscape. In the afternoon sun we witnessed hills of all colours and hues, from red to grey to brown. As we approached Medina there were palm trees and the air became cool. Most of my three days there were spent in prayers. One evening I went out walking and later sat in a restaurant, where two children aged nine or ten came by and I smiled at them. They came close to me and we started to talk. The two boys knew some English and they wanted to buy drinks for me. I told them that I had the money but they insisted that I was a guest in their city and they must offer me a drink or food. I was really touched by those little children's polite behaviour and gentle hospitality.

When I told brother Misbah that I wished to perform Hajj, he introduced me to Mr Ishaq Beg, an engineer working in Jeddah for the Italian firm Efcodella, who organised the pilgrimage for family groups at a minimum sum and was also well-versed in the rituals. As I prepared myself, I kept thinking of my mother who had performed Hajj twice. I felt prepared and happy that I was fulfilling this duty incumbent on all Muslims. As we boarded the bus, everyone was wearing sparkling white robes, reciting the *kalima* and offering thanks and praises to Allah. Tears rolled down my eyes. My heart was filled with Allah's love and glory as I thanked Him for this opportunity. I loved every minute of the Hajj. The Kaaba again filled my heart with awe. I managed to finish the Qur'an in three days in Arafat and Mina. It was hot in the day so I used to keep one mattress on top of me to avoid the sun's intensity, but the evenings were pleasant. We lived in a clean tent with new bed sheets and clean mattresses laid out in the corner. A partition separated men and women. In one partition there was a *samovar* containing water. Close to our tent was a doctor's surgery, dispensing free medicine and advice. I was happily surprised to see such good management.

There was no desire or the need to read a newspaper, or to listen to a radio or to watch TV. Everyone was thinking of their sins and mistakes and wrapped in deep remembrance of Allah. Some of my traveling companions were expecting elaborate lunches and dinners and made comments on the food but I did not find that becoming. I did not like to speak very much while I was in Hajj. I was wrapped in total ecstasy. On one rather hot afternoon someone sent a tray of fresh grapes and red apples to our tent. When my mother heard my account of Hajj later she said that it seemed like a luxury compared to hers. I admired the Saudi government for the comfort and care provided to millions during the Hajj. They made sure that there was sanitation, food and water in abundance along with the free access to the doctors and medical care. I noticed that small trees were being planted in the vicinity of Arafat. Every time I entered the precinct of Kaaba, it seemed the whole sky was lit up. Thousands of people were praying to one Almighty God and were void of all other materialistic and worldly feelings and I felt as if the sky and the stars were also praying with us. Mr Ishaq Beg did all the hard work and looked after us well. May Allah bless him.

I was unaware that the Saudis had the habit of holding their employees' passports and could not understand why we all had to wait in a queue for long hours at the end of the term to get them back. I lost my patience, which probably annoyed the male workers in the office. They then deliberately delayed the process. I was furious as I wanted to get back to London as quickly as possible since my mother was feeling quite fragile in those days. A whole week passed in waiting. I went to see Abdullah Naseef, then the Rector of Jeddah University and complained of this male chauvinistic attitude. The next day my passport was handed back to me. I refused to extend the contract at Manarat for the second year.

Later in 1983 I came to know of the demise of Dr Al-Shawi's wife. I sent a letter of condolence to their daughter Zarina, who had been one of my students. Shortly after, Dr Al-Shawi e-mailed me requesting that I rejoin the school. Though I could not take up the offer because of family circumstances, I thought it was very decent of him to respond and invite me to teach again in spite of losing my temper on all of them.

Family concerns

My daughter Jasmine was expecting her third child. It was her practice to always recite *Surah Yasin* during labour. On this occasion she told me she noticed a light entered the room during her pains. When a baby girl was born she was named 'Ayesha'. She grew up to be wise person and a comfort not only to her mother but to all whom she meets. Ayesha was also to be my right hand in various charity projects.

During that period my relative Saad came to stay with us while he studied chartered accountancy; one of the advantage of owning a big house was to be able to accommodate guests and relatives. Later I started teaching at Greenhill College in the evenings and also worked for Harrow Council's legal department as a translator. I was chosen by the community to be the governor of Anson School. The headmistress, Mrs Davies, was a very dynamic person of goodwill, devoted to the well-being of students whose mother tongue was not English.

My son Ajmal had passed his BSc in Biology and wanted to be a fish farmer. He ended up in Kent working for an old Englishman who made him sleep in the cold winter in a caravan. I was concerned about his welfare and when I went to visit him, found he had a bad cold, swollen face and did not look at all well. I immediately brought him home in my cousin's car and called my Ceylonese doctor. Ajmal had mumps as well as pneumonia and was ill for months. That was the end of his fish farming. My brother Ameen subsequently called him to Kuwait and there he found a good job. On receiving his first salary he sent me a pearl necklace and gold bangles. Later on in his holidays to London, he brought me a pure gold jewelry set with real pearls clustered in gold roses. He also worked hard and saved money. Upon my suggestion he purchased a four bedroom house in Preston Road. He then returned to Kuwait and I got down to repairing and furnishing the place. It was hard work as it had been uninhabited for some time. I loved that house and after decorations were done, lived there for some time as it was close to my workplaces in Harrow.

Jasmine's life was in danger during her fourth pregnancy as she was very ill. Her husband, as always, was not at her side during such periods and she lacked the support wives normally receive at their time of delivery. My mother prayed ardently for her and finally a premature baby girl was born at Princess Alexandra Hospital in Harlow weighing only 1.94 kg. At the time Tayyaba was working in nearby Bishop's Stortford Hospital and helped out considerably. Baby Saba's first few days were precarious but the child survived. My Jasmine was a fighter and managed to look after her children through thick and thin. Unfortunately her marriage was a mismatch and did not bring happiness to her, although both Salam and her possessed fine qualities. Jasmine later qualified as a Montessori teacher and also completed a Bachelor's degree in Librarianship. Saba remained a delicate child though she too, like her mother, is a fighter and subsequently passed her Chartered Accountancy exams.

My brother Ameen asked me to look for a house for him in London and I thought it best to buy one nearer my home so I could renovate it and furnish it before his arrival. I tried my best to furnish and renovate the property on Chatsworth Road as I knew he was used to a good quality life. I was glad that the house was large enough for the furniture shifted from Kuwait in 1984.

Tayyaba and the children moved back to St. Gabriels Road from Glasgow with their nanny Ratna. Their third child Shamila was born in the Royal Free Hospital in 1986. When I went to see Tayyaba in the hospital, she did not seem at ease. She told me that the doctors' report for the baby were not encouraging. Her hip bone and pelvis were kept in a cast but thank goodness she was not as unwell as doctors had predicted. Jamila and Tayeb started their schooling at Yusuf Islam's newly opened school in Brondesbury, while Tayyaba, Shamila and Ratna left for Burnley as my cousin Dr Syed Akhtar Ali had arranged for my daughter-in-law's GP training. We were joined at St Gabriels by brother Ameen's son Idris, a tall, blond and very gentle boy who had come from Kuwait to study at Imperial College. He graduated at the very young age of nineteen. He occupied a room in our top floor. He was an avid reader and kept his room very tidy which pleased me immensely.

Ajmal returned to London where he had started work with the Caterpillar company. We went together for a short trip to Pakistan and I used this opportunity to sell the plot of land held in my children's name in the Defense Housing Society. During this trip Ajmal met and got engaged to one of my brothers' graceful daughters. I was very upset when he broke of his engagement with her and did not want to see him or speak to him. In June 1987 my mother arrived in London, together with my eldest brother Inam. She loved Ajmal dearly and told me not to be angry and when he phoned, she asked him to come and see us.

My mother was losing weight and looked very frail. I took her to our family doctor who knew her. After examination he told me that her heart was gradually failing, but naive as I was, I still did not realise the gravity of the situation. She kept on working in the house when I was absent and prayed, as she always did, standing upright and prostrating for long periods. I wished that I had spent more time with my mother rather than on other commitments. She only had a few days left of her life which I did not know. One night at about four in the morning I found Jimmy sitting in mother's room and the light was on. He told me that she was in pain so he had come from his bedroom. Her condition deteriorated but till the last minute she went to the toilet on her own for ablution. She told us that she was breathing her last breaths. Inam Bhai held her right arm and kept on reciting with her *kalima shahadat*. I called for the ambulance. They put an oxygen mask over her but she did not regain consciousness. There was a stern nurse who was on duty in Emergency and would not allow me to go inside with her. I waited at the corridor and she came back to tell me that they tried to 'regurgitate' her but she was gone. I was angry inside me at the crude word she used for my mother – instead of using 'resuscitate'. Inam Bhai and I took her to the mortuary at six thirty a.m. and came home. In the meanwhile, Jimmy made all the arrangements for her burial. Zulekha Bibi, Jasmine and I bathed her. She had a serene smile on her face and looked very peaceful. Now I understood the reason for her coming to London and bringing Inam with her. Perhaps in her heart she knew that I loved her deeply and dearly and so she gave the last few moments of her life to be with me and with Inam to be present at her burial.

I have yet to meet a more pious, loving and God-fearing lady in my life. She would never address anyone without saying 'my dear' or 'my darling'. I never heard her utter an abusive word. Her funeral prayers were held in the Central Mosque at Regents Park the next day, on Friday 11 July 1987 at *dhuhr* and the burial took place at Chingford Cemetery. Telegrams and letters of condolences poured in from all over the world. The news of her death was printed in Muslim and Urdu newspapers in London as she had made a name in British Muslim society. She always prayed for the whole of Muslim *ummah*. The prayer on her lips was that Allah should not show her any more grief as she had already lost two children. My mother was almost like a companion to me. Anything good which I learnt was from my mother. She helped me with my children and later with raising the grandchildren. She taught us and she also taught them. She was a good and patient teacher and a wonderful person. It was noticed by many that fragrance encircled her though she did not use any perfume. I was lost without her and was plunged in deep sorrow for days. My eldest brother insisted that I went with him to Burnley to see Tayyaba and the grandchildren. Reluctantly I left St.

Gabriels home and went with him. Many years have passed but it is amazing that not a day passes when she is not in my thoughts.

Tayyaba soon returned from Burnley and started locum assignments in London. Jimmy remained engrossed in his work and other activities and did not pay attention to the maintenance of his property at Normanby Road. I used to get annoyed quite easily during the period they shared the house with me, but he and his wife seemed to bear it with patience. Another sad incident was soon to engulf us. Salam had come back from abroad and Jasmine held a Qur'an *khatam* ceremony in her house in College Road. It was getting late and we were waiting for Ameen's family to join us in College Road. We then heard that Ameen's fourteen-year old daughter Salima had to be rushed to hospital after an asthmatic seizure while spending the night in an Irish friend's home. That family had a pet cat and her asthma inhaler had run out. Her friend's parents had gone and left the two girls at home. Salima collapsed and the other girl must have called the ambulance. She was taken to Hammersmith Hospital in Scrubs Lane and kept on a heart and lung machine for three days. Salima was buried in February 1988 in the same graveyard close to my mother's grave. Her parents had also consented to the doctors' request for an organ donation of her kidneys for a Sikh patient. This made me fume inside but according to my brother Ameen and Peggy if someone else's life could be saved, why not. The couple had always been very gentle and decent, but after Salima's death their lives changed and they accepted and submitted to Allah the Almighty even more. Shortly after, my mother's sister, Kulsum, who was being cared for by her son Athar and wife Lynne, also passed away.

The remains of three relatives now rest in the same cemetery in Chingford. I realised how much I missed my mother's prayers and became aware of the significance of the *duas* of our elders.

I soon pulled myself together and became immersed in community work. I was enjoying teaching at Harrow College and also helped in organizing the World Women's Day events. On one such occasion I invited Dr Ang Swee Chai, who had been an eye-witness to the massacres in September 1982 of Palestinian refugees in Sabra and Chatilla. She arrived with a projector and screen and showed the work she had done in Gaza Hospital, at times without light and water and under shellings. Later I read her book *From Beirut to Jerusalem*. We also invited Dr Pauline Cutting, another doctor serving in the Palestinian refugee camps but she was not in London. These heroic ladies, who risked their life to serve the suffering victims, made me decide that I also must try to help humanity as much as I possibly can, which my own religion also teaches. A lecturer at Harrow College, Clare Fletcher, encouraged me to find out more about dyslexia because I had two students with this condition in my class.

One evening in July 1991 I heard of the BCCI bank closure – I had been out of London at a conference on Dyslexia. When Jimmy picked me up from Paddington station he informed me of the headlines. It was a blow as only recently I had transferred £74,000 into my account at the BCCI bank following the sale of a plot of land in Karachi. I remained awake for many nights as the loss was great. I would sit up in bed in the middle of the night and think of BCCI. My brother Misbah visited me in London and when he saw me in such a state of shock, took me with him for a holiday to Norway. We were well looked after there by his friend Mahdi Hasan, an oil engineer and recipient of a gold shield for his professional expertise, and his wife Shameem. Our hosts also took us to the glaciers and fiords that descended from the high cliffs and submerged into the sea below. We also visited Stavanger's famous ski resort that had a jump of some three hundred metres from above the mountain top. Misbah also organized a rail trip to show me Oslo, with its hundreds of statues and the art of Edward Munch, and I came back refreshed and started to think how best I could recover some of my money from the alleged BCCI crash. I had to unearth old land registry papers and have them attested. I wrote to all the MPs I knew and sent numerous letters and gradually began to recover some funds from the liquidators in dribs and drabs.

After breaking off his engagement with my brother's daughter, Ajmal met a Croatian girl. There was something odd about her: she questioned me to check whether the house belonged to my son. Ajmal went ahead with a civil registration marriage and only later was there an Islamic *nikah* ceremony, thanks to help from the director of Rabita, the Muslim World League's office in London. Ajmal soon stopped phoning me and lost contact with the family, which was very unlike him. We later came to know that the marriage had not been a happy one. In the ensuing separation proceedings Ajmal lost his Preston Road house. Alas, we learn from our own experiences and do not follow the advice given.

In 1991 the crises in the former Yugoslavia started to become more widely known. First Slovenia and then Croatia declared their independence, to be hastily recognized by the European powers, and next Croatia and Serbia together cast their eyes on the partition of Bosnia. On the second day of its independence, the Muslim population faced two historical enemies and lacked resources. Reading the news I came to know that a British aid worker, Asad Khan, had been arrested by Croats and put in the prison in Kisilijak. I was concerned and anxious as this aid worker was said to have a young family and a very worried wife. He was unlawfully detained and imprisoned for the only crime of carrying food aid inside the conflict zone. It took much effort from the British Government to obtain his release. My daughter Jasmine was able to obtain his address and took me to meet him. We were warmly welcomed by Asad Khan and his wife Nasra. I was impressed by his bravery and commitment as he described how he collected aid and took the food stuff and medicines to the war torn areas, driving in old cars and vans and crossing many borders all the way to Eastern Europe from London. In spite of his bad experience of prison he was still committed to help the suffering children and the wounded refugees. He had established a charity by the name of

Convoy of Mercy – CoM. He described to us the circumstances of his imprisonment in Kisilijak. He was horrified to hear of Croats manning illegal checkpoints into Bosnia – they did not recognise the independence of Bosnia Herzegovina and were preventing aid workers free access. The Croats demanded a toll, effectively a bribe, payable in cash or in the form of goods. What added to the injustice was that the UN and UNHCR recognised those illegal checkpoints and made no attempt to dismantle them. Seeing Asad Khan's enthusiasm and commitment, I decided to accompany him to the war-torn Balkans.

ⳍ *Chapter 6*

Venturing into the Balkans

Taking advantage of the summer break at Greenhill College in Harrow where I was teaching, my first trip to the Balkans was in 1993. I also took leave from the Legal Department at Harrow Council, where I worked as a part-time translator. We collected money from relatives and friends and packed our bags, filled with goods and clothes to take to the refugees and stranded people. On the way Asad briefed me on the situation prevalent in the Balkans. The media was portraying the war as an internal conflict then and not much publicity was given to the Russian help for the Serbs and the massacres that were taking place inside that region. It was during our journey together that I came to know the true picture and the way events unfolded from the very next day that Bosnia Herzegovina had declared its independence.

Our house in Soline near Split in Croatia was away from the many refugee camps. The view was breathtaking and I felt elated and happy. It did not seem that I was in a war-torn country or in any danger. It was only when I visited the refugee camps and saw the plight of the trapped people that I realised the tragedy taking place. There were many camps of displaced people, spread like mushrooms, and each camp spelled its own misery.

The Bosnian and Croats were supposedly allies. However when the Bosnian refugees arrived in Croatia, the Croats insisted that all Muslim refugees should have their religion stamped on their refugee cards just as was Nazi practice with the Jews fifty years ago. Let us not forget that during the communist regime the Bosnians were not given any status. When I started to teach the Bosnians English and would ask them their nationality, they all responded as 'Muslim'. I had to drum it into them that their nationality had been Yugoslavian and was now Bosnian and Islam was their religion and not nationality. They had been brought up with no sense of national identity, unlike the other communities of Yugoslavia.

While visiting the camps I noticed that there were many inter-marriages. Almost one in four Bosnians was married to a Croat or Serb. Initially the refugees were placed in the holiday camps. Those who had managed to bring some money were able to rent rooms with Croat families. The landlords were taunted by their fellow Croats so this option soon became very difficult and later non-existent. The refugees were not supported by Red Cross or UNHCR in Split at the time. I was told that voluntary organisations were supplying cooked food and clearing the sewage. Saudi Arabia was also paying rent to Croatian government for the refugee camps – four Deutsche Marks per person per day. There were other Muslim agencies working in the field like Merhamet. When I was in England I had been unaware that Muslim countries or relief agencies were doing such humanitarian work. The media always portrayed Muslims as corrupt and good-for-nothing people.

Muslim NGOs in Zagreb and Split were repeatedly raided by the Croatian police in 1993. Their funds would be seized causing delay and disruption to humanitarian effort. Documents or files with refugees' addresses would be taken away, to be used by the Croatian Police to evict Bosnian refugees from their houses and any rented accommodation that they had managed to find. This intensified the dispersal of Bosnian refugees throughout the world. The offices of Al-Taib, a Muslim NGO, were ransacked and the police took off with 25,000 DM. Soon after that the warehouse of the International Relief Agency (IGASA) was closed down and one of its aid vehicles confiscated at a police check point. The same ill-treatment was given to Muwafaq, another Muslim NGO. Its chief was caught by the Croat police and detained for 24 hours and some £45,000 taken away. Many aid workers including Yusuf Islam were robbed during this period, as most of us carried cash since banks were not functioning.

In June 1993, the camp at Promejna and Zivagosce near Makarska was closed by the Croatian authorities but no European nation came forward to take the 600 refugees. The task of showing humane and civilised values fell on countries like Pakistan, a third world nation, yet ready to welcome the Bosnians and resettle them. Arif, the son of my cousins Dr Akbar and Baigma, an American national, was in the forefront of efforts to resettle them there. Even though a poor country offered a warm welcome and provided more than what it did for its own citizens, these efforts were only to be criticized by the International Committee of the Red Cross (ICRC).

Médecins Sans Frontières was building houses in Gabela Camp in Čapljina for Croatian refugees from Bugojno while the HVO – the fanatical Croatian army, 'Hrvatsko Vijeće Obrane' – held some 12,000 Muslims in the concentration and refugee camps and prisons in one town alone. The International Red Cross had been told by the HVO that they were prisoners of war and were not given access. The HVO's 5th Brigade included mercenaries and Croats from the United States and Canada. Christian missionaries and churches were also busy in the refugee camps.

Asad Khan had written in *The Times* during this period to describe the conditions, in which even aid workers were not spared:

"I met a Muslim aid worker, one of many from all over the Muslim world. This aid worker was taking aid into Bosnia Herzegovina together with a colleague and they were captured by the Catholic Croats. They were then taken to Čapljina and badly beaten with long wooden bats. No food or water was given to either of them for four days. They then found themselves with eight hundred or so other Muslim civilians of Čapljina. They included doctors, teachers and other professionals, men, women and children. They were kept in a small hall with no space to walk or to stretch out. Small empty food cans were given to urinate and to defecate. The Catholic soldiers would then pick some Muslim girls, sit them in a row and humiliate them verbally and physically. These civilian Bosnian Muslims had been kept in that concentration camp for over two months, some were allowed to leave if they willingly signed away all their property to the Catholic soldiers. Others were not so lucky."

I soon uncovered more disturbing news: the UN was said to have used food as a weapon to bring the Bosnian President to 'negotiate' away his country. Lorries full of food and medicines were parked at Split for weeks before they could be allowed to enter Bosnia. UNHCR would only send one convoy a month while the food rotted in the warehouses. It was not a mere conflict but a large scale, planned genocide. The aid was pouring in now from all quarters and the bags of sugar and flour were packed sky high in the warehouses and at depots while the Bosnians ate grass and starved. I saw all this and more. I saw with my own eyes how the whole of Split in Croatia was being rebuilt and modernised at the very time that Bosnia was being destroyed.

The roads and highways constructed by the UN benefited the Croats and Serbs. It enabled them to move their artillery and heavy tanks, while the Bosnian army lacked vehicles and fuel. In reality Bosnia lacked a proper army – many young men were given six weeks of training and then sent to defend their country. The UN made no efforts to control the roads. The media reported that the Bosnians were not clearing the mines off the road to allow Croat casualties out of Nova Bila. The fact was ignored that every time the Bosnians went to clear the mines, they were shot at by the Croats in breach of their promise to the UN. It was an excuse not to allow

Bosnian casualties out elsewhere. The UN again made no attempt to enforce the ceasefire.

The Croats economy boomed while I was there, benefiting from the NGOs who based their offices in Zagreb or Split. The NGOs rented expensive accommodation and paid European prices for their establishments. The UN had unlimited funds and resources. They lived in luxury. They bathed in the midnight warm Dalmatian coast and had plenty of booze and food. Prices soared because UN staff was well-off, while smaller NGOs like ourselves – where the workers supported themselves through their own means – were left struggling but kept up their work.

In 1993 and 1994, Ukrainian and French UN troops were caught selling drugs and weapons in the black market and in any case UN troops bribed their way through Serbian and Croats checkpoints rather than using their mandate and superior forces to force their way through. This again meant that charities had great difficulty in getting through checkpoints as they were not inclined to waste aid or money donated to them. Joining a UNHCR convoy also did not help, as all NGO vehicles were placed at the back and if they were stopped, the UNHCR convoy just left them behind to their fate. British Asians were left to be beaten up at checkpoints even though it was clear from the vehicle registration plates where we were from. In Croatia and Bosnia UNPROFOR (the UN Protection Force) was universally known as 'SerbProFor' with good reason.

Muslim aid agencies were facing many problems getting aid into Bosnia. Anyone who was not a white European or American got no further than the first checkpoint and any hint of Islam either in the name or birthplace meant being turned back, beaten up or arrested. As a result the Muslim aid agencies were paying others to take aid in, but then they could not be certain if it reached the intended destination or just sold on the blackmarket. Caritas, the Catholic agency, and the Red Cross concentrated their aid mainly amongst the Christians. The UN merely registered surprise when one of its convoys was stopped by women and children begging for food. Another problem was the inability of some agencies to be aware of the realities. Marie Stopes from the UK decided to take female psychologists and counsellors over for the Bosnian rape victims, which was certainly a vital requirement. However this counselling also took the form of assertiveness training and free condoms. To come out with such irrelevant help! How can women be assertive when several men armed with guns were intent on rape, often after having killed their husbands?

While in Soline I attended UN briefings in order to obtain information on roads that were open or closed and for the latest news bulletin. This enabled us to direct the convoys to deliver food and medicines as safely as possible. In one of those meetings I remember the British Army Major Wolsley admitting that the British UN troops were training the HVO in 'man-management and command'. The British UN commander in Kiseljak also admitted allowing the Croats to run guns through UN lines especially to Vareš where the HVO had initiated the massacre of over 100 women, children and elderly at Stupni Do – after the Swedish UN contingent refused requests to check what was happening. I was alarmed to hear this at UN meetings and realised most of the posts at UN and UNICEF were given to the Croats at that time. The Croats were in strong position to harass any NGO that tried to take aid or help the refugees, but our young volunteers did not flinch and continued the task of delivering aid.

The so-called hero Colonel Bob Stewart was very vocal in condemnation of the HVO later, but with his 2,500 British troops, scimitar armoured vehicles, tanks, artillery and small arms, little was done at the time to stop the massacre of innocent Muslims in Ahmići and Vitez. British soldiers sat and heard the cries of the children and screams of the women while they were burnt alive in their homes. Asad sent me the account written by reporter Andrew Hogg describing Colonel Duncan's vain attempt to lead a column to Žepče. Duncan called it a day claiming he had neither the mandate nor the resources. The West Yorkshire regiment withdrew and the rampage continued in July 1993 with both Croats and Serbs united to finish off the Muslims. On one week-end almost 10,000 refugees were streaming southwards from Maglaj in an enclave of 100,000 that was surrounded by Croat and Serb forces. There was no way our CoM could possible enter besieged Maglaj.

Another typical example of the UN putting a spanner in the works was the obstruction in the delivery of the world's largest mobile hospital from South Africa to Bosnia. President De Klerk even provided a ship to transport the 130-bed hospital costing £1.3 million to the Italian port of Trieste. This was a fully fitted self-contained hospital ready to be deployed in less than half a day. All concerned authorities cut red tape and facilitated the delivery except the World Health Organisation WHO. According to one of the organisers, Dr Sooliman, when the hospital arrived in Ploče in Croatia, WHO declared the hospital unnecessary for Zenica as it had renovated a disused steel factory that was only four months away from completion! The hospital floated idly for months while the Bosnians were in desperate need of medical attention and surgery. After months of intense lobbying, WHO recommended the hospital be deployed in Mostar. By that time the donors, *Waqf ul Waqifeen*, were so exasperated that they were prepared to agree to anything.

Stobreč Camp

On arrival in Split in Croatia I met some young graduates from Oxford University who were CoM volunteers. We had rented accommodation in Soline, a district of Split. A young student, Sabina, burst out crying when we entered the Stobreč camp. She had made many friends last time she was there with Oxford Aid. This camp contained at least 350 refugees and was supposedly amongst the best looked after. It had a big hall where food was distributed. The hall had a few tables and chairs, otherwise barren.

There were units of wooden partitions in which many refugees were housed on bunk-beds. Luckily they had hot water and facilities to wash their clothes, unlike the other camps. There was no schooling or any other activity in the camps although the Croat children attended schools. I noticed the children's sad faces. They told me how much they missed their school and their friends. Some sixteen year olds were quite under stress and did not like being cooped up in camps. I still remember their sad faces and wonder where they would be today.

Asad and I both felt the immediate need to start some learning activity in each camp. I began providing English lessons in the camps' halls. I went to UNICEF and spoke to a Croat lady in charge, Nada Marasović. She was a program assistant and pleasant but had little to offer to the refugee children. She supplied me with a list of some refugee children and said that four to five children could be placed in each Croat school. She wanted to know about the CoM teaching program and I described our activity that involved bringing 15 to 20 children each day from the camps to our premises in Soline. We would teach them some English, provide lunch and then take them back to the camps at the end of the day. I also mentioned that I was temporarily managing English lessons in Stobreč camp's dining hall and needed some stationary and a black or white board. Nada was later able to provide me a small teaching kit.

When the next CoM trucks arrived I was delighted to see some colouring books, colour pencils and stationary for our children. Asad had also managed to bring two classroom boards for me. The convoy workers and drivers noted the increasing resentment and animosity of the Croat police and public towards Muslims. I met Mike and Peter who had arrived from England along with others. It used to be always fun to see the smiling enthusiastic faces of such good-hearted people who risked their lives and brought goods across the continent to save others' lives.

By July 1993, harassment of the humanitarian Muslim workers by the Croat police had increased. Asad Khan shared with me some of his first-hand knowledge: "I was sitting in the house of an aid worker who was released after 17 days in a Croatian jail, when Police from Omiš just barged in and ransacked the house. Four hundred and fifty women and children from a refugee camp at Trogir, Croatia, were thrown out by the Croatian authorities. Similarly in Split, 600 refugees in another camp were given their marching orders. Two young girls from the same camp were murdered by Croats while travelling on the bus to school."

I never thought that I would experience such harassment but was soon proven wrong. Chalmer, the reporter, and Ian Balmer had departed and the Oxford University volunteers were also on their journey back to England with Asad. I was alone that night in a flat near Soline. It was hot and the 4th of August. I tossed and turned in bed, the mosquitoes were attacking me and there was no breeze. I had opened the balcony door wide open but still could not sleep. It was three-thirty a.m.. I must have dozed off as suddenly I heard voices and door banging. I got up and looked down from the balcony. There were four soldiers carrying guns. I went down with a thumping heart and opened the door. I was in a flimsy nightie. I greeted them with a 'hello'. One of them spoke some English, but there was no reply to my greeting. An armed soldier remained at the doorway, while the three came right in. They started to look around. They saw the white and black boards and the table and chairs. There was no light that night, but they had torches. One soldier kept on pointing the gun towards me. They asked me if I had hidden the *mujahideen* there. To that I laughed and said, "of course not." Before I could ask them anything they came up to the bedrooms. I was horrified at their behaviour as they started to search all the wardrobes and cupboards. Asad's room was locked and they asked me to open the door. Trembling, I gave them the key and told them that the reason I locked that room was that I did not want the children to break the hi-fi system. They opened that door too, always pointing the gun towards me. Of course they found nothing there. I tried to relax them and asked them if they wanted a cup of coffee. I simply wanted to see the reaction to this invitation, although my legs were feeling like jelly at that moment. They gave me one final glance, this time not with much hatred, said *dobro* and left. I noticed that their guns, like those carried by other HVOs, were of German make. I was not afraid of them but I immediately remembered the information from Asad about the attitude of Croats.

The next day I informed our Croat landlord Ante of this nocturnal visit. He looked a little worried but said nothing at the time. After a few days he told us that the neighbours were threatening to put a bomb in the house as they did not like the children coming from the refugee camp. He wished that we vacated the premises, so we emptied the warehouse and loaded the vans with the food boxes and our own belongings. We moved the CoM centre to Duce and some of the injured people to Nemira, where CoM was already running a rehabilitation centre.

Among the young Bosnians coming to learn English at our centre were Amra and Alma. These girls, sixteen and eighteen years old respectively, were from Donji Vakuf, a picturesque city first shelled by the Serbs and then by the Croats. The pair would return to their single-room accommodation with their mother. Many young girls were raped at that time so they did not dare walk alone. One day the girls told me they were being harassed by the Croat police, who would ask them to sit in their cars or hurl bad language and abuse. They moved to the Stobreč refugee camp. It was safer for them to come to our premises to learn English as our aid workers would pick and drive them with other children.

My break with jobs in Britain

I resigned from my jobs at Harrow Council and Greenhill College in order to devote myself fully to the Convoy of Mercy's relief and educational work. I was often questioned on the relevance of educational work in war-torn areas and endeavoured to explain its importance in various interviews and meetings.

During decades under Communist rule the Bosnians were not allowed to travel freely, even for Hajj. They were not exposed to the outside world and their horizons were constrained to a little world of mountains, rivers and folk music. In the major cities, students were taught French, German or Russian but it was superficial. The schooling and pedagogy was poor and had not kept pace with developments. There were no coloured picture books or visual aids and English learning barely featured. They hated to learn Russian because of its Soviet associations. The war since 1992 further deteriorated the educational system and it was in a state of collapse. Many qualified teachers had fled from the country or were killed. Most school buildings and gymnasiums housed refugees or were under shelling. The remaining schools lacked basics like stationary and paper let alone computers facilities or language labs, and often operated on a two-shift system to accommodate as many students as possible. Many young persons had received no schooling for two years. Now, with the war, Bosnians realised that English was internationally spoken and if they did not learn to communicate in this language they would lag behind. They were part of Europe and could not remain excluded while many Europeans were now speaking and understanding English. I returned to the Balkans in October 1993 as a relief worker and English language teacher.

CoM transported over three thousand books and many tons of paper, stationary and computers to the schools. Wherever CoM operated, we opened English classes for children. They loved to attend and at times I had to coach fifty students at one time. The colourful books in glossy paper with pictures were appealing and they started to take immense interest in the English language. The classes gave students a place to come and assemble in an environment conducive to learning rather than remain cooped in one room with their parents and possibly grandparents in refugee camps, or roam about aimlessly on the streets when the curfew was lifted. The students with long gaps in their education found something useful to do. Understandably, the youth in Bosnia were very frustrated as four precious years had gone to waste during the war. Those who were sixteen years old had never been to secondary school. The boys in their final year had lost a great deal as desires and plans to go to university were frustrated. The twenty-year olds did not have a school certificate to show for themselves. Their education was shattered and so were their ambitions. They felt that they were without a future. It was therefore of vital importance for them to be engaged in some kind of positive activity. Some youngsters committed suicide and others suffered from trauma and depression. Education was crucial for their development, well-being and self-esteem. Moreover it was my personal conviction that language brings people close together. I did very much want the Bosnians to know there were many in Britain who cared for them and genuinely wished to help them in their plight, and that not all British and American people were evil even though some had at times collaborated with the Serbs in order to annihilate their population. Wherever possible I also accommodated some Croatian students in my class as they needed help in English. I always managed to maintain good and cordial relationship with the Croats and CoM distributed aid to Croats refugees as well, not once discriminating. Whosoever required help received it.

CoM was also committed to caring for the sick and wounded and we had a rehabilitation centre at Nemira in Croatia. Asad Khan visited Turkey and brought us the news that the camps for Bosnian refugees such as in Kirklareli were very well organised. The Turkish government had also built a new hospital for the Bosnian refugees to which CoM could bring some amputees. The hospital needed physiotherapy equipment and prosthesis which Asad later delivered. CoM organized direct deliveries of medical supplies from England. The facilities were better in Turkey than at our rehabilitation centre, or the Red Cross hospital in Split, and so some of those whom we were caring for, like Husrep Sulejman, were admitted to the Turkish hospital. CoM also managed to send patients for treatment to Germany and England as well. Three injured men – Hasib, Kapetan and Elmir – were sent to Queen Mary University Hospital in London for artificial limbs. It required great efforts on Asad's part to obtain visas for them and later provide accommodation.

CoM delivered personal letters and money from Bosnian families in England to their relatives. There was no postal service and somehow the CoM volunteers managed to deliver the mail. At times we had to hide the letters containing money in odd places of the vehicles so that this was not stolen at the checkpoints. By June 1993, the CoM had transported 1,300 tons of food, 20 tons of medicines and medical equipment along with 18,000 blankets to Bosnia. CoM's work was covered on London Carlton TV and various newspapers. Asad received numerous calls of support and encouragement. CoM was donated four big old Army Bedford vans. Many volunteers from all walks of life helped in driving the vans from Britain to the Balkans, then risking their lives in Bosnia. Most of the time they slept in their vans in order not to incur hotel expenses. They performed all manner of duties from distribution of aid and money in dangerous places to cooking at the Centre.

Many volunteers not only gave their time but also donated materials and money. Eddy Wright brought an inflated rubber dragon dingy that was loved by refugee children from Dalmatia. The gesture however was not appreciated by the Croatian fascist militia, Ustashe. Bill Croker gave up his job as a magistrate to help and made almost sixteen trips. Bill was a wonderful person in his late fifties and managed Oxford Aid to Bosnia. However his heart was with CoM and he usually stayed with us. A separate book can be written on his activities. He remained a dear friend of CoM until his demise in 2009.

Eddie Wright's efforts for refugee children, Croatia – 1993.

Convoy of Mercy team – after driving the relief vans from London to Croatia – Bill Croker is second on the right – 1993.

A young and handsome man of twenty nine, Neil Golithy from Nottingham, joined CoM as a fleet manager. On embracing Islam he adopted the name 'Ibrahim'. He had resigned from Black & Decker and arrived with lots of tools.

One thing was certain – we all had to come back to London to our homes, to recuperate and re-charge our batteries in order to go back to those war stricken zones. Working with refugees and distributing aid does take a toll on your health as well as emotions. It took me some time to adjust myself back into my own surroundings and cosy abode.

Ediba Kapić's Story

During my teaching days in Omiš and in Nemira I had spotted a bright girl. Her real name was Ediba but everyone called her Deeba. She was sixteen and was going to be seventeen when I first met her. She was a very sensible young lady, too mature for her age. I wanted to know more about her. She was a good friend of Idris, who was one of our volunteers and I was amazed how quickly she improved her English. She was regular in attending classes and was very soon helping me to manage and organise them.

Deeba's father was a well-known doctor in Čapljina, Dr Kapić. He had opened a large hospital for which he obtained an award from Germany. Once the war commenced, he continued his work and treated all the wounded and his patients with the same care and courtesy regardless of their religion or nationality. The Croats respected him well but the Ustashe picked him one day and sent him to the torture camp, like they did to everybody from Čapljina or Stolac. I had developed a special relationship with Deeba because of her hardworking nature and I also felt sad and helpless at the thought of her father being tortured in some camp without reason. She and her mother were pursuing all avenues to locate him and obtain a release. I was briefed not to reveal any details that would only serve to upset them further.

Dr Kapić was transferred to many prisons and finally to Ljubuški camp. He was among eighty others, all kept in one hall. There was hardly room to sit, let alone to lie down. They were beaten every day and given one slice of bread. The doctor was called 'the intellectual' in this prison camp. It so happened that an aid worker was also held there. Once released, the aid worker brought out a little piece of brown paper not more than an inch wide, on which was written the word 'Deeba'. One day this gentleman came to our class in Omiš and asked if we have a girl by this name. When this little piece of paper was given to Deeba, she jumped with delight and happiness. She went around kissing everybody and shouted with happiness that her father was alive. She had immediately recognised her father's writing on this torn brown piece of paper.

It was quite a lesson for me to observe how the aid worker broke the news to Deeba and later to her mother. From then on I also learnt to break such news gently and with utmost care and diplomacy. In 1993 I sent a letter from Duce to the British High Commission in Zagreb to grant Deeba a visa to enable her to study in Greenhill College. When she arrived in London, MWA chairperson Mrs Hassan welcomed her and made arrangements for her stay in Medina House, situated in Baker Street.

The Rehabilitation Centre at Nemira

CoM's rehabilitation centre had already been functioning at Nemira with a doctor and three full-time nurses when I arrived there. It had seventeen beds crammed in six rooms with young people – some without limbs – and also trauma victims. Nemira was a seaside resort on the Croatian coast but its scenic beauty could not hide the ravages and sufferings of war.

The wounded civilians wore soldiers' uniforms as they did not have any other clothes. When the neighbours started to kill them, they acquired a gun from somewhere and tried to protect their families but being neither experienced or trained soldiers, were soon injured and caught. The Red Cross hospital in Split and elsewhere in Croatia would perform some surgery or plaster their broken bones and then seek to get rid of them quickly. In any case the Croatian medical staff was mostly unsympathetic to the Muslim wounded or injured, who had no place safe to go or to recuperate, and so they landed in our rehabilitation Centre.

The sick beds were on the top floor, together with a room for storage of medicines and bandages. We had a kitchen and dining area and a drawing room of sorts on the first floor and the ground floor was occupied by CoM workers. We conducted English classes in one room which was suitably equipped for learning. We lived in the other three rooms and the toilets stank at one stage when the sewage system was not working.

In addition to the doctors and nurses, there were two helpers, Jure Palcic and Idris. Jure was a Croat but it was remarkable to see his dedication and friendship. He was often taunted by the Croat soldiers for helping us but he carried on his duties and served humanity. When Asad and I were invited to his house we found his wife Natali to be equally sympathetic. Idris was from South Africa but he had been brought up in England. He had long, dark hair and sported bracelets on his wrists. This young man drove around fearlessly, looked after sick and wounded and was full of life and fun. Amongst volunteers from Britain who came to Nemira were Rashidah Butt and Shabana. Both sacrificed their precious holidays in the service of refugee children and the teaching continued with their help.

One of the doctors at the Nemira Centre was Emira, a Muslim married to a Croat who worked for the charity Caritas. The three nurses were on shift so there was cover 24 hours a day. I acquainted myself with all the patients and staff and sat with Dr Emira for an hour daily. She would brief me and I prepared lists of the medicines to be acquired by Asad in London. Dr Emira was from Mostar – the pearl of Bosnia. She loved Mostar but after the town was bombed she moved to Omiš with her Croat husband and child. Her only brother was killed in Mostar. She wept bitterly as she not only loved her brother but also Mostar, a beautiful city being bombed and destroyed.

Some of the patients at the Centre

Shera's real name was Sharif. He was nearly 19. His stomach wounds had not healed. He was thin and frail. Dr Emira told me how his parents were caught. His mother was raped in front of him and later when the HVO shot her, he fell on to her body and screamed: "Please do not shoot her, take me instead". The bullets went through him. His mother was dead and he lay over her. HVO thought that he was dead too and threw them both in a ditch by the river. Dr Emira dressed his extensive, weeping stomach scars every day while the nurse Munevera assisted. His bed sheets had to be changed daily and sometimes twice a day because of the weeping wounds. At times the electric supply was cut off and we had to wash the bed linen by hand. Later on we had a generator. Unfortunately I could not speak to him or other patients very much at that time as I had not yet picked up the language, but my heart was filled with sadness at the cruelty of fellow human beings. I received news from Fadila Memisević that thousands were massacred and their bodies thrown into the rivers Drina, Lim and Sana – people were horrified seeing the rivers red with blood.

I also remained busy in teaching but whenever I could I would go to visit the wounded upstairs. I often found them smoking and drinking and since I was neither a smoker nor an alcohol drinker this behaviour disgusted me. However, when Dr Emira told me Shera's story and how he used to sit up and shriek in the night, I could only feel sorry for him and prayed for his health.

There was Mo. His real name was Muhammad and he was 21 years old. I was told later that he was a soldier. He was tall and strong and spent most of his time with Shera. He had a neck injury. He played excellent chess and each time gave me a checkmate. He sang beautiful melancholic songs and pined to go back to Bosnia. He twice attempted to do so but was caught and not allowed to go in and turned back at the checkpoints, as most Bosnians had no papers or passports.

Suleman was called 'Sulio'. He was a forty-year old father of two from Doni Vaquf near Bugojno, where he lived with his family and parents. The Serbian onslaught in May 1992 and eventual capture of the town made his family refugees. They arrived in Bugojno as total destitutes. In August 1992 he was injured by sniper bullets and lost the use of his left arm. Even after treatment his left hand could not function fully as his fingers did not open. Sulio played the accordion before and even now loved music. He was always jolly and smiling and would sing while mopping up the Centre's floor with one hand. He tried to help in whatever way he could. He thought all the time about going back to his family in Bugojno. Efforts to evacuate him for treatment abroad had failed. It was heart-breaking to see this big and gentle man longing for his home and family. There was no physiotherapist when I arrived at Nemira so I decided to massage Sulio's arm myself daily with warm mustard and almond oil. While I messaged I recited a prayer – *Surah Fatiha* – for healing. One night there was no electricity and as I was applying warm oil on his arm, Bill Croker came and took my photo in the candle-light and nicknamed me as 'Florence Nightingale of Balkans'. After fourteen days a miracle happened – Sulio could move his three fingers! Achievements like these come from God alone but the thought that He does listen to our prayers gives comfort. It motivated me further to help those in need of help and also reinforced my belief that God Almighty does listen.

Hasib was badly injured by a mine. This twenty-seven year old truck driver had to have his leg amputated and was sent to a hospital in Croatia. His wife had given birth to a baby boy named Alim whom he had yet to see. Croatian authorities did not allow Muslims to go back into Bosnia. CoM managed to send him to England to be provided with an artificial limb and was subsequently able to walk. His wife Alma and six year old daughter had gone to live with her parents in Hrasnica in Bosnia. While Hasib was receiving treatment in London, Asad would deliver food parcels and money to the family. I once accompanied Asad to their bomb-damaged house without electricity or heating. When Alma read the letters from Hasib, tears kept rolling down her cheeks. One could see how much this couple was in love, though torn apart by war and its misery. Alma and her parents welcomed us warmly in spite of their own troubled lives. There were many others who received treatment at Nemira. Something about each one of them has remained with me that I cannot forget even if I tried.

While based at Duce I used to buy freshly baked bread from the local bakery. The shop keeper was a Croat lady who was quite friendly towards me. She had a young son who was a doctor and suffering from pains in his stomach. She called me at home one day and in tears, told me that the news had spread in the village that Sulio's arm was better and that I was a good woman. She requested me to pray for her son. She showed me the pictures of Virgin Mary and Jesus on the wall. I told her that I did not pray like her. I pray differently and directly to God and in my own way. She begged me to pray for her son and insisted that I went from the shop to her house where her son was lying on bed. I placed my hand on his stomach and very humbly and sincerely recited *Surah Fatiha* nine times daily and begged Allah *Jalla-Shanuhu* for his health. I did this for about three or four days. The son's name was Dino, I think. He got better by the grace of Allah and the mother kissed me and gave me freshly baked *kifle*. I told Dino not to drink any alcohol as perhaps he had ulcers. In turn he told me that he was treating many wounded Muslims at the hospital where he worked. I was embarrassed as many people started to call me 'Florence Nightingale' and my cheeks would burn with a sense of humiliation to Allah for accepting my humble prayers. With all my failings I never considered myself a good *Muslima*.

An unpleasant encounter

Marion Sabic, the owner of the building where Nemira centre was based, would frequently come and speak to the occupants. I was told that his twenty-two year old son had committed suicide and that his wife too had died. He was not liked as the neighbours thought that he was evil and some even considered him a psychopath. I was told by Jure that four years ago he went to the telephone office and threatened to dynamite the place when he was refused a reconnection of his phone because of non-payment. He was said to have spent some time in prison for that. He always smelled of strong drink. He was living a lonely existence with only his dog for company. His younger son was also charged for stealing. I was amazed to note that in spite of all this, the crowd at the Centre would call him in and ask him to eat meals with them. They told me that they felt sorry for him and knew that he was not well.

We tried to tell him to get the septic tank cleaned but he would not get any repair work done. The toilets were broken and there were cockroaches and mice everywhere on the ground floor where we volunteers lived. He was only interested in increasing the rent, so we gave notice to vacate. It was then that we really saw his spiteful side. He locked up our warehouse, which was in his basement, and would not give the keys. He asked us to pay him 6,200 DM for repainting the walls that he said we had damaged. He also called in the Police and told them that some 'fundamentalists' were living at the Centre. It dawned on us that Idris had draped a green flag with the *kalima* on it in his room and this was considered a big crime in Croatia. Luckily Jure handled the Police and they left without interfering with us. Idris was told straightaway to remove the flag from his bedroom wall.

There was something odd about Marion. As soon as he saw Asad he melted away. Asad somehow knew how to tackle him. Asad brought the required paint and other materials and we all gave a hand in making the place look better than it ever was. To my surprise, Marion brought cold drinks for us and he did not ask for the Deutsche Marks. He even kissed us all farewell and returned the keys of the warehouse so we could retrieve our aid goods.

This was not all. Marion asked me up in his flat one evening and tried to chat me up before we left, but I ran a mile. I just could not take to his alcohol-smelling breath. He always tried to speak German with me and though I had told him that my fluency in German was limited, he still insisted speaking to me in that language. The next thing I came to know was that he was spreading rumours that I came to him one night in a lace nightie and tried to seduce him. I just laughed at this fabrication and no one believed him. Marion tried to keep contact with us even after we had left. He came to visit us in our new premises in Duce near Omiš. Not only that, he once even came to pick me up from the Split airport. He told me then that he had been very ill. He said he had suffered a heart attack and had not touched drink since. I only half-believed him then. Later on I came to know that his second son had also died. When I returned to Split with Asad after a gap of three years we asked people about Marion and were told that he had passed away six months previously.

Further trials

I was very tired packing and moving from one place to another, along with the wounded soldiers and sick Bosnians. On arriving at our rented premises in Omiš, I felt happy as we could occupy two spacious floors. Downstairs there was a big hall with a kitchen and store room and a spacious courtyard. In the past it had been a luxury hotel and a popular holiday spot, but now it was not fetching any money. The landlord knew Jure and hence we were happy with the arrangement. The landlady had a son of nine called Ante. I also asked him to attend our English classes and to join us in various games, which he gladly did at times.

Our clinic was established on the first floor and Dr Emira was still with us as well as the old nurse. We all had separate bedrooms with functioning, clean toilets. The kitchen was well-stocked and Alma and Amra's mother continuing to work and cook for us. The sea glistened in the sunlight and the view from the hotel was breathtaking. At such moments I feel close to God and earnestly prayed to Him to remove enmity and create peace and love towards each other.

I carried on teaching children, who were picked up from their camps early in the morning to spend the day with us. I used to hold the classes downstairs in the big hall that also served as a place for prayer at *dhuhr* time. We gave the children fresh milk and sandwiches for lunch and played games with them, and they were dropped back in the evening. The police would not say anything to our Quaker volunteer from America and only occasionally stopped us and looked inside our vans.

Suddenly one day my Croat landlady Dragica came down and told me to vacate the premises. I spoke to Jure and he told me that many Croat soldiers were coming back to their homes and some of them were threatening landlords that they would bomb their building if they kept Muslims. I was horrified as it was not long that we had shifted. I came down with a solemn face and told the children not to come the next day. One boy from Bugojno had a beautiful voice and he liked to call the *adhan*. Apparently someone had heard the call of prayer and was angry. One boy, whose name I do not recall, stood up and reminded me that I had once told them that in difficulty we should make the prayer of *Salat ul Hajat*. I bent down and kissed him and performed this special *dua* with my young innocent students. They all left with sad faces. The next day was a Sunday and I told them not to worry, maybe something good would come out of it.

I had a sleepless night. The team had gone to deliver aid and I was alone in the big house with six wounded patients, one on dialysis machine. Dr Emira had gone home. Asad was in London and I did not know what to do or where to go. I was tired of shifting as it was quite tedious to pack and carry not only my personal luggage but also all the heavy cartons of aid. I had a late breakfast and wrote poetry in Urdu about my plight. Then in the afternoon, Jure came and knocked at my door. He said that the landlady called him and he had come to interpret. The landlady gave me fresh milk and figs from her in-laws' garden and smiled and offered us coffee. I was still dreading that she would give me a date to vacate, but she told Jure to tell me that if I prayed with the children in the bedrooms on the first floor and not downstairs and drew the shutters, it would be alright. Then no one could see us praying. She took me to the first floor and showed me the room to use for prayer. I thanked her and thanked Allah that we did not have to move. Finally when I went to pick up the children from the refugee camps and broke the good news, their faces were lit and they all came running to board the van. Their belief in prayers was reaffirmed, that Allah does listen when we seek His help.

Hotel Lav also housed Croat refugees who had fled from Zadre after Serbian bombardment. The mainly Croat teachers in the school established on the ground floor were paid for by UNHCR and UNICEF. The relief agency IGASA met the transportation costs for the Bosnian children coming from the camps. The school had a Bosnian principal with little say in its running and seemed intimidated by the other staff. The older Bosnian children resented being taught by Croats. They also felt anxious seeing the Croats carrying their Kalishnikovs which they would shoot for fun. One day when I arrived to take my class I noticed that the hotel's crystal chandeliers were strewn in bits on the floor and being cleared up by the cleaner. I was told that it had been destroyed by the Croats who said that if they did not have chandeliers in Zadre, there should not be any here!

I was advised by my kind landlady that if I allowed the Croat soldiers to hold their wedding parties in the big hall they would perhaps feel friendlier towards us. I needed the money so I agreed to let them use our hall for a sum of 100 DM. I also made it a point to go and greet the bride and the bridegroom. It worked as the ice was broken and I received quite a few smiles from the guests as well.

The Croats' wedding parties were noisy. They liked to fire Kalashnikovs into the air – which caused our patients, particularly the wounded Bosnian Julage to tremble with fear. One such night when the wedding ceremony was on and unable to sleep, I composed a poem and named it 'The Wedding':

Lovely marble mountains
Slabs of black and grey
Mingle with the white
and slumber cosily by the sea
Sea is here, calm with a gentle flow
Sunset bathes in the crimson glow
Somewhere a soldier is wedded
The music begins
The flag is hung with a live cockerel
Tied on to a pole
Seven shots are fired, luckily into the sky
Leaving a pattern of red stars go by
Kalashnikov's thunder echo
The music is played
Amidst the flow of whisky and gin
The dance is on the swing
The wounded Bosnians hidden here and there
And the wounded soldier Julage trembles with fear
At each shot they hear
I look at the happy couple
And at the live hanging cockerel
Still tied to the flag and the pole
Its wings flap in the air
Still alive in despair
Yes the dance music is on

> But my heart sobs
> At the cockerel and at the frightened soldier
> He was man once!
> I glance back at the lovely mountains
> And the beautiful sea
> And at the Dalmatian deceitful beauty
> Full of hate and cruelty
> Oh Allah! forgive us and show Thy mercy
> Just then a silent moon rose beyond the hills
> And witnessed it all with serene humility.

One evening, our poor patient on dialysis loaded his car with his belongings because he wished to visit his family. He had been going daily to the Red Cross hospital. Overnight he passed away, leaving a desolate car in the car park. Neil arranged for his funeral. I often wonder whether his family ever knew of his death and in what circumstances he died, longing to be with his family.

Jasmina Cosić

Asad brought a tall, young and elegant lady who was suffering from severe depression to our Omiš centre. Her name was Jasmina and she, together with Ryan Grist of UNICEF, had helped Asad when he was arrested by the Croats in Kisilijak. Jasmina had been sent to United Nations in Geneva but on the third day of her arrival, she was taken ill and sent back. She had nowhere to go. Her marriage to a Serb had failed and her only son was in Sarajevo with her ex-husband. Asad was contacted and he brought her to us to be under the treatment of Dr Emira. Jasmina was a vulnerable person slowly recovering from a nervous breakdown, but always took great care of her appearance and would visit the hairdresser and dress fashionably. She was the only person looking glamorous during the times of bombings and attacks.

One day, Ryan came to visit her while Dr Emira was away on a week's holiday and they had a long conversation. Later on in the night, while Neil and I were sitting in the kitchen having a cup of tea, we heard a thud that came from Jasmina's bedroom. We rushed to investigate, but the door was bolted. Neil somehow kicked and pushed the door open and saw Jasmina lying on the floor next to a glass table. Neil and I both tried to pick her up. It was not easy but somehow Neil had the strength to pick her up and carry her on his back. I tried to get her bedroom slippers and wrapped her in her dressing gown. We rushed to the hospital, honking at all the checkpoints, and shouting 'emergencia' to the Police. Neil drove with speed while I kept on trying to wake Jasmina up and kept on speaking to her but the situation was tense. We rushed straight into Emergency of the Red Cross hospital in Split. Luckily the doctors immediately took her in. We desperately waited outside in the cold corridor for hours for the news and prayed for her survival. Jasmine had a lot of talents and was an intelligent young person. Finally the doctors asked us to return home as they had washed her stomach out and hopefully she would recover. Anyway she was out of danger. It was 3.30 am when Neil and I returned to our beds at Omiš. We then realised that Jasmina had taken the clinic's keys, quietly opened the locked cabinets and helped herself to as many tablets as she could lay her hands on in an attempt to commit suicide.

Neil and I brought her back from the hospital after a three-day stay. It took me days to counsel her. I took her for long walks and tried to speak to her about God and His commands against taking away one's own life. I tried to make her recite the small *surahs* of Qur'an and slowly and gradually she returned to normal. She started to take interest in translating English into French. She missed her son Albin very much but Sarajevo was under siege. Jasmina and I became very close – we used to pretend that we were at the Ritz in London having afternoon tea. We used to walk along the shore in the evenings and watch the crimson red sun drowning into the sea. She used to marvel at my capacity for work. I hoped and made efforts that she could face hardships and challenges ahead and perhaps learn to survive in chaos like some of us. Above all, I wished that she applied her education and talents in useful pursuits. Many years later my wish did come true, as she wrote many books. She not only fought with her sickness but faced the terrible tragedy of losing her young eighteen year old son and later her parents. She was left alone but that beautiful and courageous woman gained her strength back to face life and its turmoils.

* * *

On one of my travels back to my home in London, I saw the newspapers were now reporting the details and images of terrible atrocities, torture cells and destruction. The world was eventually waking up to the fact that the Bosnians were the victims of aggression and that it was not an internal conflict or civil war as previously reported. Credit goes to many of our brave British reporters who risked their life and ventured into those horrifying places for reporting the truth – but better late than never. The penny finally dropped and many more people volunteered to help the Bosnians. Our Government also decided to change its attitude towards the war in Yugoslavia and the sympathy for the Bosnians increased thanks to the British media.

Jablanica

Aid workers found their way to the Balkans via various routes. Some would fly to Zagreb and stay in this Croatian capital city, but this was not of much use in helping the Bosnians stranded in various pockets besieged by Croats and Serbs. On one of my visits I preferred to go to Vienna, then enter Slovenia and make my way along the Dalmatian coast. The only way in or out was with the UN or its UNHCR convoys, but this depended on the whims of the Serbs. The situation inside Sarajevo, Banja Luka and Gorazde was desperate and although people were not starving to death, malnutrition was rife.

I felt an urgency to work inside Bosnia. Some of our volunteers, like Asad and Sadakat, had ventured into Sarajevo via Hrasnica by passing though the muddy and frosty underground passage called 'the Tunnel' in freezing weather. The consensus within the CoM team was that we had all come to the Balkans to help and we had known before leaving home in England that there were risks, so we decided to go in. While studying all the maps obtained from BRITBAT and UNPROFOR, it was clear that the dotted lines of the convoy routes were very close to the Serbs' line of fire. We were lucky to have British Muslims who had not changed the names on their passports as well as our good friends and volunteers who were non-Muslims. This help was invaluable in driving trucks through the checkpoints. The road to Hadžići was a dangerous route with snipers hidden on both sides of the mountains. The NGOs were taking risks and Asad did not want me to go through that danger, but the plan was agreed to go ahead.

Finally, we were on the way to Bosnia. It was fun travelling with Asad Khan and we were often together in a truck. Neither of us minded driving without frequent stops, and we ate little and never felt tired. Asad could quite easily sleep on any parked place on the wheel. We both loved to listen to old favourite songs, and I would make tea while he was still driving, on his home-made tea machine attached inside the vehicle. It was hard for me to sleep. I would walk in the parking areas during the night travels or do *tasbih*. We both prayed during our long journeys wherever we found a parking place. We never thought of spending charity money to go to a hotel for rest or sleep.

The Boona checkpoint was particularly notorious as the Croat soldiers prevented any goods or food entering Bosnia unless they were given money. Asad somehow managed to tackle them, while I chatted with the Customs and the Ustasha police in English to provide assurance that we were not locals but British. In any case we had Convoy of Mercy painted boldly on all our vehicles in black letters. I would break the ice by asking the soldier who was pointing his gun at us for coffee for me and other travellers! Asad looked at me in a bemused way.

Friendships in Jablanica

I felt a thrill of happiness in my bones as I touched the ground of Bosnia at Jablanica in January 1994. The winter sun was glistening on the snow-capped hills surrounding this little town. A white minaret of the mosque was welcoming us from the green surroundings in the early morning sunlight. Asad and I entered tired and sleepless after journeying for thirty-two hours, but seeing the morning sun-bathed little city, we both felt fresh and happy. Senad Velić, the Imam of Jablanica, welcomed us and we put our luggage inside the little *jamia*. We spent the later part of the night there while Imam

Senad Velić gave war news to Asad. In the morning we went to his house for a wash and a good breakfast provided by the Imam's wife Marjiama. Hot food used to be a luxury in those days of travels and adventure.

Many people came during the day to the *jamia*. We enquired about any accommodation but without much success. We took a tour of the little city but could not find any, as the refugees kept pouring from everywhere. All shops were closed and there was no electricity at night. Just when we were venturing to sleep a second night inside the *jamia*, we were invited by a bright-faced girl, Sanela, to her house. She commenced helping us in Jablanica. She was an eighteen year old who learnt English very quickly. Her father's name was Becir and her mother, a Serb, was Selveta. They were originally from Crne Gore, also called Montenegro. Their house was burnt and they were dumped on the outskirts of Čapljina. They had walked all the way to Jablanica. Someone had provided them with a room for shelter near Jablanica mosque. Sanela was drawn towards learning Qur'an and attended mosque daily for all prayers even though the father never prayed. I was impressed to see how hard her mother had worked. She welcomed us in their one room and we spent the night with them. Only God knows how she managed to take out spotlessly clean linen and gave us a warm bed while they slept on the floor. They had one makeshift toilet outside in the open grounds covered with curtains. It was quite daunting to go out in freezing cold and use the outdoor toilet without a flushing system or light.

Over the next few days we searched for a place to live. Asad spoke some Bosnian but I could only utter a few basic words, that too in Serbo-Croat picked up in Croatia, not Bosnian or Bosanski.

I was moved by the hospitality of these simple country folk. Selveta knitted woollen socks – *papuche* – which the Bosnians wore inside their homes, as no shoes were allowed inside. She also knitted woollen sweaters and cardigans for sale. One day she came to me and said that she had taken a bath and she was ready to accept Islam. She had seen Muslims from England had come to help the stranded people, risking their lives and bringing aid. I was pleasantly surprised and took her to Imam Senad Velič who asked her to recite the *kalima*. There were tears of happiness everywhere. Sanela came over and gave me a forceful kiss. Selveta said that she wanted to be called Sadeta. I was not familiar with their names. In any case names do not matter – it is the person carrying the name and his or her actions that count.

* * *

We were invited to Jablanica TV. The interviewer asked me many questions about our work and Sanela interpreted. We were the only foreigners and civilians there other than UNPROFOR and logistics personnel. I explained how the British people felt for the Bosnian victims. This was important because most Bosnians resented the British Government's policy of the arms blockade.

The priorities of UNPROFOR however at the time often caused me to wonder. For example, while people were starving and being killed, special envoy Yasushi Akashi placed importance on ceremonies to light candles and arrange flowers at crossing points! In an UNHCR bulletin in 1994 he was quoted describing such gestures as an "important symbolic humanitarian step in creating greater understanding between the parties in this tragic conflict". Was visiting graves more important or saving those trapped in Banja Luka, Bihać and Žepče? Not only women but men were raped and tortured in camps. Moreover by UNHCR's own accounts there was a massive shortfall between the pledges made for the delivery of aid to Bosnia and actual practice. The town of Bihać in the east needed about 2,000 metric tonnes of food deliveries during a month in 1994 – the actual food delivered was 126 metric tonnes.

I met Alma Sefo. She was only seventeen years old but a remarkably intelligent girl. Her father, Sead, an engineer, was in Sweden while Alma and her mother Ayesha were left behind. Alma asked me to come and meet her mother one day after the class. I came to know that they had lived in Stolac. Sead was an engineer who had been held in a concentration camp after the Croats' heavy bombing of Stolac. Alma's father was rescued from the concentration camp and somehow found his way to Sweden with his brother-in-law. When he had a chance to come back to Bosnia, he drove a van and Asad helped him cross all the checkpoints so he could bring a few things safely without having them confiscated by the checkpoint police. Alma worked with us and would be with me from morning till late at night. We used to prepare boxes of aid and bind them with tape. She was a good interpreter and travelled to various towns with Asad Khan where refugees were stranded to deliver food parcels, money and letters that the refugees sent to their stranded families. Asad did what most of us could not do and God protected him.

We kept on looking for accommodation while I continued to teach English in the mosque to children and teenagers. I spent the whole day in the mosque. We had brought stationary for the schools but these were all shut and refugees had occupied even the gymnasiums. The director of one of the closed schools asked for our help and Asad Khan and I visited the premises and made an inventory of all that was needed. We supplied the school with the necessary stationary, typewriters and a computer. The people of Jablanica were delighted as they were realising the importance of learning English. There were no shops and no businesses. The only work to be found was to interpret for various NGOs and UNPROFOR. An UNPROFOR official, Douglas Castle, spotted me distributing leaflets for the opening of classes at the school while he was having his morning coffee in a high street café. He told me that news had reached him that I was only interested in teaching Muslims. Instead of helping the masses he was putting a spanner in my volunteer work. I was not getting any money while fat cats like him drove around in luxury cars with drivers and satellite TV. The poor CoM volunteers were not even getting proper accommodation! I retorted back and asked him that if he was a doctor would he differentiate treating his patients? He kept quiet to that. Even in that small town there were many mixed marriages between Christians and Muslims and our English classes and aid was open to all.

On one of UNHCR meetings held in Jablanica I informed the American coordinator that the tunnel nearing Početelje was closed by the Croats because the four hundred old beautiful Počitelj mosque was being destroyed. I had hoped that by mentioning closure of the tunnel some notice would be taken but instead she shrugged it off saying that no official information had been received. Such was the indifference. The next thing we knew was that the mosque was bombed and a shopping arcade erected in the mosque's garden. When I reported this to UNPROFOR at Jablanica, they claimed to be unaware. In reality they were not bothered. A month later, the tunnel was opened. All the Bosnians could do was to print the mosque's picture on a calendar. Thanks to Arab money and help from Indonesia and other Muslim countries, some mosques are now rebuilt, including the one in Počitelj.

We finally found accommodation in one of the chalet bungalows owned by a local entrepreneur, Dino. When it rained we could hear it dropping on the tin roofs, at times clattering all night but at least we were comfortable there. We were also given a big warehouse by the *Opstina* and the town mayor welcomed us. Sanela's father was made caretaker of the warehouse. Rachid Benaïssa dispatched a large consignment of chocolate biscuits together with other aid from Paris. He also visited us in Jablanica. Neil Golithy, Julie and other aid workers would bring boxes of aid that were unloaded into the warehouse for distribution among the stranded refugees. The CoM drivers would then proceed to other destinations. Asad Khan's mother, Mahmooda *Apa*, also came and stayed with us in the small chalet. She was remarkably loving and caring and always made sure that I ate something nourishing. When Neil and his team would arrive she would quickly get busy and cook something for the lads to eat with their coffee. Sometimes we would go to Dino's restaurant for a meal. All shops were closed as there was no

Convoy of Mercy team's stop in Dino's restaurant in Jablanica –Neil Golithy (Ibrahim) Shaheed third from the right – 1994.

merchandise to buy or sell. We lived largely on food cans brought from England.

CoM's aid reached where no one else would venture – zones that were termed 'centres of death' by the Press. Our team workers were called dare devils as they risked their lives and went to those dangerous places in their ex-army Bedford MK trucks. CoM was gaining respect and was commended for its efforts. Many ex-army British soldiers helped us and provided Asad old pickups and ambulances. We also worked in cooperation with other groups such as Caritas and the Oxford Aid Committee. The Bedford trucks were individually named by Neil: one was called 'Sarah Jane', another 'Princess'.

Asad brought tons of aid on each of his trips. Some would first be unloaded in Dugi Rat for distribution by the boys to different areas under Neil's guidance. They would then proceed to Jablanica and then further inland. The route to Sarajevo was via a network of tracks that led over a mountain from Tarchin to Hrasnica, a suburb of Sarajevo distance of some 20 kilometres from Mt Igman. It was impossible to get to Sarajevo by the normal road routes without crossing Serb lines. Even if they gave permission to cross their lines, the Serbs invariably confiscated half the load. The Serbs were then able to feed their troops and the civilian Bosnian Serbs who lived in territories connected to the outside world via the Brčko Corridor to Belgrade and Serbia proper. Their actions were a way of reducing the amount of food reaching the surrounded Bosnian Muslim civilian populations in the enclaves. Knowing the difficulty with which the food was collected and brought over, it did not go down well with us that any should be handed over to Serbs.

CoM's entry to Sarajevo

Over dinner one evening at Dugi Rat, the volunteers started talking about the hazards of delivering aid to Sarajevo. In the discussion and banter the question arose: "how can we take forty tons of aid inside the besieged city?" How one could go from the sublime to the ridiculous! Sarajevo was under siege by the Bosnian Serb Army and had been so over two years.

In early April 1994, the CoM trucks were loaded with forty tons of food parcels and chocolates donated by Sweden and held in the Caritas warehouse at Split. Our brief from Caritas was to make it to Sarajevo and if we could not, to divert the aid to which ever distribution centres we thought fit. The CoM convoy took the Dalmatian Highway, drove past Omiš and Ploče and then to Metković where the trucks crossed the old Croatian-Bosnian border and then moved on to Doljani. Neil Golithy negotiated the crossing with the border guards who were always reluctant to let us cross. They regarded the recipients of the aid as their natural enemy and begrudged them every ounce of it. Neil would play his trump card: that if we were denied access then the guards would have to account to the UN – we were acting as agents of CARITAS, a Catholic aid agency and the Catholic Church was a powerful force in staunchly Catholic Croatia. The convoy then passed ancient Mostar and then to Jablanica for a stopover at our base. Neil was always in a hurry to get to Konjic before dark, as no one travelled at night in Bosnia. The electricity was cut off and bandit gangs haunted the deserted areas adjacent to the confrontation lines. Even a large convoy like ours, unless it was armed, could easily fall prey to the modern day highway men with their AK-47s. It was to their relief when they entered into the sandbagged and barbed wire gateway of the Malaysian Battalion (MALBAT) camp in Konjic. One felt relatively safe in that camp – it was an oasis of sanity and military order, only occasionally threatened by a 105mm howitzer landing nearby. The Malaysians always welcomed us. Neil and his team were given sumptuous hot chicken curry and rice. Morale was restored after a long tiring day. We were allocated two large tents well equipped with hot showers and a couple of camp beds. Our boys carried their own sleeping bags. It was important that these daredevils rest a little and feel fresh for the oncoming hazardous journeys.

Next morning after breakfast in MALBAT camp, the vehicles were checked and topped up with engine oil. The convoy then moved off towards the mountains of Bosnia. It was a warm and sunny as we passed slowly through to the village of Lokve. The small mosque battered by artillery fire stood beside the road and many small houses clustered around it bore witness to the shots and shells of this unholy war. Unsmiling, frightened children clung to their mother's long dresses and some young men and the elders eyed us suspiciously as we passed by. The only trucks that ever came that way were the engines of war, bent on destruction and death. It was after reading the lettering on the doors of our trucks

– *Humanitarna Pomoc* – that the look on their faces softened a little.

We did not notice some activity going on in the backs of the trucks. Two young men had climbed on the back of the last truck and cut the sheets to get inside. They must have thrown about a dozen of food parcels out and settled down at the back of the truck. As the convoy climbed up the mountainous terrain, the clear sky became overcast and grey. Our ten-ton four wheel drive trucks managed the rough mountain track. In the back the two men devoured as much of the Swedish chocolates as they could. It started to snow gently at first then with great intensity. The team had not come prepared for the sudden change in weather. They daringly drove up the rocky slopes of Mount Igman that had ice on the bends. One truck slid gracefully off the road and settled down comfortably with one wheel hanging over the edge of a small slope. It was just a drop of few feet but enough to keep the team busy with shovels and tow ropes. The snow chains were fitted on. There was not enough room for the trucks to turn around as on one side there was a steep cliff and on the other a drop of hundreds of feet below. The two hitch hikers still remained undetected!

The trucks inched forward. While Keith was manoeuvring one truck, the rear wheels slid on an ice-covered rock, bringing 'Victoria' and the rock face-to-face, ripping the canvas from the sides and spilling several boxes of Swedish generosity on to the snow-covered ground. When Keith dismounted to survey the damage, John Cox, who had been witnessing the scene from the mirror of his truck, came down to assist. They found the boxes stripped open, the food spilled all over and the two men crouched in the back. The whole team stopped and asked them to get down immediately. The aid workers were disgusted by their dishonesty, but then when people are starving they can stoop low. The snow had stopped falling, leaving the road with a treacherous combination of ice and wet snow. 'Sarah Jane' started to slither to the edge of the precipice and her rear wheel sank into the soft shoulder of the cliff edge, poised between the hellish highway and the beckoning valley. Keith, Mike and Ibrahim with other helpers unloaded the truck and piled the aid on to the remaining trucks. That was not all. The now rain-soaked boys found that 'Vera' being driven by Guy had slipped five metres below and luckily was stopped by a huge cypress tree but completely turned upside down. The lads shouted and came running towards the vehicle as they feared worst had happened to Guy. To their relief he was found leaning against his toppled truck. They all said a prayer of thanks but in their heart they knew that Igman had exacted revenge for trespassing it. That was how CoM managed to bring food inside Sarajevo via Hrasnica. They proceeded with determination and zeal, slipping on ice, and continued their journey down the mountain with no ignition and no lights otherwise they would be under Serb fire from either side of Igman. The Serbs always gave us a hasty and inaccurate welcome with their guns. Neil had gone ahead to survey secure parking for the night. The people were surprised to see him, but when they saw the rest of our trucks they could not believe their eyes.

The CoM convoy was taken to the Chief of Police who welcomed us to Sarajevo and thanked the team. The French UN Control post could only take them in the morning so they parked their vehicles in the Police Station and cooked their meals in its compound – sardines and baked beans which they had with hot coffee and soup. Every few minutes they could hear 30mm gun and mortar fire. The next morning they made their way to the airport. They were allowed to cross the runway only and after much discussion and examination of papers. The French Foreign Legion sergeant kept exclaiming to them: '*It ees eempossibeel to drive over zee montagne!*' to which the boys would retort, 'OK then how did we get here?' The sergeant would say: '*Maybee, you are in zee disguise, no?*' Then Neil would say with a smile, 'Aye, maybe these thirty five tons of food we bought from your local shops! Don't be a prat, man!" That was the first non-UN convoy to the besieged city for six months. The boys were jubilant; they phoned me to say that

My class in Jablanica – 1994.

CoM had broken the siege of Sarajevo. Of our eight trucks only six made it through, but they did it. On reaching Dugi Rat on the way back we learned that the Serbs had arrested a French UN-affiliated convoy the next day.

* * *

Seeing the number of students increased, the young mayor of Jablanica and the well-known official Sefer Hamdo both suggested that I held a class in the *Opstina* in the evenings for adults. The municipality building was in the centre of the town and luckily not shelled. It was surrounded by a garden and one could see the granite busts of Stalin, Lenin and Garbachov on the front facade. I was amazed at the tolerance, or was it still fear, in the hearts of local people that the statues were not destroyed, knowing fully

Seed distribution in Jablanica, next to me is Murveta and her mother and two sons – 1994.

well how they massacred the Muslims during their regimes? I also admired their tolerance for not desecrating the churches in revenge while witnessing the destruction of their mosques and the killing of imams. We had forty-six students in that evening class. Sefer Hamdo and his wife Murveta also attended the class and had become good friends.

It was the custom of that town that notices of deaths were pasted on the trees outside the *jamia*. The Imam held a burial ceremony almost every day as many people were killed and soldiers' bodies came to the *jamia*. The *shaheeds* were not bathed according to Islamic customs, but the *janaza* prayers were held in the same manner for all. Most of the cemeteries are situated on the heights in Bosnia. The procession would climb up with the dead body, partly by car and partly on foot. *Surah Yasin* was recited three times and the Imam would say the final prayer before laying the body in the ground. I attended two burials of my young students' fathers.

One of the bereaved was a ten-year-old student and she was very sad in class. The week after her father's death we heard a loud bang during class in *Opstina*. The whole building shook because a bomb had fallen five hundred yards away. The faces of the children turned white with fear. The girl started to scream and became delirious. I held her tight in my arms and took all the children quickly to the basement of the *Opstina*. Once I thought they were safe, I ran into the office of UNHCR where I found two of its employees. One of them, Mike, was trembling and holding a drink in his shaky hands. He told me that a bomb had just hit outside Dino's bungalows where I was living at the time and offered me a drink, to which I declined and thanked him. I came back to the basement and stayed with the children for an hour. When all seemed quiet I sent them home. The bomb happened to fall on a huge six-ton lorry carrying food aid. Luckily the drivers had gone inside Dino's restaurant and no one was hurt. The bomb created a huge crater and the six tonner's pieces were spread everywhere. What a sight!

Asad left me a much needed Suzuki van, though obtaining petrol was a big problem. Neil had told me of the help provided by the Malaysian army's MALBAT contingent, so I also ended up carrying a plastic can to them requesting for some fuel. The polite Malaysian major would usher me in the canteen while someone would fill the container full of fuel. Warm food and a can full of fuel was a luxury in those days. While other forces would not welcome outsiders in their camps, MALBAT was the great exception.

We moved from Dino's bungalows to Ciglana Ulica or the 'Gypsy Lane' as it was named in Communist times. One of the Communists' good actions was to provide land for the gypsies on which they built their own houses. We rented a spacious first floor flat while the owners lived on the ground floor. I was able to store a lot of cartons of aid as well. It had a decent well-furnished drawing room and most importantly a proper bathroom and kitchen, which I had been missing since I left London. My students would follow me home sometimes, though the owners did not seem to be keen on children. The flat was close to our interpreter Ehdin's family and I was invited to their home quite often. As we sat in their balcony I admired the view of the mountain range. Ehdin's father was a small built well-dressed man and seemed to be a product of communist culture. He had three sons and two daughters. One son was married to Zehra who was from Montenegro and the other to a Serb who was quite interested in Islam. However her Muslim husband was not inclined towards religion. Both the sister-in-laws of Ehdin attended the English class. I noticed that only his mother prayed.

On one of Asad's trips to Ciglana we decided to invite the Jablanica's dignitaries to thank them. I had locked my bedroom and the flat and left for Dino's restaurant. When we returned later in the evening we noticed that the flat had been ransacked. My bedroom door was also broken open but luckily none of my things were taken. A note lay on my desk next to the computer which read, 'We don't take things belonging to Super *Baaka*'. I was thankful for their consideration, though they took all the food stuff away.

A few days later our warehouse was broken into and pilfered. When the goods were being unloaded a lot of people would come and stand by and watch. The news spread that the warehouse contained chocolates and hence a lot of boxes were taken away along with other food items. I was told later that the pilfering may have been carried out by a local Bosnian Muslim warlord, Zulfikar Zuka. No one was ever caught.

During my stay at Ciglana I met Harun Imamović, a remarkable young man who had lost an eye during a raid but continued to work night and day. He would arrive at odd hours in the night to pick up boxes of aid to distribute to the stranded people in trenches. The aid boxes contained spaghetti, beans, teabags, coffee, and sugar along with a toothbrush, toothpaste, soap and shaving kit with a small box of first aid and of course a match box and candles. Candles were most important as we had no electricity. The boxes for women had items for babies and hygiene kits along with food. Each box was packed and marked with great care till the late hours in the night and we noticed that the mums were happy to receive pampers and the sanitary towels as well in their aid boxes. Ehdin and Alma were a big help.

The afternoon English communication class concluded after three months. Imam Senad Velić and the director of the high school, Mr Lepara, were invited to present certificates prepared by CoM to students who achieved good grades. One student, Dunya, the wife of the mayor of Jablanica, played the guitar and we had quite a festive afternoon. The Bosnians baked excellent cakes and loved music. I was glad that the class terminated as I hated going out in the hot sun at two thirty in the afternoon and then again to teach at the *Opstina* at five thirty. It was quite tiring but their enthusiasm made me forget the conditions.

Later in 1994 I needed a break. I visited Rachid Benaïssa in Paris, where he provided accommodation in his home annexe to a Bosnian family. A son had a broken nose and scarred face due to shrapnel wounds. When I got back home to London, the Conservatives were losing ground and the trend started in support of Labour. I wrote a letter to Tony Benn about Palestine and Bosnia and the poor coverage given by the newspapers and media. He responded favourably, but of course when a Party is in opposition, they can easily speak up for the truth. The test is when they are in power.

Anyhow here I was, a most insignificant creature of God Almighty, worrying for each drop of blood being shed and praying to God to give us peace and love on the planet. While in Britain, Asad and I travelled to many cities, including Bristol and Sheffield, to make communities aware of the situation. We were able to encourage many volunteers to help in the work. My son Jimmy offered his Normanby Road house to a Bosnian family who had fled from Prozor. Meanwhile Yusuf Islam sheltered many Bosnians who managed to escape from the war in two buildings in Keys Road close to my own house, so while in London I made contact with them.

I arrived back in Jablanica in summer 1994 determined to help as much as I could to remove the pains and suffering of people. The famous *Stari Most* or Old Bridge of Mostar, originally build in 974 and then rebuilt in 1566, had been destroyed. We had to come by raft from Pula, with all our vehicles filled with aid. The British ex-army officers sold us fifty-year old army jeeps. Those came in handy as we faced roads in Bosnia that were often no more than goat tracks and the terrain was rough. Sturdy jeeps and vans were needed to traverse the partly bombed-out roads with huge craters. One jeep was converted by Asad into an ambulance. I was stopped at the Croat checkpoints, thoroughly searched and asked if I carried arms. I laughed and told them that ambulances do not carry arms. By this time my Bosnian language was quite good. I noticed that a smile or a laugh did help a long way.

On 24 June it was my daughter's birthday. I tried to call her but there were no telephone connections. I went to the post office but it had been shut for months, and then to the Military and the Police. I was told they had an old Morse code telephone. They tried to help me but there was no signal. The whole city was plunged in darkness. I was lonely and missed my darling daughter. I strolled down the empty lane which led towards the hills. It was past eleven at night.

There were thousands of glow worms decorating the silent and dark hills on a hot summer night, with their lights on their backs. There was no breeze and everything was still and silent. I walked slowly in the lonely wilderness and suddenly felt as if all the coniferous trees were silently bowing down. It seemed to me that even the hills in front of me were all bowing in this silent star-lit night and

Eid Festival in Jablanica – 1994.

---

performing *sijda* to Allah. I stopped short for I was in awe for a minute or so. A slight fear overtook me and all of a sudden I uttered an ayat from the Qur'an, *wa najmo wa shajero yas judaan, fa bay ayyeh 'allaa i rabbekuma tukazebaan* in the stillness of the night. I slowly walked back to my flat in Ciglana Street. I realised then that I was not alone. My Allah was my Protector and because of this belief I never felt scared or afraid. In the morning Ehdin told me that the lonely road led to the Serbs pockets behind the hills and one must actually avoid that road at all times.

The Ramadan of 1994 was spent in Jablanica. By now I had come to know almost everybody in that small little town. I was invited by the Chief Imam to attend the *Bairam* or *Eid* ceremony. It was conducted in a most organised manner in the open grounds of the gymnasia hall. I was officially introduced to all the dignitaries there. The whole of Jablanica population came to hear the *nasheeds* and Qur'an recitations. A packet of hot meat sandwiches was given to all by courtesy of Merhamet, the Bosnian NGO. In war times this was a special treat.

I was thrilled to see such a well organised *Eid* party. People gathered after the prayers and the mountains were in the background. Carpets were laid and a stage set up from where the whole programme was conducted and relayed to the audience. In spite of the war the children seemed to wear the best clothes they had. Everyone greeted the other with *Assalamu 'alaikum*. The ceremony was conducted by the Chief Imam and it started with a most beautiful recitation of Qur'an. The sound of the verses echoed and floated across the wild flower-scented valley of Jablanica. Even those people who did not understand a word of what was recited felt as if they were in a trance. There was complete silence in a crowd of a few thousand. Local dignitaries, the NGOs and the press were given the best seats in the front row. The Chief Imam welcomed us all and gave a small sermon. The ladies sang *nasheeds* in the course of the programme. At the end of the ceremony I met Commander Nazim Halilović, a hero whom the young Bosnians adored. I wrote an account of this *Eid* celebration in the magazine of the Muslim Women's Association in London, that was later published.

While still teaching in Jablanica I made frequent trips to London to collect funds for CoM. I was helped generously by Yusuf Islam, who was then a patron of Muslim Aid as well as by my friends Nusrat Gatrad and Ruqaya Hoosen. MWA's President Fatima Hassan managed to collect funds for CoM and also helped in delivering hospital equipment which was given to Jablanica hospital. In those days one carried cash as the banks were not operating and all business was at a standstill in Bosnia. Rachid Benaïssa came from Paris bringing with him a large consignment of aid, including warm clothing and chocolate biscuits. We had tea at Dino's, who never charged when he spotted me in his restaurant.

Students with presents for wounded patients at Jablanica Hospital – Dr Shuko, second from right – 1994.

Many refugees came to Jablanica from Prozor in the north of Bosnia. Some of them were lawyers and doctors. It was a pleasure to teach them English. A small number of refugees had a clannish mentality and each one of them thought that they had suffered most. I wanted to imbibe in them a spirit of solidarity at this crucial time. The classes were expanding in numbers day by day. One day I asked the students if we could pay a visit to the patients in Jablanica's hospital. This was a novel idea for them as under the communist regime such humanitarian activities were unheard of. The class agreed and we all decided to bring some baked cakes and flowers to the hospital patients. Upon our arrival Dr Shuko, the director of the hospital greeted our students with a big smile.

We all walked in and saw the hospital was full of injured soldiers everywhere. Each one of us carried a piece of cake and started to distribute these. Other students placed flowers on their bedside tables. I went to a bed where a very handsome young man was lying covered with a blanket. He looked at me and smiled while his blue eyes twinkled at seeing the cake and flowers. He asked me smilingly to put the piece of cake in his mouth. I was young then and it embarrassed me. So, I said to him: "No, you eat it yourself. I am not putting it in your mouth I am leaving it on the table." I was getting red in the face as he looked at me again with his enchanting smile. Then he removed the blanket by his head

Convoy of Mercy's medical supplies arriving for Konjic hospital – 1995.

movement. I will never forget what I saw. He pulled out both of his bandaged hands that were blown out by the bombing. I ran outside the room. Tears just could not stop and for days, I kept on thinking about that young man. How he must be coping, unable to feed himself, bath or go to the toilet? I just could not wipe him from my memory.

Asad Khan continued taking convoys to Bosnia and visiting various hospitals to deliver aid. He also visited Konjic Hospital and provided lots of medical supplies and surgical instruments, while I relaxed at home for a whole month.

Many students who had escaped the bombing did carry with them the anxiety and the terrible effects of war but at least their limbs were safe and sound. The visit taught us to value our faculties and the perfect functioning body that God Almighty has given us. He alone provides us with food in hunger and safety amidst fear and danger. There are also those among us who cannot take stress and suffer from depression or turn to alcohol and drugs. After their visit to the hospital my students managed to save whatever they could and brought home-made juices and cakes to the hospital patients a few times.

Food was in short supply in those days and the shops were still closed. The travel routes to Hadićži, Pazarić and Tarćin were impossible to cross because of the constant shelling. A journalist was hijacked between Tarcin and Konjic. However I managed to go to Tarcin and met the Imam Tergic who invited us in his small dwelling close to the *jamia*. I was asked by the commanding officer to speak to the young soldiers who were given a short training of six weeks and had to go to defend their families. Mudderis and Harun both were doing an excellent job along with the Imam in keeping the morale of people up and by telling them to be calm and remember God Almighty who listens to all prayers. There was Ajsa Hasimbegovič who was working and helping in the so-called little army of Bosnia. Cemila of Konjic worked and helped the local community of Butrović Polije who were in distress. Many men who escaped torture in the camps or were imprisoned and later released had emotional problems.

The daughters of the landlord of the Ciglana flat had returned and we had to vacate again. Dr Shuko of Jablanica Hospital showed us a newly built bungalow close to Sefer Hamdo's house with a garage, where I could park my Suzuki. We were often invited to Safar Hamdo's house during our stay in Jablanica. We used to sit by the fire warming ourselves while eggs were fried and hot soup was being served – typical Bosnian hospitality. They had two boys of age nine and ten. Murveta's mother had also come to live with

A class opened in an abandoned school, Butrović Polije – Cemila is seen standing – 1995.

them as her house was taken by Serbia and totally destroyed. Their small house also was partly shelled and the gap in the roof was sealed by plastic. I had often wondered how they coped in this small bungalow of two bedrooms.

One day Cemila, the aid worker, came from Konjic and requested me to visit Butrović Polije. Sanela and I went to see the village along with Asad's mother. The road from Jablanica to Butrović Polije was full of craters and mostly damaged by bombings. Driving in the mountain's winding and broken roads was not a joke. On arrival Cemila met us there and showed us the local school that had been closed since the war. She requested CoM to provide some form of teaching. I was busy during the weekdays and only had the weekend left, so I promised her that I would undertake to come on Saturdays and Sundays. Cemila was delighted and soon the local Imam also came to thank us.

I was driving to Butrović Polije one Saturday morning with Alma. Suddenly the Suzuki's tyre got stuck on the few wooden planks of a broken bridge. It was a big struggle to extricate the car as it was loaded and also contained winter pullovers for the elderly. To my relief I saw the Imam of MALBAT, whom I had once met in the Jablanica mosque. He stopped his vehicle and helped us push the Suzuki out. From then on he volunteered to take us to Butrović Polije in his jeep. The school hall was filled with students of different ages. An Arabic class was held by the MALBAT Imam and I took the English class in the main hall. After the class, we all prayed and packets of biscuits were distributed to all. CoM was also able to provide warm sweaters. MALBAT also distributed aid to the village.

A poignant episode – Hesiba's story

One day, I was called by Dr Shuko to Jablanica Hospital. There was urgency in his voice and he wanted me to come immediately. Upon arriving there he led me through the corridor. He asked me to counsel and console a rape victim who was released from the prison and had walked back to the hospital. Her name was Hesiba and her husband, a local man of Ostrožac had been shot dead right in front of his house by a Serb. She was terrified and ran inside with her one-year-old child. The next day the Serbs came and took her away with the child. She first refused to speak to me but later on she opened up and with the help of the interpreter she told me a little, but mainly insisted that she did not want to see this baby conceived as a result of rape.

Hesiba lived in that notorious camp with other women. One mother had a nine-year-old girl. Two Ustashas came and took the girl away in the evening. Her mother wept and begged them to take her away instead of the little girl but they used abusive language and forced the girl away as she was trying to hide behind the mother. The whole night the girl's screams were heard in the building and the next day she was found dead. Hesiba noticed the blood squirted on the walls of the room where the poor girl was held. Hesiba was dragged in the following evening, in the same horrible room and every night since.

She broke down in sobs and requested me to do away with the baby she was carrying. I tried to pacify her and take her mind off the birth. I came home exhausted from the hospital to get some sleep. I had never done any counselling and did not know to whom to give the baby. She did not even want to see the baby. She kept on beating her stomach with fists and pulled her hair in desperation while in pain. Doctors tried to sedate her.

I asked my team to advise me as how can we help her. Ehdin and the volunteer Daniel 'Danny' Bronkhurst from London, both said that they would look after the baby if I brought it home. The next day I rushed to the hospital. The corridor was full of wounded soldiers but Dr Suko came running towards me when he saw me passing through the wards. He told me that Hesiba was delirious and now in the labour ward. We waited outside and when allowed in I told her that she must not be worried and that I would look after the baby.

I went to see her afterwards and again she asked me to take the baby away. I told her that I would do so but in the meanwhile she should feed the baby which she refused. I told her that she would get milk fever if she did not feed the baby. She started to cry and pull her hair again in anger. I brought in her first baby boy. When she saw him she stopped crying and kissed him many times. The not quite two-day old boy put his little hands on her mouth and eyes trying to stop her crying. Gently and slowly I recited some sura from the Qur'an, stroking her hair slowly and she fell asleep.

I came home and filled a carton full of groceries, tin foods, spaghetti, tins of tomatoes, chocolate biscuits and baby's pampers, milk, milk bottles and all toiletries which were brought from London for distribution. I went to Hesiba and told her that I would bear all expenses for her and for the baby if she would keep him with her for some time. I also told her that I would take that baby away if she so wished. She was calmer but did not reply to me and turned her face away from me. I told her that I would come again to see her and would like to know of her decision. I went to the Jablanica mosque and requested Imam Velić to come and give the ritual *adhan* in the baby's ear. First he declined saying that he could not give *adhan* to that 'snake's baby', but I told him that he was our Imam and the baby was innocent and had harmed no one. Finally it dawned on him that one cannot take revenge on an innocent baby. The Imam agreed to come to my house in the evening so we could go to the hospital. I had barely arrived when Dr Shuko came in a panic with the news that Hesiba and the baby had disappeared. The doctor was sure she intended to commit suicide and was trembling with fear. His face was white.

So we went looking for her all over the place, enquiring whether anyone had seen them. Finally we were led to a house perched on top of the hill. Hesiba was up and greeted us and asked us to come in. This was her sister's little house. She accepted the cartons full of food and baby things. I placed some money in her hands and was relieved that she agreed to keep the baby and was not seeking any more to commit suicide. I told her that in Islam it was *haram* to end one's own life. Luckily she listened. I found her much calmer from then on. She finally accepted the baby and promised to look after him. Later she joined our rehabilitation centre and worked as a cook but I noticed that her health was failing as a result of her ordeal in that wretched concentration camp. She must have been a blue-eyed beauty once.

* * *

With Imam Senad Velić at the *Nishan* commemorating the *shaheed*, Jablanica
– 1995.

I was contacted by the Jablanica *Opstina* that the marble and granite
nishan – a memorial stone – that Asad had suggested and also
designed, was finally ready. It was erected in the centre of Jablanica
in memory of the *shaheeds* of Umliani and Čihovici. A day was
chosen and all the local dignitaries attended the placing ceremony.
The Imam recited *Surah Fatiha* and all the people gathered around
and prayed for the martyrs. Later the dedication on the memorial
was extended to include all the *shaheeds* of Bosnia.

In August 1994 we heard the tragic news of Neil Golithy's death.
They had been driving a relief truck over Mount Ingman on a dark
and wet night and the tracks were slippery. As was the practice,
they were driving without lights trying to pass unnoticed of Serb

snipers. An arc of tracer bullets flashed in front of them destroying their night vision. The Serb gunner missed but the damage was done. The truck's off-side front wheel dropped over the edge of the road and despite Neil's attempt to get her back on to it, 'Samantha', the latest addition to our fleet, plunged over the cliff and crashed five hundred feet to destruction. The French found Neil and Tony the next day: two more victims of the war in Bosnia.

Alas, we lost our Ibrahim Neil Golithy, a thirty-two year old young and handsome man, a rugby player fond of the bagpipes. He was a true Scot as was his colleague Tony Richards. The two *shaheed* at Igman gave their life to serve humanity. Ibrahim's body was transported for burial to Glasgow where a lot of people attended his funeral service. Ibrahim Golithy still remains close as ever in my thoughts. May God Almighty give them both peace and Paradise in their eternal life. *Ameen.*

Kulsum, an accountant from London, came to help me to teach English. The house was small but became very uncomfortable as winter approached because there was no heating. There was a wooden *pec* in the hall but since we had never seen one before, we did not know how to make it function. One day Murveta carried wood logs to our house and tried to help us by heating the old *pec*, but since there was no outlet the smoke filled the room. The person from whom we had rented the house came and told us rudely that we were destroying the house by burning wooden logs. He asked us to vacate the house immediately. It was Christmas time and heavy snow covered the grounds. Kulsum was from Singapore and not used to the extreme cold. We did not know where to go. I had been away from home a long time. We explained the situation to the MALBAT commanding officer. I left the Suzuki with Sefer Hamdo and we moved in to the MALBAT camp by the permission of its CO. He broke the Army rule to accommodate us by giving a tent next to the boiler room. Kulsum fell asleep as it was warm but the noise of the boiler kept me awake. The commanding officer came quietly and told us that we could go to his camp-site and eat and relax in his tent while he was on duty if we so wished, but we did not want to take undue advantage of his hospitality.

Kulsum spoke Malay and the major and other staff in the dining area welcomed us. All transport was at a standstill. The next day one bulldozer was leaving for Split and so we climbed on to the high seats. Kulsum was of smaller stature than I and she managed with difficulty. We sat with the driver. The sky was overcast and so were our spirits. The river Drina was covered in white snow and the beauty of the scenery uplifted me. There was nothing moving except our vehicle. Kulsum chatted in her mother tongue with the Malaysian driver. We were always happy to head home. From Split we went to Pula by ferry and took a coach for London, as all flights were suspended due to the weather. My heart was filled with happiness as I greeted a happy new year to our Passport Control and Customs officers – it was the first day of January 1995.

ଔ Chapter 8

Ostrožac and Sarajevo

COM's activities were now well established in Jablanica where the authorities recognised our work and the zeal of our volunteers. We needed a more permanent base to serve as a rehabilitation centre and were shown an idyllic location by the hills and a lake in the outskirts of the Bosnian town of Ostražac. The building was dilapidated and roofless with trees growing in the ruins. The owner, a Serb, had to flee after his son killed a local man.

Asad gave me a thousand pounds to get the work started. I looked at him and wondered how long these one thousand pounds would last. He left for London the next day, leaving behind a young South African to help. This person was a disaster – swimming in the lake and enjoying an easy life without lifting a finger. I became frustrated with him and personally took charge of the work. After taking my classes in Jablanica, I would drive the Suzuki van daily the five kilometres to Ostrožac, passing through broken roads with huge craters and five tunnels. The Police had by now become quite friendly with me. MALBAT at Konjic came to help and dug and cleaned the rubble from the place. At Asad's suggestion I also located a helper in Konjic named Aziz and the work started.

Asad asked Aziz to find a flat for me. He offered a room in his flat where I stayed for a short period. It was also occupied by his cousin, who would lock herself up in the bathroom and cry for hours on end because of difficulties in obtaining the right papers to allow her to join her mother in Germany. I gave them money as I could not help in any other way. I was getting fed up with the girl's attitude so one night around midnight I shifted to the partially built Ostrožac centre where there was practically nothing except an electric kettle and a few utensils. I slept on a sofa bed that Asad had brought from my home in London. However I was happy to be in my own premises. The next day Aziz brought my luggage to me. I had stayed seventeen days in Aziz's flat and every evening almost at the same time the shelling started. The windows shattered and the window glass panes broke. After the raid, five minutes later, the reconnaissance flight came maybe to assess the damage. This was July 1995, after the announcement of the so-called peace. Whenever the curfew lifted I would go to the local post office to make a call to London. My children were relieved to hear from me, as they must have heard the news of shelling at Konic. Once I noticed a woman's brain splashed on the pavement, right outside the post office. Luckily the body was removed.

Our centre was located near a refugee camp run by the Merhamat relief agency. Families from the camp would attend my English classes. This is how I came to know Idriz, a ten year old boy who quickly became my shadow. He would help me with distribution and sit with me in the car and tried to look after me as if he was a man. Other children, including Tono, were great helpers.

A team of workers came from Konjic and material for the roof was purchased. The weather started to change and the clouds on the horizon were giving us the warning signs of winter snow. It used to be extremely cold at night as October was coming to an end. I wanted the roof to be finished before the first snow. At the end of every evening I would look up and count the remaining tiles to be fixed. Luckily I had the kettle which allowed me to make tea for myself and also boil some eggs. We were providing hot cups of tea to the builders on the roof. I sat and prayed and it so happened that the snow began to fall just when the last tile was placed. We all clapped happily – the workers on the roof and

Completion of roofing work at the Ostrožac centre – with Tono on my right – 1995.

Students at the English language class, Ostrožac. Idriz is first on the left – 1995.

I below. As per Bosnian custom a clothes line was set up on the newly-completed roof.

The electrical work was also soon completed but it proved difficult to find toilet seats. The carpet was laid, replacing the relief blankets and a cook and cleaner were hired. Beds were brought in and the bedside steel cupboards washed and cleaned. While work was still underway several young persons also had started to gather for an English class. Their schools were closed down. Aziz found some garden furniture from somewhere and a white board was placed on the wall in the ground floor. The youth enjoyed coming to the Centre as biscuits or chocolates with a drink was also served after their lesson and in between I would also try to teach them prayers.

* * *

Meanwhile I was still going to Jablanica in the Suzuki to conduct the English classes at the *Opstina*. I would bring back food and other items from the warehouse. I also provided regular reports to Asad in England. I was soon surrounded by many children who tried to help in whatever way they could. My helpers in Jablanica, Amela and Ehdin, also started work at the rehabilitation centre. The South African man who was with us at the beginning ended up in prison after a brawl with an intruder in his house. We did not really want him as he never came to the Centre and I did not have time for such people.

My darling daughter Jasmine also came to see me for ten days and took delight in meeting all the young students. She took them for drives in my VW car which I had brought from London and they loved her. Jasmine and I went to the nearby villages and distributed seeds to the families for them to restart their farming. My students included Hashim, the son of the local baker Ramzo, who supplied us with bread. Each time I would stop by the bakery, I was given a hot bun or a cake to take away and would not be charged. We would sometimes sit on his terrace in the evenings and I would try to converse in my broken Bosanski. I used to keep all cash with them as thefts were commonplace. Our warehouse was broken in several times and goods taken away. My car's rear window was stolen twice, which I then purchased back from the local market! The second time I picked my glass pane, I told the vendor, who was probably the thief, that if he needed money I would give it to him but he should not touch my car. His face turned crimson red. What annoyed me was that the Police never found the culprits.

I went for a short visit to London to purchase necessary items including kitchen tops for our centre, to be sent with Asad Khan's convoy. It was also a pleasure to see my grandchildren growing up.

* * *

I was alone in the winter in Ostrožac. One day, when the weather eased a little, I came out and seeing the Serbian neighbour Milutin clearing the snow, I thanked him. People had passed by without bothering to help, yet here was someone prepared to do something. Later his wife Bianca came up to the Centre's first floor, panting, with a freshly baked Swiss roll. I noticed that she wore several layers of thick woolen socks and she told me that her leg was swollen and very painful. I asked her to come again the next day, which she did. After removing all the layers of socks, I was horrified to see the lower part of the leg black and weeping with numerous small ulcers. I warmed some water and washed her wound. I had nothing else at the time except antiseptic Dettol, cuticura powder and Vaseline. She had perhaps braved herself with strong brandy before coming to me with the painful leg. I kept on reciting Sura Fatiha while dressing her wound. It became a routine for nearly ten days and I was happily surprised that although the leg remained black, the ulceration had stopped. Thanks to Almighty God who provided the healing power in *Surah Fatiha*. Bianca was of course very happy as her pain had eased and she was walking better, but some local people, including my helper, Alvir, did not like her coming to our Centre. The villagers knew that her son had shot a

Bosnian and had run away to Serbia. CoM ignored such remarks and continued to help whoever needed it.

I was missing my daughter and wrote this letter to her:

My dearest Jasmine

I have been trying to phone you the last seven days but it has not been possible as the satellite connection is not working efficiently. I am sitting in my bedroom which is nearly finished. It has a balcony and I can see bunches of grapes on the vine, the pear and peach trees and then the lake. So this is Ostražac. The doorbell rings every minute and I have a stream of visitors whether I like it or not. I am distributing pampers, oil, milk, spaghetti and other food stuff. We also have clothes to give out. Asad has very kindly hired a man from Pula to help me and ensure I am not alone here. But this Suleman has one problem. He likes to sleep a lot and doesn't work for days. He then turns up and says he is sorry. But when he works he does so very well. So I just shut up and put up with him. The trouble is that Bosnia is very much short-staffed. Men are on the front. There have been a lot of killings. Bihac is being ground down daily, but here it is relatively calm. There is a curfew here and in Konjic but I didn't get to know about this till I got stopped by the Police. Next to our Convoy house there is a small house where all the things are stored and Suleman loves to hold on to the keys. Almost all the women wear shorts and swim and sunbathe. They wonder why I don't ever indulge. I have been going daily at 10 am to Jablanica and then I come back at 12.30 to start my class here. After the class, *Dhuhr* prayers are held and then at 3 pm I come back to the flat to have my food. We have a woman helper who comes every alternate day to clean, wash and cook. This place gets very dirty. It is dusty and lime is flaking off the walls. The moths come in the evening and are found dead in the morning. The place must be swept daily. The classroom must be cleaned. All the students make *wudu* and fresh towels are also needed daily. Cobwebs are also formed within two or three days. Lizards creep around freely. In the evening though it does cool down. I still get the 6 o'clock sun on my face when I drive to Jablanica in the evening. The time I enjoy most here is after my return from Jablanica when the setting sun illuminates the surrounding hills, there are one or two clouds floating above and a fragrance of natural flowers and trees hangs in the air. The local people offer me *lipa chai* – an herbal tea. They also bring me rose drink and milk, and make cheese for me. They are always inviting me for dinner. In the evening I go to Tono's house for dinner – Tono, Idriz and Mersudin are my three pals…

I noticed that men normally do not like to discuss what happened to them. Our dentist, Mr Irfan Malik of Abbotabad in our Ostrožac centre, would sometimes tell me of their plight. They would often tell him how their teeth were knocked out and the abuse they suffered, leaving deep scars hidden inside them. They did not even want to share these experiences with their own wives. Like Irfan, Dr Shayan also arrived from Pakistan as a volunteer to help. The two were kept constantly busy. Hilmo was in charge of the wounded and invalid soldiers, brought from Hrasnica. Dr Shuko from Jablanica Hospital was provided bandages and other sterilised items like needles and injections along with supply of medicines. The services of our doctor and dentist were much appreciated. The Bosnians needed dental care, apart from the losses when their teeth were pulled out under torture. The poor diet during the war and the consumption of a lot of sugar in their coffee also led to dental problems. I noticed that almost all Bosnians smoked and most of them suffered with bad teeth and presumably the children's teeth decayed due to malnutrition. Dental clinics were shut or had disappeared. The local population that had initially been wary was now quite happy with us. We provided them some jobs and essential services.

A CoM truck with a Bosnian family, Umliyani – 1995.

My little children would spend long hours with me. They planted flowers in front of the Centre and often helped me wash the patients' bedside tables. Old people were particularly happy to be attended by the doctors as they could not go to the hospital in the cities due to lack of transport at the time. We had an ambulance which was used by the doctors and the dentist to go to the surrounding villages in their spare time and treat the sick and the elderly in their homes. The Centre was running smoothly and there were fruits and flowers all around us. Ehdin had put up an iron fence which was admired by all.

'Danny' Bronkhurst and Philip from Glasgow stayed with us for months. Danny prepared a brochure about the rehabilitation centre, also describing the details of war that had cost over 200,000 lives and left thousands of people with severe disabilities and psychologically scarred. Both military and civilians suffered from sniper fire, mortar and grenade explosions, shrapnel and mines. The severely wounded with amputations needed some length of time to convalesce with physiotherapy and nutritional care. There was an overall shortage of rehabilitation centres and hospitals were overflowing.

We distributed aid to Umliani and Čehovici. These were remote places with refugees in a terrible plight living amidst bombed out houses. CoM managed to reach to those far off places where no one else ventured. Later the inhabitants of that area presented us a certificate of appreciation. Thanks to Asad's zeal, CoM had continued to deliver relief items to villages and towns and also medical aid to hospitals in Konjic, Jablanica, Zenica and Hrasnica and at the institute for the mentally handicapped in Pazaric.

I met Dr Elaine Laycock OBE, the medical director of SOS Bosnia and a committed Catholic. As we both were involved in the same sort of work a warm friendship emerged straight away. On her visit to the Ostrožac centre I told her of the urgent need for a kidney

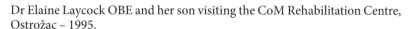

Dr Elaine Laycock OBE and her son visiting the CoM Rehabilitation Centre, Ostrožac – 1995.

dialysis machine, which she promised to obtain. She also met our Dr Shayan and discussed his interest in ophthalmology. When Asad next came to Ostrožac the dialysis machine sent by Dr Laycock was delivered to Jablanica Hospital under care of Dr. Shuko. On her second visit, Dr Laycock was accompanied by her son Richard and brought special eye testing equipment for Dr Shayan. Essential instruments were also provided at my request by Dr Abdullah Hoosen for our dentist Irfan Malik.

One day a UN car stopped outside Ostrožac centre. Major Oly from BRITBAT emerged with a Bosnian interpreter Senada. He was from the Midlands. He had heard about us and wanted me to help forty stranded families in Prozor who were surrounded by the enemy, to which I immediately agreed. I told him that it was difficult for me to go as snipers targeted the Muslim NGOs. He returned the next day and we loaded his van with the aid boxes prepared by CoM and a Belgium charity with whom we worked. Once in Prozor I noticed how much the major was loved by those stranded Bosnians as they realised how much he cared for them.

Asira's story

One evening I received a phone call from Dr Majid Katme that he was sending an Englishman over to see me in Ostrožac. A large burly looking Andy then arrived, with a request to bring a girl living in Mostar to our rehabilitation centre. He worked for an NGO in Mostar and did not want to disclose her name. Asira was brought to me the next day, a very pale looking girl of twenty accompanied by her elder sister. She was engaged with Ibro who had gone to the front after a little training. The Ustasha were watching her movement and one night caught hold of her, tied her mouth, raped her and threw her in the ditch beside the road. She lay there unconscious. She later got up, dusted off her clothes and crying all the way, walked to her sister's home. The parents were worried as Asira had not arrived home. Her father was a respectable Imam in the area where they lived. She did not want to face any of her family members from a sense of remorse and shame. The sister phoned the parents to say that she was not feeling well and was staying with her. It was a normal thing as she often had stayed with her elder sister. When Asira skipped her period, she became very upset.

The parents were still unaware of what had befallen their dear daughter. Asira was approaching five months of pregnancy and could not abort the baby, so the sister begged me if she could stay with me till her delivery. She did not want her parents or anyone else to know about it. Even during the days of war, there was such admirable dignity in the Bosnians. Many NGOs tried to help the rape victims, but the Bosnians strongly objected. They did not wish to be reminded of their torture and their ordeal and wanted those poor girls to pick up the threads and start afresh.

Anyhow I was left with Asira. Gradually I tried to make her accept the grief and tell her that she had to be strong and come to terms with life. She was constantly in touch with her fiancé Ibro on the front line. It was very difficult for her to tell him what had happened. When she was seven months pregnant, Ibro came home for a break and found out that Asira was not with her parents, so he went to her sister's house in Mostar. The sister told him the whole story. He immediately came to see Asira. It was a meeting of two lovers. They embraced each other with tears rolling down their faces. Ibro thanked me for looking after her and said that he would pay her costs. I smiled at that and told him not to worry. He assured Asira that his love has not diminished a bit for her and that when he returned, he would marry her. Asira's pregnancy soon started becoming apparent. As is typical in small towns and villages, I was often asked who she was and from where she had come from. Such uncomfortable questions made Asira very nervous. I tried to protect her as much as I could from those inquisitive people. The beautiful hills of Konjic and the surroundings looked so peaceful and yet so much of sadness was hidden in them. There were a lot of rape cases committed by the Serbs and by the Croats.

Discussing care of a newborn baby with Danny Bronkhurst – 1995.

We however did not hear of any Muslim or Bosnian soldiers who raped the enemy women. Ibro came to see Asira and brought loads of fruits. When he left Asira told me that Ibro was requesting her to give the child away as soon as he was born. I tried to tell Asira that no child deserves such a fate, but this was their choice and my persuasion did not help so I kept quiet. Luckily Asad was with me when her labour pains started. Asad was extremely good to Asira and was rubbing her and messaging her back. This was the other tender side of Asad. He took her to the hospital and we both stayed there. She delivered a boy and the next day and was ready to give the baby straight to a Children's Home. The severe lady in charge interrogated Asira with all kinds of questions. Asira was in tears as she explained to her the whole story. She requested that the baby be adopted in a Muslim home. We brought Asira home the next day from the hospital. After a few days when Asira felt better, she returned to her own home. A few months later Ibro returned from the military service and they were happily married. I understood then why the Bosnians did not want publicity of rape victims.

Jasmine and I went for a trip to Turkey in 1995. We loved the minarets and palaces and the Turkish hospitality. It was a welcome change for both of us. We stayed at the flat of Bilge, who was brother Ameen's good Turkish friend from his days in Kuwait. Bilge's mother was a refugee from Bulgaria. We took a trip from Istanbul to Bursa and visited the one thousand-year old Ulu *jamia* mosque with its full grandeur and an indoor, refreshingly cool water well.

I returned to Bosnia by my preferred route via Vienna. I was carrying a lot of cash in my brief case. I needed to go to the washroom, where I heard the announcement that the plane was ready to take off for Split. I ran towards the boarding gate, but just as I was entering the plane, I realised that I had left the briefcase in the toilets. I was panic stricken and broke into a cold sweat. I ran all the way back at full speed, remembering the look on the airhostess's face. Luckily I found the money intact and ran all the way back just to catch the plane in time. I shot in just as the doors closed and the plane took off and all the passengers cheered. I then realised that the charity and zakat money was saved by Almighty God as it was destined to reach the needy.

Close Encounter with Serb Soldiers

I was invited to Alma's place one evening but was late in returning to Ostražac. I was only wearing a pink blouse which was adequate during the day as it was nice and sunny but in the evening it turned freezing cold as I sat in the car. There were no lights and the curfew was on. I drove through the first tunnel and entered the second tunnel. I knew there was a big ditch somewhere along the way, but could not see in the dark. All of a sudden I landed in a huge crater and my Volkswagen stopped with a thud. I had never changed a tyre in my life. It was pitch dark and there was no movement of any kind in the tunnel – only the wind howling and the water dripping into the crater from the roof of the broken and bombed tunnel. I did not even have a torch. I waited helplessly for some time which seemed like hours. All of a sudden I saw a light. It was a car coming slowly into the tunnel from the opposite side. I stood right in the middle and waved frantically with both my hands. The car stopped and two soldiers came out waving their Kalashnikovs towards me. They saw the situation I was in and smiled. In my naivety I thought that they were Bosnian soldiers, so I started talking in my broken Bosanski, while they took out their tools from their vehicle and pulled the car out of the crater. They started to replace my tyre with the emergency tyre. I told them how brave they were for fighting the Serbs, whom I hated.

They listened but kept on working and changed the tyre. One of them wiping his hand spoke to me and said, "Lady, I should take this car first thing in the morning and get the tyres changed. This is only an emergency tyre." I thanked them and approached to shake hands with them, but one of the soldier's faces reddened. He then told me he was a Serb soldier. Pointing his gun towards me he said "If I wanted, I could have shot you and thrown you in this ditch, but I have heard that you are a good woman – they call you super *Baaka*. So I did not shoot you and have repaired your car. But I will not shake hands with you or would accept your thanks". I realised then that one of them was Coco, the Serb soldier. I came home tired but thankful to my God that He saved me.

Haris Silajdžić was elected as the Bosniak member of the Presidency of Bosnia but the shootings and Milosovic's atrocities continued. On 28th May 1995 we were sad to hear the news that Irfan Ljubijankic, the foreign minister, was killed when his helicopter was fired on by a missile from Serb-occupied Croatia while he was returning to Zagreb from his home town Bihac. Planned assassinations were continuing all the time. Only a month earlier this young man of forty three years had attended the VE Day celebrations in London.

Srebrenica

In July 1995 troops from Netherlands were stationed at the central UN base at Potočari. Their service in Srebrenica earned them double pay. Their mandate was to protect the inhabitants from ethnic cleansing. As UN could not be seen as taking sides, the Dutch peacekeepers were also to ensure that the Muslims remained unarmed. On 6 July the Serbian army began the offensive on the town. On 11 July the Dutch peace keepers handed over Srebrenica to the Serbs, which was described by the media as 'the fall of Srebrenica'.

Not all the news was known in Bosnia at the time but when I read *The Guardian* of 25 October 1995 I could comprehend how Srebrenica was the victim of a high-level UN plan to abandon the enclave to its fate and the eventual massacre of civilians. The same newspaper report quoted one Bosnian commander, Ramiz Becirović, who fled over the mountains and arrived in Tuzla: "if the enclave was sold out deliberately to the Serbs then I think Akashi and Janvier [the UN envoys] too should appear before the tribunal in Hague to answer for the Serbs war crimes committed in Srebrenica".

In *The Independent* on 21 September 1995 Robert Block reported the words of a sergeant in the Dutch army at Srebrenica, Johan Bos: "I found myself standing on a ridge with the Muslims behind me and the Serbs in front of me. Well, I wasn't going back. So we waited, and after a while the Serbs came and told us that if we surrendered we would be well treated and we would go home as soon as possible. So we gave up our arms and equipment and that was that, they took us away".

The Muslims were led away and were all killed. This was considered by the United Nations as the worst act of genocide since World War II. Forty thousand Muslims were expelled from Srebrenica. Some eleven thousands were said to be missing, presumed all shot dead and killed. Men were separated from their families, were locked up in the nearby warehouse right under the noses of UN peacekeepers and blue helmets at Potočari. Ratko Mladić visited them the next day and informed them that they would be exchanged for Serb prisoners. They were then taken away to be killed. Six mass graves were found in the nearby fields and woods at the time, but further excavations continued even later.

I went to Srebrenica in the freezing cold when our friend Mr Cheema was posted there and saw the warehouse and the location of this massacre. Some years later, during the course of my teaching English in the evenings at Buce Potok nursery, my lessons were attended by two brothers originally from Srebrenica. I was invited to their half-built house in the suburb of Sarajevo, where I was welcomed by their mother and Elvir. While enjoying delicious home-baked cakes and sipping tea without milk, she showed me the photograph of her eighteen-year-old young handsome son, Muriz. Tears rolled down her cheeks while I could also not stop my own tears. She herself was injured while escaping from her home to Tuzla while her husband Zuhdija and Muriz were separated to be killed. They were two of the nine thousand victims massacred. Many years later, in February 2008, they received the news that their son's bones had been identified. Zuhdija's remains are still not identified. A black bag full of Muriz's remains was handed to the family. I accompanied them for the burial which was among six hundred others taking place on 11 July 2008. A grave for Muriz was dug by the two brothers while we watched him buried in a small green coffin. We then held the burial prayers and I arrived home exhausted at night.

Back in 1995, I met many of the UNHCR staff and other aid workers: I remember Peter Herbert of the International Rescue Committee who worked closely with UNHCR and repaired the roof of a Konjic bakery factory; Kristine Peduto worked with the Solidaritas agency and distributed aid to over three hundred mentally handicapped persons; Adis Jujo took care of Serbian minorities in Konjic. I noticed that UNHCR and UNICEF looked after the minorities in Bosnia but to a lesser extent those in Croatia or Serbia. I had to go to Mostar and then to Medjugorje to get my United Nations registration card. It was not an easy affair; some obtained the UN card without any hassle but others like me had to wait and fulfill all kinds of formalities. Finally I managed to get the UN card which allowed me to move freely inside all 'Yugoslav' territory. During that period weeping and crying women were taken by bus to Kladanj near Tuzla as they had witnessed the horrors and the loss of their husbands and children who were shot in front of their eyes.

I continued my English classes and supervised the rehabilitation centre in Ostrožac. The invalids were happy to be by the beautiful lakeside, even though we did not have all the equipment they needed. I had made it a point to mix freely with them, playing chess and seeking to console them through the recitation of some Qur'anic prayers whenever I had a few moments before going to bed in my apartment upstairs. It is not easy to lose one's limbs or hands and perhaps time alone could heal the inner scars. In the mornings I noticed many empty brandy and beer bottles placed quietly in the rubbish bins. Upon enquiring I was told that some of the invalids resorted to drink because they could not face their handicaps. Knowing the harm they were causing to their already fragile health, all I could do was to silently pray for them. I could not stop their drinking habit.

I asked Hilmo to get me an official certificate for helping and bringing the invalids from Ilidza to Ostrožac for recuperation. He was able to do this promptly. The certificate was needed to register the rehabilitation centre and CoM in Sarajevo. This registration had to be renewed every year. A ceasefire was agreed in October 1995 under the Dayton Agreement, which Alija Izetbegović called 'a bitter pill to swallow'. In February 1996 the siege of Sarajevo was lifted. The city had been under constant attack with only two tanks to provide defence.

I had to go to Sarajevo in order to register CoM. I made my first trip in our white CoM van with Dr Shayan and Senada. We stayed in a

A glimpse of Sarajevo's tragedy – 1996.

room in a football teacher's small flat. She said that she burnt her dining chairs and books in order to keep warm in the severe winter. There was no electricity and water system was broken down, and people gathered water in bottles and plastic cans. I was shocked to see the destroyed mosques and the bombed, burnt and looted library. There were no children playing and it felt like a ghost town. The cemeteries were filled with recent graves – I was told that 10,000 people were killed in this city alone.

One day after *Juma* prayers at the Begova Jamia I saw a crowd of people around Alija Izetbegović. I stood there to catch a glimpse of him. He seemed frail and sad and there were tears on his cheeks. When he approached nearer I shook his hand. I introduced myself in English, "Saida from CoM". He undid the watch on his wrist and gave it to me and said, "thank you for helping Bosnia". This very brief meeting was the first and last I had with him.

Though there was ceasefire, shots were heard now and again in different areas. I met Amrudin Nurak, a Bosnian official, and with the Egyptian Ferid was able to register CoM as a charity in Bosnia. I also registered myself with UN in Sarajevo in order to attend the monthly NGO meetings. The CoM name started appearing in the directory of the International Council of Voluntary Agencies.

While walking in the centre of the city I spotted the scene of the market square massacre of the preceding August, when Serb shells had landed killing forty three and maiming numerous others. There was red paint to mark out the original blood stains near the bakery. We returned to our rehabilitation centre the next day heavy in heart but determined more than ever to help the Bosnians in Sarajevo.

In 1997 on request from Muslim Aid in London, I visited Tuzla where the Charity had been funding a rape victims' camp project. I had to meet and interview the doctor treating traumatized women and check on the use of resources. Later I submitted a written report to Muslim Aid.

Teaching in Sarajevo

Yusuf Islam was approached by the *Reis ul Ulema* Mustafa Cerić for an English teacher for the Ministry of Religious Affairs – *Riasat* – to teach English to the staff. In this way I found myself with an additional teaching responsibility in Sarajevo. I left the centre at Ostrožac under the care of Danny, Ehdin and Alvir. I sold the car to Mladen Bosnijak a Croat who worked for Asad for a meager sum of 800 Deutsche Marks. Dr Shayan also returned to Pakistan after giving his valuable service to CoM free for seven months. I found him very courteous, noble and well-respected by the Bosnians.

I was fascinated by Sarajevo with its famous Begova Jamia, *hamams*, *morchekhana* and *madresa*, surrounded by the old shopping arcades. The city centre was badly bombed though one could see Turkish architecture underlying the bombed buildings. I used to cross the bridge to go to Careva Jamia which was also partly bombed but functioning. Both the Reis ul Ulema's office and MINA – *Muslimanska informativna novinska agencij* – were housed in a wing of the Jamia.

The Director of MINA, Amir Hodžić, had organised a class of twenty four adults. Two of them were later posted as ambassadors. I enjoyed teaching the Bosnians. Muhammad Alija, Mela and Ibrahim still remain in contact. Mustafa Cerić said something very nice to me that I still remember: "Mrs. Sherif, if you teach one word to a person he/she becomes the slave of yours the rest of their life." Indeed I noticed the amount of respect the Bosnians showed towards a teacher. I had seen the malpractices and bad behaviour of our students back home and was glad that Bosnians were different. I was also approached by the Principal of the newly-opened Turkish College to teach their English language teachers and 7th grade students.

Sarajevo was waking up slowly from its deep gloomy slumber. One did not hear children's laughter. The river flew silently while people walked on its six bridges. The old books were paving the broken footpath. People sold anything in those days, including old spectacles. I looked for a house to stay but there was none available. The best properties were taken on rent by the Americans and other agencies. Many refugees had also come from the surrounding areas. Water and electricity was intermittent. Soldiers were seen walking everywhere. Most shops were shut. The bakery in the centre however was by then supplying fresh bread daily.

I stayed in the *madresa* of Begova Jamia in a room given to me on the first floor. There was only one blanket and no heating. The toilet was at the end of a long corridor, some three hundred yards away. It was a hard struggle to hold oneself in the cold till one reached the toilet and find it locked. Luckily my room was close to the offices of the Centre for Islamic Architecture (CIA) and the director Mr

Kemal Zukić and his assistant Mela Mlivo spoke English. They kindly provided me the key to the CIA's facilities. Before that I used to pee in the emptied apple juice cartons.

I used to go every morning from the *Madresa* and have breakfast in MINA before starting my English class. I was in demand then and taught at other places as well but always returned in between to the MINA office and became good friends with Amir Hodžić. He was a TV journalist before the war but after the TV centre was bombed, he commenced working for *Riasat*. His house in Vogosça had been destroyed and he was living temporarily in a Serb's flat, which he had to vacate quite soon. The Serbs had killed the Imam of Vogosça, Hasib Ramic, his wife and children including a three month baby. Their bodies were found close to the mass graves in Vogosça. Many imams were killed and decapitated during this war.

Vasvija's story

One day I asked the students in my MINA class to write about their war experiences. Most Bosnians did not want to speak about it and they had shut it within themselves. I wanted to bring out their feelings in writing so their anger of the injustices could be reduced. One girl, Vasvija, poured out her heart through the written English homework. I sat and read her story and then understood why she was always sad. Here is her real life story:

"I was a young kid of sixteen and had a brother who was a year older than I. Sarajevo was bombed by the Serbs in 1992 and 1993. One bomb fell on the workplace of my father. He was taken to the hospital with shrapnel in his head and brain. My mother and we children waited frantically. Finally we heard a phone call from our father's colleague that he was admitted in the hospital and was unconscious. There was curfew but with difficulty all three went to see father and recognised him among many dead and wounded people lying in the hospital. Two days later the curfew was lifted and so my brother went outside to throw the rubbish in the bin on the street. Suddenly a bomb fell and every one panicked and came out to see who was hit. It was the boy who had gone to throw the rubbish- my brother. There were no ambulances and no cars. Mother and I both stood crying and did not know what to do. We fetched the wheel barrow and put my unconscious brother in the wheelbarrow and finally reached the hospital, where my father was already fighting between life and death. My brother was immediately taken in by the doctors. He came to life only to say good bye. The father came round after a week but we did not tell father that their son had died. The doctors told us not to tell him. Later on his insistence we broke the news. The father lived for another six months but then died later. He could not take the grief of his son."

Vasvija broke into tears when she handed the written account of this dear brother. When I read her written work even I could not hold back my tears as I knew how much she missed her brother. The Bosnians did not have very many children and I thought of the poor mother.

* * *

I often went to Ostrožac in the car provided to me by the courtesy of Mustafa Cerić. The fruit trees were laden with prunes and apples. Later one could see the grapes being ripened by the sun. Bosnia is beautiful with its abundant natural beauty, war or no war. The principal of the Turkish College and his wife invited me to go to Blagaj, a *kuca dervisa* or *darvesh* house near Mostar with a history dating back to 1466. The road to Mostar was treacherous and bombed out, but these scenes were forgotten at Blagaj. The hill is split and water gushed down from under the gorge to a green blue ravine. The *tekia* overlooked the river. It was carpeted and furnished in the old Turkish style. The room possessed serenity and tranquility which could compel one to bow down and pray. There were two graves in the room next door. Could there be a more peaceful place to pray to God than this!

I always returned to London for Ramadan as I did not want to miss the *taraweeh* night prayers at Regent's Park mosque in London. However it was snowing heavily and Sarajevo airport had been taken over by SFOR and Americans were in charge there. I had to go to London. The military plane was standing ready to leave for Frankfurt. I took my chances and got talking to a US army major working in logistics. When he knew that I was stranded and needed to go home, he asked me to sit in the military plane with others. That was my first time in an American military plane. It was very unlike a civilian plane, with hanging red nets, on which we sat. On the way I spoke of the Bosnians' plight and he listened. I asked him some frank questions about American attitudes towards Muslims. As he listened his face was getting red, but he knew that I was speaking the truth. I knew that he could not throw me out of the plane so he listened and I talked. He did say however that it was the media's coverage and that an average American was quite friendly towards Muslims. Anyhow we parted with a kiss and I felt that he was quite genuine. I did not know much German and was told that Frankfurt civil airport was quite far away. Luckily a bus was going to Frankfurt which I boarded and went to the airport to take my flight home.

The Buća Potok project

One of my students at *Riasat* was Ibrahim Ahmetagić, who never did any homework but was good fun and could chat easily in English. He took me to Buća Potok, a town very badly affected by the war and the fighting in the forests of Jugge. I was introduced to the school headmaster and it was agreed that CoM would start a summer course in his school as there was shortage of English teachers. Luckily my grandson Tayeb and my two granddaughters Jamila and Ayesha, and Amina Halilović, along with other undergraduates volunteered to come and spend their summer holidays to help out. We ran a successful program with morning and evening classes, teaching some 400 students for twelve weeks.

At the end a certificate giving ceremony took place and I had asked Asad and his wife Nasra to attend. The Minister of Education, Rizwan Begović, also attended the ceremony. It was a delightful experience. This was the beginning of CoM involvement in Buća Potok.

* * *

On one of my visits to Ostrožac I contacted our good friend Ramzo, the town baker, whose son and daughters had been my students and whom I had taught to pray. Every time I visited Ramzo, the table was set and I had to eat with them. While sitting in his terrace outside the shop, I gave him the news of Sarajevo and explained how hard it was for me to find a suitable place to live and have an office for CoM as I could not pay the huge amount of rent like some other NGOs. Ramzo had the answer. He told me that he had a house in Shvrakino – some refugees were living in the bottom flat but the top flat was empty. So I took up his offer and with Danny's help shifted to that flat. Amir picked me up every day to take me to MINA office to teach. The flat needed repairs which I undertook. Ramzo refused to take any rent so I tried to renovate his flat instead.

I brought Asira to Sarajevo to stay with me in that flat. Shvrakino was on top of a hill. It looked like the peak of Mount Everest. I could not ask Asira in her remaining pregnancy days to stay there. I moved house once more to a rented place nearer the centre of Sarajevo in a very prestigious locality next to the Austrian Embassy. Asira was also happy in that beautiful flat. I wanted her to get registered quickly and be seen by a doctor. The maternity hospital was also quite close from this flat. My English friend Simon often came and we would go out for a coffee sometimes or walk in the town after my class finished in MINA. He was good company and as I was starved of some British humour and good spoken English we enjoyed each other's company. Simon had told me that I could be perfectly safe with him as he was not interested in women physically which suited me fine.

The Hulusina Obdanica Project

One day during a lunch break I walked up the hill from MINA and passed by the huge orthodox Franciscan Church which stood unharmed but noticed a bombed out building right opposite to it. I was told that the bombed building had been an *obdanica* or nursery school before the war but two children were killed there during the bombing. I wondered to myself if I could open an English nursery school there and with this idea in mind I went back to MINA office and made enquiries with Mr Amir Hodžić and also discussed my idea with Mela Mlivo. Mela knew Amira Kapitanović, who was a Minster in those days and later posted as ambassadress to Hungary. We had a pleasant meeting. She gave me a letter and immediately arranged for me to see the director responsible for Bosnia's early learning *obdanište*. I was given an *odgovor* or contract to be signed and was absolutely thrilled with the idea. I phoned Asad who came to Sarajevo and we signed the contract in July 1997 to build and run a nursery for five years.

In this way I had the pleasure of meeting Rizwan Begović, the Minister of Education. He was from Stolac and his house there – a heritage site – had been destroyed. I gave him a copy of the nursery and primary school curriculum that I had prepared incorporating the Bosnians' needs. The bombed-out three-story building looked haunted but I was fascinated with the idea and started the plan. There was no roof and a tree was growing on the second floor. I did not realise that there could be a danger from the mines in the basement and here I was, walking quite freely and fearlessly. I tried to contact the mines' removal team at the UN meetings held every week in Sarajevo and was directed to the Italian division of the rescue committee of UNPROFOR. They told me that I was on the waiting list; in the end my turn never came.

Here I was facing the unending task of clearing the rubbish along with two of my aid workers. Shahed Saleem, an architect from London, had come to draw the plans. Suddenly one day a UN van stopped outside to see what was happening. A white-uniformed gentleman stepped out and I told him the CoM has taken over the building to repair and rebuild the previous ill-fated nursery. He looked at me, shovel in hand, and then at the size of demolished building, with heaps of rubble, broken glass and the dumped rubbish outside. The officer smiled and said: "You have the courage, lady! I am coming back." With that he left. I was still there one hour later when I saw him coming with the shovels and four men. To my surprise they started to clear the debris and took two truckloads in one day. The gentleman was not an angel though he acted like one. His name is Afzal Cheema, a UN security officer, who took pity on a small person like me. He reminded me of Major Oly from Ostražac. It goes to show that there is no shortage of good people in this world.

Convoy of Mercy was always short of money as we did not have an office or paid personnel to raise funds and promote the work. I had the experience of building in Ostrožac and thought that with Asad's help we could do it and we did. Yusuf Islam gave money. The *Opstina*'s Mayoress Halima Hadziamacović provided a lot of assistance and with friends' contributions we finally completed the restoration to every one's delight. From England, Mr Omar Zabadne and many family friends like Mr Parvez and others helped financially. Leila Aksami, Alija Izetbegović's daughter, at the time patron of the Prvi Gymnasia, also provided some old window frames. That was how we managed. We did not live in hotels or eat out at expensive restaurants. We spent our own money on travel tickets and hoped that God Almighty will accept our efforts to lessen the suffering of people.

My very able friend Dr Azra Jagajnić was then at the project implementation unit (PEU) at the Ministry of Education, where I also conducted English classes. She managed the funds from the World Bank to reconstruct schools and a heritage centre with library. Azra took me to the heritage centre and we drove some four hours from Sarajevo passing through the magnificent mountain range. We stopped enroute near a high mountain where a dervish was said to have made prayers for water and the mountain was subsequently cut open making a gorge. Azra is still busy writing books and attending conferences on environmental issues. While searching for accommodation in those days Azra had offered me her flat. I kept my luggage and furniture there, but due to shortage of water could not stay in her flat.

I fell sick in the winter as I decided to live in Hulusina in a damp room full of water. I wanted to supervise the construction work personally. I did not like the builders hired by Asad, who travelled daily from Ostrožac to Sarajevo to work on site. I caught cold and had high fever. My kidneys were affected as I passed blood in my urine. Luckily Samija from Ostrožac had come to help me in Hulusina. Each day she took a sample of urine to be tested in Ilidza hospital. She looked after me and my health soon improved.

The two men assigned to care for the Ostrožac centre had left leaving the place empty for months without informing CoM and the Centre was ransacked. All the equipment was smashed to pieces. This was sad as we had built the rehabilitation centre with much pain and effort. I had no one to share my feelings of sadness. Asad worked on impulse and at times I did not agree with his decisions. I received a call from Jabalnica's *Opstina* that the Serb who had originally fled from the property was back and making a claim. The Jablanica Municipality officer, Mirsad Babić, was standing at the premises waiting for me. Upon arrival I noticed that the Serb had given the top portion to a family and wanted to take possession. The local authorities had to comply with the UNPROFOR ruling to hand the Serbs their property. The reverse was not done in Croatia, Serbia or even Bosnia for the returning Muslims. I managed to get hold of Aziz, hired a van and brought a few things to Sarajevo. That

Bosnian children at Hulusina Nursery school, with teachers David Horsfield and Amela Puskin – 1997.

was the end of Ostrožac and it pained me for days and even more to see it go to a Serb, whose son had killed a local Bosnian.

When the children's nursery opened in Ulica Hulusina the local newspapers published a photograph on the front page. It was described as the Bilingual Nursery School and the first English nursery on the soil of Sarajevo. The Nursery was established on the ground floor. Our residence was on the third floor and my children visited me occasionally. My grand-daughters Jamila, Ayesha and Saba, all talented artists, helped to decorate the nursery walls during their summer holidays. Farid was appointed the manager of the school. Children's swings were in place, flowers blossomed on the grounds and the fences were painted. In 1998 Asad had hired a couple Shazia and Shabbir from Pakistan to our Nursery as teachers. The young couple did not know one word of Bosnian but they worked willingly and learned quickly to teach children using modern methodology. The very gentle Babar Mirza from

London, known to us as 'Bobby', was a pillar of support whenever I needed help.

When I look back I realised that in those days I was teaching for nearly nine hours daily. How did I do it? Only Allah knows. Morning class from 9 to 11 at the Mechanical Engineering Faculty for the professors; at 11am at the PEU; at 1 pm to MINA staff; from 3 to 5 pm to some forty mechanical engineering students; from 6 to 8 pm at Hulusina to the adults, while Shazia took the beginners. I also taught English at the beautiful brand new Turkish school for two months.

During this period, one of my fourth year mechanical engineering students travelled to Vareš to see his house from the outside. While there, he was shot and killed by the Serbs.

The nursery was getting popular and more students kept enrolling. A young teacher, David Horsfield from Yorkshire, came to teach

Bosnian Army soldiers on a visit to the Nursery – 1997.

and stayed on the top floor with us. David was a blue-eyed and fair young man and a vegetarian. When the ice was broken he told me that he had a Muslim girlfriend and that they had married in secret. When I asked him why he had not brought her along, he explained that racial prejudice was not one-sided. The girl's brothers could have English girlfriends and mistresses but objected to their sister's friendship with a white boy or 'gora', even though he was a Muslim and prayed while they themselves drank alcohol and did not pray. Being in love, David and Shameem married in a mosque in Dewsbury but he could not live with her as he was threatened by one of the brothers who did not approve of their relationship. I found this bizarre as in my own family we have many mixed marriages without any qualms. He loved Shameem and missed her, so I told him to call her to Bosnia for a holiday. He went over the moon and decorated his bedroom to receive her.

Amela's Story

One of my helpers at the Hulusina nursery was Amela. This is her story:

"In 1992 I had left home to come to study at Sarajevo University. We heard that the first victim of war was a medical student, Suada Dilberovic. She died on the bridge by a Četnik sniper fired from Holiday Inn. By the way that bridge is remembered by her name now. From then on I kept on hearing the shootings off and on. No schools and no colleges. Everything was shut and at a standstill. I left Sarajevo and went home. It was after days that I got a proper lunch. All the shops were shut and not much food was available. My mum was a nurse in a health centre and my father was working in a building company. After work instead of going to friends like before, they stayed at home as everyone did after six pm. They asked me about my health and I told them that the [Serb] army has surrounded Sarajevo. They kept quiet and did not want to hear about it. After five months, I got a message from my brother from a concentration camp at Manjaca – *dobro sam* – just two words. My tears did not stop. I went from door to door to find the whereabouts of that torture camp. My mother told me to keep quiet and not talk about my desire to fight against the Čhetniks as our street was guarded by the Serbs keeping their thirty army tanks in our amateur fliers' airfield. No flying for sport now. The Army was flying their planes. Our coffee shops, cakes shops all were flattened by the Čhetniks as if those buildings never existed. One neighbour Nedim Imanović who wanted to go with me to fight soon disappeared, never to be seen again.

I sat in my room for days and did not even talk to my mum. I kept praying *nemaz*. Perhaps prayers only saved me from becoming crazy. My mother, a qualified nurse, asked me to go to Sarajevo on 27 April to get vaccines for the children. Nobody in those days wanted to go to Sarajevo, so I went. A journey which normally takes only five hours by train took nine hours. At every hour the train stopped and the Army took the boys and men out. I did take the vaccine parcel but the train conductors told me to mark it as 'glass' and they placed it in the carriage. It could happen that they would have taken me and also the vaccines, but somehow Allah protected me. The parcel in the box arrived safely to Prijedor but I stayed behind in Sarajevo as was instructed. There were no more trains to Prijedor from Sarajevo. Soon there was no telephone and the food which I had kept with me was all gone.

Somehow I managed to go to London and was united with my mother, but there were no news of my father or my brother Alan. Later some journalists wrote about the torture camp where both were held. I must tell you about my father now. My father also was taken in 'Keraterm'. In May the Yugoslav National Army with tanks entered. It is still a stronghold of Čhetniks. Armoured tanks passed our street and the soldiers caught all boys and men and held them at one place while the women were taken away to be held separately. If anyone disobeyed they were finished off with a bullet in the head.

Muhammad Puskar, my cousin died in front of his house while still in *wudu* as he prepared for prayers. He was a *shaheed, insha Allah.*

The Red Cross saved some people and my brother was able to come to London. But there was no news of my Murat, my childhood fiancé. I was miserable in London and wanted to come back. I wanted to fight the enemy. Asad Khan brought me back on one of his aid convoys. I met Saida and later on started to work in Sarajevo Nursery in Hulusina, in 1997 and remain a good friend of COM even today. My Murat came back and we got married. I have three lovely children now. But I cannot go to Prijodor even now.

 In Prijedor they killed 2000 university professors, doctors and engineers. All together nearly 30,000 people were killed according to the official record. What is alarming is that even after six years of war, those who killed us still live in our houses and we are not able to go in. The UN is allowing all criminal Serbs to return to their houses we have to vacate those premises. We are not able to go back to our homes even now as there is no protection for us in those areas. We live in a small place in the suburb of Sarajevo, without a bathroom. Every penny we save, we build one room."

* * *

In May 2000, my brother Misbah phoned me in Sarajevo and broke the news of the death of our eldest brother Inam. He had been working to his last day as the Director General of Punjab Libraries. He was also a retired Air Commodore. He had written many books of verse and his memoirs in English and Urdu, which he characteristically entitled 'Memoirs of Insignificance'. A few months earlier he had posted me his book of poems with the note inside: "To my dear sister Saida, the last of my poems." He was a great scholar, a first-class tennis and cricket player, deeply religious and a loving personality. Those who came in contact with him always said that he was one in a million with an unforgettable personality.

"One did not know where to begin"

I had been totally involved in my relief work inside Bosnia while the Serbian government had been busy in ethnic cleansing in other regions as well. One day all of a sudden I noticed the arrival of many refugees in Jablanica from Albania and Kosova who were housed by the Municipality. I visited their camp and heard accounts of torture and imprisonment. One mother cried as she told me how her six year old son was killed in front of her own eyes. It dawned on me that ninety percent of Kosovars were actually ethnic Albanians. At the time I managed to provide some cash to help the municipality's efforts. On one of my trips to London my elder son introduced me to Shaikh Zymer Salihi, a religious leader of Albanian Muslims in London. Thanks to the efforts of such respected scholars, many Kosovars had fled across the border to neighbouring Albania. By 1998 there was an increased awareness in Britain of the hardships and persecution faced by the Kosovars.

In April 1999 Asad Khan and a team of volunteers traveled 3,600 miles over 8 days to reach Albania where they visited numerous refugee camps including those in Peskopia, Durres, Tirana and Shijak. They were able to distribute $55,000 of cash to 45 families, as well as books and toys for children. While I was setting up the Halusina Nursery in Sarajevo, Asad made a further fact-finding trip. On my first visit I flew to the Greek island of Corfu with him. We did not see any of the sights of the island such as the grand castle on the shoreline, but headed straight for the ferry for Albania without any rest or leisure. Albania looked totally different from any other East European country and much less developed. Asad told me to keep the windows shut which I would have done anyway as young men scrutinised us and even tried to look inside the car. The office from where we obtained the visas was messy and the grounds were full of mud. We collected our visas and drove away as fast as possible. Mosques had been closed down during his long regime in power and a whole generation grew up unaware of Islamic essentials such as prayer.

Shaikh Zymer Salihi came to meet me and told me that he had made arrangements for me to stay with Mr Bazil Pico, the Secretary of State for Religion in Albania. We arrived in Pristina and the city on the whole looked quite organized, with a well-built central square. As arranged, Asad and I went to meet Mr Pico and I was welcomed in the family's small apartment. Asad decided to sleep in our rented car. The highlight of this visit was an opportunity for us to meet and interview the Grand Mufti of Albania, Hafiz Sabri Cochi, at a mosque and Islamic centre under construction in Tirana. He was in his seventies, of tall stature and polite and humble in manner. He had been imprisoned for 23 years under the Enver Hoxha regime. The following is an extract from our interview:

CoM: What was the situation of Muslims during the communist regime of Enver Hoxa?

SC: The Islamic scientific and religious schools and other institutions were closed by official order. All Islamic thought was banned and Islamic leaders were exiled or imprisoned. The waqf and other Islamic properties were confiscated. Before the communist regime there were 1700 mosques these were made 'shaheed' by the regime and some turned into clubs and restaurants after destroying their minarets. There were anti-religious laws

Mufti Sabri Cochi with Asad Khan and myself – 1999.

passed and anyone found praying was imprisoned for 10 years. Similarly prison sentences were imposed for anyone found with religious books in their homes. Religious values and education could not be passed on to the children and they were forced to keep non-Islamic names.

CoM: How have things changed for the Islamic community since the death of Enver Hoxha?

SC: There is now democracy in Albania but due to its secular nature it does not represent any religious groups. A very small proportion of the waqf property has been returned. Some cases are going through the law courts now. It may never be possible to regain all the lost land and property as high rise apartments have been built to house state workers on waqf land.

Some 50 new mosques have been built and a further 300 repaired throughout Albania. New madresas have been opened by the Albanian Muslim community and now there are many copies of the Qur'an and Hadith in the Albanian language. The Muslim community is given 20 minutes a week on television to air their views and news. The Islamic community also publishes its own newspaper. In Albania the danger for Muslims is now from other religious missionaries; there are missions of Bahais, Jehovah Witnesses, Evangelists, Catholics, Christian Orthodox and many others. Muslims of southern Albania have been forced to change their names to Christian names by the Greeks if they wanted to continue working in Greece.

CoM: What help is provided by the Islamic countries?

SC: [So far] little help has come to the Muslim community or from other Muslim countries. However many Islamic charitable societies are working in Albania.

CoM: What kind of work are these societies involved in?

SC: There are more than 40 such charitable societies. Fourteen of them have now formed a coordination council. Their activities are repair and building of mosques, starting up of madresas, sponsoring and running orphanages, providing money and food for the very poor in society, [running] language and computer schools, translation of religious books, [providing] audios and videos in Albanian language and other self- reliance programmes.

CoM: What is the religious composition of Albania?

SC: There are some 75% Muslims, 15% Christian Orthodox and l0% Catholics.

CoM: What in your view is needed for the welfare of Muslims in Albania?

SC: We need money to propagate Islam on a bigger scale. The people need jobs so investment in industry from Islamic countries is also needed. Since Albanians are looking to the West to solve their financial situation and provide a role model, we need Muslims from Europe to come to Albania and work in the Muslim community.

CoM: Finally what would you like to say to the British Muslims?

SC: Muslims in Europe have reacted quickly to the plight of their brethren in Bosnia and Chechnya and we hope they will do the same here in Albania. We need British Muslims to come to Albania and work in the Muslim Community bringing their technological, analytical and scientific approach to Islam.

The Mufti's comments strengthened my resolve to contribute in some way to the education of the young people in this region. We went to Besanet and I cannot forget my encounter with a lady in the market selling embroided linen and other items: I said *assalamu alaikum* to her and she burst out crying and embraced me. It was the first time she had met someone who greeted her with an Islamic greeting. She told me that she remembered her mother praying *namaz* when she was a child but afterwards it was banned. During our travels we came across a very old and dilapidated mosque. Peeping inside we saw a man cleaning it up. He told us that when they came here it had been filled with dirt and used as latrine and a place for cattle. He was a Pakistani who lived with his wife in a nearby apartment. We were invited to his home and saw his wife teaching the Qur'an to six or seven girls in their flat devoid of any luxury. There were four sewing machines in a row in the small room where the Albanian girls also learned to sew.

We all sat in that room and they extended their generous hospitality, offering us a tasty, hot meal – one encounters people who are like jewels hidden in the corners of the world, doing good work. In the town of Besanat we met an Arab who worked for an NGO and was married to an Albanian lady. She took us to meet her grandparents who gave us an account of the turmoil in their land. They took out a torn Qur'an and showed it to us very proudly. They said that they had to keep it hidden as no one was allowed to read the Qur'an or go to a mosque until recently.

To help us in our travels we had purchased a road map. Following it, at one point to our amazement the road came to an abrupt end and a huge mountain glared at us. There was no road but one was indicated on the map! We headed back from where we had started and finally saw a few houses and at six in the morning and hired a room. So this was Albania! En route we noticed steel and cement-built strong bunkers at every five hundred metres. I could not imagine its purpose or was it just a lunacy of Enver Hoxha? Maybe he thought that someone will attack this country. First a Soviet-dominated Communist regime and then Serbian control had led to years of neglect and deprivation. The people were deliberately kept behind in education and deprived of knowledge of their culture. Moreover the Kosovars and Albanians hated to learn Russian. They were not even allowed to go to Hajj. Its warm seashores and natural beauty was being smothered, I dreamt how beautiful this country could become with little effort.

Asad and the CoM team organized the delivery of food and medicines to Kosovar refugees in Albania. We also opened a centre for vulnerable women and children in a former factory in Shkodra while I was involved in raising funds in London.

* * *

On my next visit we entered Kosova via Podgorica and took a break at Pec. While we drove from Pec onwards, one could see graves covered with flowers along the road. The war had stopped but the plunder, destroyed buildings and many badly bombed mosques were an indication of the Serb hatred. The roads were in bad shape particularly from Pristina to Prizren, partly neglected by the previous government and partly due to heavy bombing. Finally we arrived in Prizren in the middle of the night, driving in total darkness on damaged and half-built roads and alleys. There were no road signs or numbers on the houses but Asad finally located the house of Mohiuddin. I was introduced to Mohiuddin who was educated in the famous Sarajevo Madresa. We were able to communicate as he could speak Bosanski and also knew English. The family home had three wings, occupied by himself and his two brothers and their families. One was an artist and the other, Shamsuddin, had experience of construction work.

In spite of the late hour, Imam Mohiuddin's family welcomed us. One room was vacated for the males and I slept with the ladies. I was astonished to see their hospitality as they got out of their beds, cooked and served us with warm food at such late hour. All three brothers were hired by CoM. We sat on the floor around low tables and had a meal sharing our plates. While we ate, Asad organised the work itinerary and designated the tasks for each of us. Mohiuddin was to be the manager for Kosova projects and Shamsudin responsible for all construction work.

The next morning we set out on our work. We visited the six bombed houses in Pirana, Landovica, Grejkoc, Leshane, Drenica and Terna. CoM supplied the material and Shamsudin helped to build and repair. I was to visit the sites and supervise.

English class for Albanians, with Asad Khan (wearing cap) – 1999.

Kosova had been part of the Ottoman territories for centuries until 1912 when it was partitioned between Serbia and Macedonia, and then was incorporated into former Yugoslavia. Many of its people still spoke Turkish and there was a Turkish college in Prizren that had been closed down. There were many Ottoman buildings, fountains and beautiful mosques and *hamams* to be seen, mostly in ruin. I liked Prizren perhaps because it resembled Bosnia a little. There was even a neighbouring town perched on a hill called Jablanica. The surrounding mountains seemed to whisper to the blue sky, while the river flowed at its feet.

I commenced my English classes at the request of the imams of the community. A hall was located in the same neighbourhood as the CoM offices. I also supervised the rebuilding of four bombed mosques and a few houses which CoM had undertaken to restore. Shamsuddin proved to be a good manager for the construction work. The hall on the first floor of Nikola Stella 14 was furnished with desks and chairs and a big board.

The morning class was for the younger students while the *hodjas* – community imams – and older youth, who were mainly unemployed, came to me in the afternoon. In absence of any heating, one could freeze in the big hall but never the less the learning was going on continuously.

In order to save funds I did not rent an apartment but decided to stay in the small office provided to CoM by the Islamic community and sleep on the sofa. This was also preferable as I did not like the idea of going to a far off flat in the evenings as most nights there was no electricity due to the curfew. I preferred to stay close to the town centre and in any case there was a lot to do.

I decided to make the office a habitable place. I had the old Turkish-style toilet knocked down and managed to get a proper toilet and a basin with taps installed in a small alcove with a mirror and a handle for the towel. I bought an electric kettle and powdered milk and tea. There was a café two doors away where I could get boiling

Bombed out mosque in Prizren, next door to where I stayed – 1999.

water when power was off. It was run by a rotund Kosovar who always offered me tea and to my surprise mentioned the famous Urdu poet Iqbal and his *Javed Nama*.

Next to the café was an old Ottoman mosque in ruins – a heartbreaking site. I noticed that men in the café continued with their cups of tea after hearing the call of *adhan* from the adjacent

Qur'an ceremony in a village near Prizren – 2000.

mosque. When I asked them why they did not attend to the prayers the response was that Allah was in their hearts and that they were sufi and *darvesh*. I did not understand this logic and wondered if mosques were destroyed because they ceased to be used for worship.

The director of the International Monitoring Office (IMO) in Prizren was quite sympathetic to war victims and we became friends. I would often use the facilities in Jacque's warm office because it had its own electricity generator. I used the office's computers and photocopiers to prepare material for the lessons. I was given hot coffee as well, courtesy of IMO. Life can be fun, if we enjoy the work we do. The IMO was also happy with CoM's educational work because there was a need for translators.

I was invited by an imam who was one of my students to a ceremony for boys and girls who had completed the Qur'an. I sat up the night before preparing presents for each of them. It was a wonderful site to see twenty six young women all dressed in white satin dresses while a similar number of boys wore dark suits. The ceremony took place in an old Ottoman period mosque and it was packed with proud parents and the students.

CoM helped in the rebuilding of the Emergency wing of Prizren hospital and I participated in the opening ceremony with the doctors.

I attended the meetings at UNHCR every Tuesday and desperately tried to obtain some fuel for heating the classrooms in the extremely cold winter. Wooden logs were hard to find and we were not rich enough to purchase big generators. In the end a few logs arrived with a *pec* and the hall was heated. The UN Mission in Kosova (UNMIK) informed me that I could not get a telephone connection unless CoM was officially registered as a charity in Pristina. So I set off and by chance met Asad on the road. We proceeded together and obtained the registration within one day.

With staff of the Emergency wing at Prizren Hospital – 2000 .

The UN distribution of aid to the Kosovars was mainly undertaken by networks linked to Mother Teresa's missionaries and the Catholic churches. The Kosovars did not like receiving aid from these sources. It was a regular site to see the big tanks of UNMIK guarding the main roads and bridges though it seemed to me they had come to an understanding with the Kosova Liberation Army (KSA). There was also a tank on 24-hour guard just outside the church as the Serbs were afraid the Kosovars would take revenge for their destroyed mosques.

The fruit market venders were always generous when they knew that I was a Muslim from Britain and had come to help them. They would always give me an extra bunch of grapes or an extra banana which I accepted on their insistence. Many were happy to see a foreigner and would attempt to recite sura Fatiha. It is difficult to remember one's religion when kept away from it for two or three generations.

The roads to Pristina were a nightmare with ditches and big puddles with mud. I did not have a car or transport because Shamsuddin and Mohiuddin were busy with the reconstruction work. I found it necessary to hire a young Kosovar interpreter. I stayed on my own most of the time and often had to leave for London or Bosnia. There were occasional volunteers from England such as Farhana and her young son who came from Woking to Prizren to help. She distributed aid and spent two months in the extreme cold and snow, driving on icy roads. She also took over the English classes during my absence. While serving in Prizren I also met some Turkish aid workers and a very gentle Pakistani British doctor who had come to help with a mobile ambulance.

* * *

My daughter Jasmine had planned a visit to Spain in September 2001 for our holidays as she knew of my interest in history. We flew from London to Malaga, accompanied also by my granddaughter Jamila who spoke Spanish. My friend Surayya who had come to stay with us at the Halusina nursery school provided us some contacts in Granada where we might be able to rent rooms. This was very helpful and we found a flat near the city centre belonging to a staunch American *Muslima* married to a Spanish Muslim. She was a craftswoman in leather goods and souvenirs. We were very happy to be living with her for it fitted our budget. The gardens of Alhambra and the palace transported me back in centuries to the era when the Muslims ruled Spain. I walked among the fountains in the royal gardens surrounded by hills. From Cordoba we travelled to Granada. The huge mosque of Qurtaba with carved Qur'anic *ayats* decorating the immense halls reminded us of God's message to mankind. I was sorry to see that part of the mosque was transformed into an unbecoming chamber of Catholic symbols. This did not really fit in the surroundings as one tourist exclaimed to me while we were walking there. On one corner of a wall hung an old picture showing a chained Arab bending in front of the Catholic emperor.

Hundreds of thousands of Muslims were tortured and killed during the Inquisition that started in the late fifteenth century. All children born had to be baptised Catholics or they were thrown into the sea. Many Muslims escaped to North Africa while a few hid themselves in the mountains of Orgiva, north east of Cordoba. We were amazed to learn that some Muslims had survived the Inquisition by fleeing to the mountains where they kept to themselves. Our trip by coach to Orgiva was equally interesting. We met a group of sufi Muslims. Apparently they had opened Qur'anic schools and small madresas to educate their children about Islam. The sufi gatherings were attended by many young persons with the ladies covering their hair with a small scarf and wearing loose blouses. This was quite acceptable in Spain as most women covered their head with a scarf anyway.

We walked happily along the village's cobbled roads and saw the grape vines and I discovered the familiar sweet scented flowers of Delhi covering the side walls. There was an abundance of pomegranate trees in bloom. We then decided to visit Morocco. The bus route was very picturesque as we passed along the rolling green hills of the Mediterranean coastline passing Alicante, Torrevieja, Cartagena, Aquilas Almeira, Malaga and finally reaching the tip of Spain to Alceziras – many words and place names were of Arabic origin. We boarded the ferry for Tangiers and in the distance the sight of Gibraltar reminded me of a trip by sea with my husband some years ago. Some memories do not fade. The ferry was full and the blue Mediterranean Sea was as warm and friendly as the people on board. We basked in the sun and watched the dolphins dance and jump in the waters. I looked at Jasmine sitting across me, wearing a white sun hat, her smiling face to be retained forever in my mind. Like my husband, my children liked the sea while I was a mountain lover.

We were welcomed in Tangier and Rabat by Karima and Mahjouba, a Moroccan family friends. Mahjouba had stayed at my brother's house in London. Karima's brother picked us from Tangier. A dinner of *kous-kous* was served in a typically Moorish-style home. The mother was absolutely charming and the father spoke a lot and appeared quite jolly. We spent the night in their home and the next day driven to Rabat. I noticed the poverty in Tangier, though it seemed that Rabat was only for the rich. We visited the *kasbah* and were taken to see the Atlantic Ocean coast line. We came back to Tangier and spent one night in our host's house. In the morning we went out towards the *souks* of Fez. We saw the inner city's covered markets full of people and goods. The covered market was a blessing as the sun was quite strong. There was an exquisite mosque inside the high gates of the covered market where we cooled our faces at the cold *hauz* fountains and offered our prayers. We returned to Spain on a date that the Americans will not let us forget.

Oblivious to all news, we arrived at the airport to take our flight from Malaga for London on 11th September 2001. I had purchased a little knife to slice some Spanish peaches during our journey. My daughter and my granddaughter were both wearing scarves – I seldom wore one at that time. The custom officer looked in my bag and was horrified to see the knife. I could not see why he looked so serious and insisted that the little knife should not be in my luggage. I was still in the dark and did not know of the Twin Towers. The queue of passengers looked at us sceptically because my two companions were wearing head scarves and here I was carrying a knife. Quite naive, I was still joking with the custom officer not realising people's gazes and said, "I bought it to eat your delicious Spanish peaches, please do not confiscate it." Jasmine pointed out to me the waiting queue and told me to let it go. It was only when we arrived in the waiting lounge that we saw the TV images and I read on the screen 'America is attacked'. We then realized that the New York World Trade Centre was brought down by an attack. It was unbelievable that a super power which showed its muscle to the rest of the world could be hit, not at one place but at several places by airplanes that smashed into the buildings, killing nearly three thousand people. The TV pictures showed many Muslims' relatives crying along with others at the scene of that merciless attack.

Upon our arrival in London we saw the news in English and only then understood the gravity of the whole story. The US was stunned and in a state of shock. Within a short while President George Bush identified Osama Bin Laden as the prime suspect and Afghanistan was attacked in revenge. In other words, America was ready to kill thousands of Afghans and destroy an already war-ravaged country in order to avenge the 9/11 attacks even though there was no Afghan participation in the events of that day.

* * *

I felt that the international media was out to condemn the Taliban who had ruled Afghanistan from 1992 to 1997 after the withdrawal of Soviet troops. No mention was ever made of the good they had achieved inside the war-torn country which the US had abandoned. The Americans had armed the Islamic militias to fight the Soviets, but when the war was over they walked away doing nothing to restore peace and economic stability. It is true that the Taliban did not allow women to study in schools and colleges, but perhaps this was because there were barely such institutions in place even for men. The Taliban at least burnt down poppy fields and sacks of cocaine because they wanted Afghans to work instead of taking drugs or selling them abroad.

The country was already devastated after the bitter confrontation with the Soviets. It never was a prosperous country in the first place with its rugged mountainous regions, climates of extreme summer and winter and fluctuating temperatures between night and day. The useless ex-king Zahir Shah would fly in his private plane to have lunch in Italy but did not improve the education or the well-being of the populace. Strict clannish customs and a different language kept the Afghans away from its neighbours and from the rest of the world. However there were some people well-aware of this land's mineral resources and strategic location, which could also be used to attack a neighbouring country like Iran and provide access to China via Tajikistan.

The veiling of Afghan women was severely criticised by the media but let us not forget that even in King Zahir Shah's time Afghan women wore the shuttlecock type of burqa. They observed strict segregation and women did not mix with men even then, but all of a sudden their centuries-old culture was ridiculed and the Talibans were blamed for enforcing such laws. Saudi Arabia on the other hand was never criticised for the same adherence, even though this strict type of Wahabi Islam was brought in by the Arabs who brainwashed youths and turned them into *mujahideen* or Taliban later. The Taliban did not want American interference in their country and were seeking to rebuild Afghanistan according to their aspirations and understanding of religion. The Taliban had their failings as well, but to my mind if they were left to themselves then there would have been no bloodshed and no need of a prolonged war with immense loss of life. The enmity therefore increased instead of decreasing. *The Guardian* newspaper noted that more bombs were thrown on Afghanistan than the two world wars put together!

I felt deeply sorry for the poor Afghans and once the second wave of US bombing over Afghanistan started I decided to leave immediately for Peshawar to help the thousands of refugees pouring in the borders of NWFP. Four million Afghan refugees migrated to Pakistan and a million sought sanctuary in Iran soon after the raids. I was picked up by my niece Safia, a gold medalist and lecturer in geography at Peshawar University. The thousands of tents spread miles on end, most of them supplied by UN, presented a devastating scene. There was no electricity and no water taps. The tents were pitched on sand and the children and babies played on rough pebbled, grounds. One did not know where to begin.

Before leaving London the charity Muslim Aid had asked me to prepare a report on the Dar-ul-Shifa hospital run by the Afghani doctor Dr Bakhter Amin Yusufzai and his team in Canal Town, Peshawar. I visited the hospital and started helping refugees and the sick pouring into the clinic. In return, I was able to use the hospital's premises as an office and also for the distribution of aid provided by CoM. I also had to obtain permission for these activities from the Commissioner for Refugees, Mr Nabi Baksh. I could only venture into the refugee camps once this permission was obtained. I was warned that it was not a joke to distribute aid to thousands of hungry refugees as one could be looted and robbed even injured in the process.

The influx of refugees had changed Peshawar completely. It became over congested and dirty with the traffic in chaos. I used to leave early in the morning for the camps and would help in the distribution of clothes, baby food and vitamins. All the food items like flour, rice, beans, tea, sugar, soap, powdered milk and cooking oil was bought in Peshawar and was collected. Pakhtoon trucks were hired and loaded. My car was escorted by the Police which I resented at that time but later realised how important it was to have this protection.

The aid was coming in drips and drabs and many in need did not receive any. The Police along with our volunteers went to the Shamshatoo refugee camp and issued a coupon to those families that had not received aid from UNHCR or from any other source. The head of the family was then asked to wait in a queue at a distribution point. In spite of the barbed wire and enclosed boundaries controlled by the Police there were riots at the gate and refugees had to be beaten back to stop those without coupons from gate crashing. I realised that supplying aid to 550 families was not enough when there was a sea of refugees. We managed to deliver by calling each name with the coupon number. The distribution of aid was finished but many hungry and angry refugees surrounded my car and tried to block the way and kept on demanding food. They would have smashed my windows if the Police had not rescued me. An angry and hungry person, male or female, is no less dangerous than a hungry lion.

I used to return home dog-tired and thankful to Allah for the care and comfort provided to me by my dear niece Safia and her caring husband Amjad. My first task would be to soak my clothes in a bucket full of water and take a shower. The bucket would be half full of sand. The poor refugees had to spend months and some of them years living amidst sand and dust while I could have a bath and become human and fresh again. The tents provided by the UN were torn by the end of three months and there were no further ones available. The refugees started to make mud houses and mud toilets. They queued up with containers to collect water once a day.

I started fund raising in Pakistan and was helped by my adopted son Dr Tariq Solaija who lived in Wah. Blankets were needed so we collected quilts from many households and also purchased a few hundred. I became quite friendly with the Afghani Refugees Commissioner, Mr Nabi Baksh, and on hearing my story of the last

Convoy of Mercy's food distribution point in Peshawar – 2001.

distribution, gave me permission to dispense the aid from the safety of the Police compound and in the shade of its trees. My face had become quite sun burnt. I thought of those lovely Afghan children whose faces were sundrenched and parched. I bought loads of Vaseline jars for distribution. Most Afghans are of fair complexion and a lot of them had skin problems due to living constantly under the strong sun and in the dust. What a contrast these refugee camps were compared to the camps in Bosnia.

I also organized a further distribution in the compound of Dr Amin Yusufzai's hospital. It was Ramadan and I noticed that many of the refugees did not fast or pray. I wondered at that and perhaps, alas, is it not the case that when afflicted by sorrow we seek comfort in the remembrance of Allah? As the lorries containing food approached the hospital, a police officer tried to stop the convoy with the pretext that the Pathan lorry drivers would disrupt the telephone and electricity wires. He would not let them pass. I went out on the street and gave him an earful, loud enough for everyone to hear: "Who is stopping those trucks! Get me the mobile. I will just call the Deputy Superintendent of Police and if he knows what is happening he will get rid of those rascals." Everybody noticed me shouting on the street. There was a hushed silence and after five minutes the lorries passed through. The trick worked. Later the same police officer tried to please me, at the same time requesting for some food rations for his employees. I knew that most of it would go to his house. After the distribution he again tried to stop the trucks passing though the street as he wanted some money from the drivers. I had a sense that this might happen and so waited at the end of the street. When he saw me sitting in the red car he retreated quickly and the vans and lorries went on their way.

* * *

One day when I was shopping in the main centre of Peshawar I noticed a good-looking boy of nine or ten trying to sell me fresh coriander. To my surprise he spoke English. I asked him if he went to school. His eyes welled up in tears. He said that he used to go to a school in Kabul but now he was selling vegetables as his father was very sick and they did not have much money. I then wished that I could return to Peshawar and open a school for all those lovely looking Afghan children who either begged or sold things instead of gaining an education.

I did try to open a school in the camps but did not succeed. The sun was too hot to bear even in a tent. In the evenings it used to get freezing cold and there were no lights. The camps were also far away from the city and it was not safe to drive late in the evenings. I met a young Afghani doctor who took me to his camp hospital. He had managed to build a two-room hospital out of mud and was helping the refugees. He had a Bunsen burner to sterilise his instruments and a gas cylinder. Water was kept in a *samawar*. A small cupboard was holding medicines. There were no doors as the curtains did the job. My immediate reaction was to supply him with all the medicines and vitamins that CoM had.

I also visited the Hikmet Yar Hospital in the outskirts of Peshawar. There were some amputees resting but the hospital was in terrible state as the Government of Pakistan was not providing financial support. The following day I returned there with lots of detergent and soaps and towels and food supplies. There was no female nurse and men did not care much for cleanliness. I decided to clean their toilets but the men did not let me and said that they would do it. I did put them to shame though.

The once well-organised city of Peshawar was now in a bewildered state, a far cry from the accounts to be found in the old travel books of its springs and gardens. The canal banks that I used to pass everyday were full of rubbish and litter. The people were also washing their clothes in that dirty water. There was a centenary celebration of Peshawar and I could not help but pen down my thoughts in a poem published in English newspaper, the *Khyber Mail*:

> Peshawar is lit
> The night has spread its shawl
> Heaps of rubbish and dirt hidden in its falls
> Jashne-Sarhad the century of all
> What do we celebrate? I recall
> The canal board so terribly unclean
> The dirt, squalor everywhere is seen
> And I dream
> The rubbish is picked and flowers bloom
> Beggars are refused
> So this profession is defused
> Thousands of illuminated lights
> Like shiny studs in a shawl

Yet electricity is scarce, I recall
Water level is low and energy wasted
What is to be celebrated?
What has happened to our brain cells
My conscious yells
The massacre of Kashmiris and Afghanis
And our incompetence to stop Israelis
Daily we see the innocents killed
With remorse and sorrows our hearts filled
Yet thousands lights are lit
And Jashne-sarhad is on
In anguish I lose my wit

* * *

I returned to London to my comfortable home, relaxed and thanked Allah that we were not suffering like the poor Afghanis. My house in London was always a busy place as it was now occupied by both my sons and their families. We always had a stream of visitors and my garden always looked splendid in summer, with roses in bloom in the front and a vine in the back porch bearing grapes for the first time. I recharged my batteries and after a few days travelled to Sarajevo to check how the nursery school was functioning. It was a pleasant change to return to Bosnia's green hills after the arid and barren landscape of Peshawar. Our teachers at Halusina, Shazia and Shabbir were by now fluent in Bosanski and managing the nursery well. On my visits I would bring with me a computer, CD player or some other item and the smiling children were always delighted to see me.

I was now visiting the projects in Bosnia, Kosova and Pakistan regularly. CoM assisted Imam Mohiuddin in purchasing a three-story building that provided space for a library, class rooms and living quarters. Asad also delivered a printing press to this Centre. We invited Mohiuddin to London and many friends and volunteers collected money for him to use for relief work in Kosova.

Convoy of Mercy's distribution of notebooks and stationary to Afghan refugee children in Peshawar – 2001.

I also raised funds from my relatives attending the wedding of my brother Nayar's daughter Bushra in Karachi who had won nine gold medals and was invited to the United States. Later in 2002 I was in Peshawar to assist in the distribution of educational materials and food packages.

While in Peshawar I received a call from Asad with a request that I should travel to Chaman in Baluchistan. He had been there himself recently and the Pakistan army unit told him of the need for a school. I flew from Islamabad to Quetta and stayed with the family of one of our dear friends in London, Qazi Sahib. While I was well cared for and given their guest room, the nights were freezing cold. I also felt sorry for an invalid in the household, who would be locked up in his room when everyone was out.

I received a call from the Army major's wife, who in a well-spoken voice told me that she would be coming with a car to pick me up. We drove around the barren hills on a small, winding road

At Spin Boldak, Afghan-Pakistan border –
2002.

towards the Chaman army base. The altitude was high and there were no trees in sight. After a while it started raining. It was pleasant to converse with the major's wife, who spoke English faultlessly. When we reached her bungalow I noticed the greenery. This was due to an age-old method of irrigation based on wells and underground channels called *karez*. After breakfast the next day we headed for the military base close to the border with Afghanistan. The Pakistani border police and army contingent exercised a strict control on the Afghan refugees crossing into Pakistan. The area was cordoned by barbed wires. I was then invited to a meeting of the local elite, army officers and the military Scouts unit and introduced as the representative of Convoy of Mercy. Chaman's only dilapidated school had been built by the British in 1926 and its windows had no glass panes and the roof was shattered. I would have rather helped rebuild that school but the major was more interested in showing me a big plot of land where they wanted to build an academy. I just could not visualize myself or a school there. Everywhere there was fine sand and not a blade of grass or a tree in sight. Nature can be harsh at times and I, a lover of trees and greenery, backed out.

I noticed two large refugee camps adjacent to each other near the border. The major who was driving told me that there were often clashes and tribal disputes and the army was called in to solve their problems. The major agreed to my request to visit the camps in the restricted border area and arranged an escort. The refugee camps were full but somehow in better shape than those in Peshawar. Perhaps this was because some trade was still quietly going on, even with the help of young children, for example bringing in vegetables. Cloth smuggled from the Chinese borders was also sold there in spite of the severe police and army control. I was able to visit a hospital for refugees in the Afghan border town of Spin Boldak, where there seemed to be a US military presence. At the hospital I met Dr Surbland, who invited me to his house for dinner and I met his wife. I could not return as it was nightfall and spent the night in their office-cum-house. The next morning I visited the doctors' residence and met a team of Chinese nurses and Malaysian doctors. Among this team was a Malay lady, Dr Fatma and her husband Dr Yusuf Asmodi. They were all ready to leave for inside Afghanistan. So why couldn't I? I pleaded to the team's leader, wrapped myself up in chador like Afghani women and took my place in Dr Surblund's powerful jeep for the journey to Kandahar.

With the medical team from Mercy Malaysia – Dr Fatma on far right – 2002.

The road was treacherous but later on I discovered that we were just driving along a track. The windscreen was wrapped in dust and sandstorms swirled around us. Kandahar's PIMA (Pakistan Islamic Medical Association) Hospital was quite clean and well equipped. The Mercy Malaysian team got to work straight away to attend to the waiting patients – mostly women with bundled up babies in their arms, while the doctor-in-charge showed me around the hospital. Next door was an amputee hospital run by the French, but unfortunately I could not visit it as the doctors were away to collect artificial limbs. I saw many beautiful children with tree stumps attached to their blown off legs. The innocent victims depended on boxes of food aid and were invalids for life because of the land mines and bombs.

We returned late in the night, quite exhausted but glad to be back in comparatively good accommodation. I was amazed at the calm and gentle conduct of the Malaysian team. All the eight ladies slept on the floor in one cold room and the men slept in the other room next to the kitchen. One Chinese nurse complained to me that the Afghan women were very dirty and the babies were wrapped up in urinated clothes. The following day, en route to Zalor we noticed the Usama Bin Laden mosque standing aloof in the desert without a road or a house anywhere to be seen. There was no water and one man wept when he told us that his orchard once brimming with apple trees was today barren due to the bombings and a breakdown of water supply. He also mentioned that the Russians killed and destroyed more than the US forces. Once we reached the little town of Zalor the team set to work drilling a well. Soon water was found and a hand pump installed. The children were full of joy and washed and splashed themselves with water. I then realized the reason why poor Afghan women carried dirty babies at the hospitals was due to a huge shortage of water for washing and cleanliness. On my return to London I discouraged Asad from initiating a school project in Chaman.

* * *

In autumn 2002 I was ready to return to Peshawar. My neighbour Valerie met me in the driveway and wondered where I obtained all my energy. We had a little chat and off I went. I revisited the Hayatabad's orphanage which cared for 80 children including 14 blind girls. A blind teacher was hired for teaching them. The orphanage building was located within well- kept gardens but the institution faced financial difficulties. The gas supply had been disconnected because of non-payment of bills and as a result a single electric heater was used to cook some lentils. My niece Safia and I collected the necessary funds and also provided quilts for the resident children for the coming winter. In CoM's name I later donated three lakhs rupees to the orphanage. By now I had many friends in Peshawar. These included Dr Bakhter Amin Yusufzai of Darul Shifa hospital, whose wife was studying at the Peshawar Medical College. He told me that now most Afghans were realising the importance of education particularly amongst women and Afghani men preferred to have an educated wife.

What I particularly missed while away from London were the British newspapers such as *The Guardian* and *The Independent*. I searched for the British Council but found that it was shut for security reasons. I managed to meet the director who invited me to tea at her residence in a posh University area of Peshawar. During our conversation I was surprised to hear that she suspected the madresas were training *mujahideen* and consequently a list was being drawn up. I was flabbergasted to hear her comment and told her that these religious schools were the only cheap way of obtaining education in this poor country. The madresas kept the youth from loitering and provided them a good religious environment.

* * *

My granddaughter Jamila was in Malaysia completing a medical elective. She wrote to me to visit her. I hesitated but since we were always very close to each other I decided to venture further East. October 2002 found me sitting in Kuala Lumpur's modern airport terminal where I was met by Jamila and Dr Yusuf Asmodi, whom I had met during the visit to Chaman. Resourceful as she is, Jamila had managed to contact doctors of the Mercy Malaysia Group. Malaysia was lush green though hot and humid. After a night in a hotel room I was pleased to move to the home of Dr Yusuf. However I could not sleep and my throat also kept disturbing me. Dr Yusuf organized for an air conditioner to be installed in my room. I was amazed at the efficient and tidy manner the workers completed the job within two hours. I was made very comfortable by his wife Fatma in their house and loved their children. Dr Yusuf told me that they had a son of twelve studying in Anyar in Indonesia and asked if I would like to go and see that school and provide ideas in the methodology for learning English as a language. I reflected for a moment and reminded myself of these doctors' own sacrifices of travelling to Afghanistan to help displaced persons and refugees. Helping in Anyar gave me the opportunity to repay their kindness. Dr Yusuf purchased my ticket and we boarded the flight to Jakarta.

The differences between Kuala Lampur and Jakarta were immediately noticeable – organization and efficiency on the one hand, and disarray on the other. We managed to find the gentlemen who were to take us to Anyar, a four and a half hour drive. We crossed many fields and some greenery but the shops and dusty roads reminded me of Pakistan. Indonesia was bigger in size and in population compared to Malaysia and a lot poorer. We gradually left the city and headed towards more picturesque country. Finally we arrived at the holiday resort of Anyar. I noticed quite a few hotels and bungalows by the seaside but beyond this there were no roads. Instead we saw small houses made of bamboo with palm trees along the track. The school was built on high grounds with a vista of the blue sea shimmering in the sunset light. I was introduced to the head master of the Anyar Nurul Fikri School where I spent nineteen days. Dr Yusuf met his son and the same night as we had dinner he told me that he had to leave early the next morning. I was quite shocked as I thought that he would stay at least for a day with me in this totally new place!

I was housed in a dormitory that accommodated six to eight girls. The place was spotlessly clean. Everybody sat on the tiled floor and cooked food was brought from the main kitchens by motor bike. Each dormitory had a married couple, both teachers, living with the girls as wardens. I had difficulty in using the squatting down toilet. I was also not accustomed to sitting or sleeping on the floor. The next day a modern toilet and a hand basin were placed in the attached bathroom.

There were separate dormitories and mosques for boys and girls, but they attended mixed classes. The school had vast grounds and I discovered the kapok trees with seed pods of silky-cotton as I walked from the dormitory to the class rooms. I put aside my prepared lectures on the methodology of teaching as I had realised that the teaching staff would find the data difficult to

Nurul Fikri School in Anyar, Indonesia – 2002.

comprehend. I therefore started to teach them basic English in the evenings and in the mornings I helped the English language teachers in their classrooms.

It was hard work and the heat and humidity at times unbearable. Luckily we had a fan in the room. The Indonesian staff saw to all my comforts. When they noticed that I could not always stomach their cooked food, I was given fish and chips. I noticed that bacteria in the food grew very fast due to the humidity. If any plate was left unwashed in the morning tiny worms crawled in the leftover food by the evening. On Sundays the staff would arrange a trip to the beach. The locals lived in small bamboo chalets and spent most of the time in the open under shade of trees. I found the Indonesians to be practicing Muslims and polite.

While in Aynar, I received an invitation to attend an international conference in Kuala Lumpur. I was asked to present a paper on how women could be helped out of poverty. I decided to attend even though I was not an economist. I started writing the paper mainly from the Muslim women's point of view as I had noticed that they were comparatively poorer. I arrived at Kuala Lumpur's airport to find Dr Yusuf and Jamila waiting for me at 11:30 at night. Their hospitality surpassed all bounds. We arrived home in an hour's time and Dr Yousuf helped me prepare a PowerPoint presentation as I was not able to use a computer to its full advantage. After typing my paper I went shopping in a huge mall to find something more suitable to wear than what my meagre wardrobe possessed. The three-day 'International Conference on Poverty Alleviation for Non-Governmental Organisations' was funded by the IMF and the Islamic Development Bank and hosted in the luxurious and air conditioned Ritz Hotel in Kuala Lumpur. Each of the participants from over forty countries was allocated their own separate rooms with attached baths. What a luxury after the hard work at Nurul Fikr – Allah *Jalla-Shanuhu* has always provided me so much comfort after a little trial and hard work, *subhan Allah*!

Of the various presentations, the one I particularly appreciated was a paper on microcredit presented by a lady from Bangladesh. One afternoon the conference participants were taken to a few model villages to see how the women collected small amounts of money and were able to utilise this to promote cottage industries and sell products. I admired the way each village had its own community hall, a small mosque and a playground along with a school. The women used the community hall for their meetings and organised everything by themselves. I also attended a dinner reception hosted by Malaysia's Minister for Women & Family Development, Datuk Seri Shahrizat Abdul Jalil in the Saloma Theatre Restaurant, after which there was a cultural show of song and dance. I found Malaysian women occupying a variety of professions and careers unlike most other Muslim countries. I was warmly invited to go to Cambodia and nearby areas but I overcame my instincts and firmly said 'No' to myself.

I was also privileged to witness the festival of *Umm Misaali* in Kuala Lumpur, which honours one woman as the 'ideal mother of the year'. The Queen, the Minister for Women's affairs and other dignitaries were seated on the decorated stage. There were about ten thousand women present in the huge hall which was well decorated with fresh flowers. Complete silence prevailed. Men sat on the top balcony and women in the main hall. The chosen lady of the year was awarded a black velvet cloak with gold embroidery and two tickets for *Umra* or Hajj. The Queen rose and placed a diamond brooch on her cloak. The mother than spoke of her eleven children and how she had managed to educate, feed and bring them all up as good citizens. She described her struggle bringing wood on her head from the forest for cooking, as there was not much money. In spite of it all each of her children went to college and graduated as doctors and scientists. I have yet to see anywhere else an Islamic gathering of that proportion so well organised. No children ran along the corridors and there was hushed silence throughout the ceremony. The program ended with a troupe of girls dressed in apple

With Muslim Aid team near Čajniče, Bosnia – picture includes trustees Mahboob Kantharia, Farooq Murad and Iqbal Sacranie – 2003.

green costumes singing songs in praise of motherhood. Malaysians thus each year relive that hadith of the Prophet Muhammad, peace be on him, that teaches us to respect our mother the most.

I left Malaysia and its gentle people and headed towards home. I always experienced a sense of pleasure as the plane taxied into its landing bay in Heathrow. Is it really my home? Why do I feel happy entering the country? These were questions not quite resolved in my mind.

After a couple of months' rest, I returned to Sarajevo to our little nursery school in Buce Potok which was being built adjacent to a mosque. Many Bosnian friends helped out – my friend Majida Mulić's husband, Amir, installed the electrical fittings without charge, while Mu'amer Kafader, one of my former students, helped in the printing of our brochure. Iqbal Sacranie (later Sir) and a Muslim Aid team came to Sarajevo and I went with them to a small town near Čajniče where this UK-based charity had built forty-three homes for refugees.

* * *

Back in London, a young friend – whom I will call 'Hamid' rather than his real name for his protection – requested help for the Chechen refugees in Baku, Azerbaijan. I had been following events in Chechnya for some years, thanks to the efforts of Dr Kalim Siddiqui and the conferences organized by the Muslim Parliament. Some of us were aware of Stalin's slaughter during the 1940s, when he deported some two million Chechens and Tatars in cattle wagons to Siberia and central Asia, to perish from cold and hunger. The Muslim Parliament conferences discussed the brutal Russian invasion and attack on Grozny of 1994-95. I felt very sorry for the Chechens, who had been denied their right of an independent state unlike other former Soviet republics. The Russians did not even wish to recognize the Chechens fleeing the fighting as 'refugees' but referred to them as 'displaced persons'. Baku was now accommodating not just Chechen refugees but also Azeris expelled by the Armenians from Nagorno-Karabakh. I immediately agreed to Hamid's request, though it was not straight forward to obtain a visa. We had to show a confirmed booking in a hotel. British Airways carried many English passengers to Baku and then on to Bashkish. Naturally petrol and pipelines interested both British and Americans in that area. On arrival I noticed that wherever we went there were Russians observing the movements of people. An American school was being established in Baku on a grand scale and upon meeting its teachers I realised that most of them came with the missionary zeal of spreading Christianity and with loads of Bibles for distribution. I noticed later that a whole American community was set up in a secluded area of Baku with well-built roads and freshly planted trees. This was a city of immense contrasts.

We managed to find a dilapidated flat of a friend where we spent the night with a Chechen family whom Hamid was helping. The bathroom had a bucket of water instead of taps. When I peeped out of the broken glass window in the morning I saw we were in a flat that formed one of the blocks built around a rectangle, leaving a small space of greenery in the centre. Once we stepped out the weather changed abruptly and it started to snow. Luckily I had brought my fur coat which saved me. Taxis were easy to get and we grabbed one. I noticed some very well-decorated shops and Turkish-style buildings. Everybody wore western clothes and spoke Russian. Hamid and I walked into an alleyway in search of the school for Chechen refugees that we had come to help. I could not see any sign of a big gate or a school sign. Hamid noticed my expressions and just smiled. The school was housed in a two-room rented place in a rundown area in Nizami Street where many

A class for young Chechen refugees in Baku – 2003.

refugee families lived in small rooms rented from the locals. The school had two shifts of eighty students, one of adults and the other of younger kids.

They were taught Russian, maths and science by their teacher Hawa and two other ladies. The Principal was called Kheva Zakaeva. The second shift started after a break of one hour. Luckily the staff was well qualified and taught efficiently without regular income and resources. We managed to pay them a meagre amount of 300 dollars per month for some time from the funds that we had brought with us. The children were very happy to see an outsider who spoke English. Some of them understood English and many were keen to learn and wanted to make pen friends with English school children. They drew pictures of their mountains and showed red blood flowing on white snow-covered hills and smoke and bombs. I brought those pictures and their letters back home and passed them on to some schools. Very few people in England knew of the massacre of Chechnya and Ingushetia. I adored these children and started teaching straight away. I was determined to help them. I went to UN office housed in a spacious building near Baku's stadium. The gentleman who received me knew the plight of Chechens and that the refugee children were not allowed in the state schools run by Azerbaijan's government. He promised to help in obtaining some remuneration for the teachers and also for the supply of free milk to the students.

I was introduced to the Minister for Education and one of his high ranking officials, Gurban Sadigov. They drove me in their car so that I could see for myself the plight of the Azeri refugees who were living in terrible conditions. Over a million had fled from Armenia. It seemed that the world's media was ever ready to highlight the Armenians as victims, but little was said when they acted as aggressors. Some of the refugees I met would start to recite *Surah Fatiha* to show that they were Muslims. An elderly refugee told us that she was from Khojaly and that her city had been destroyed in 1988 within one night, More than six thousand people were made

Azeri refugee camp in Baku – 2003.

homeless and driven out or killed by the Armenian Forces with the assistance of the Soviet Army. The military aggression led to the occupation of some 17, 000 square kilometres of most fertile land and destruction of numerous cities and villages. This ethnic cleansing continues from as early as 1905 and is still is ongoing. In 1990 the Mesketians, people of Turkish origin, were also exiled from Central Asia and landed as refugees in Azerbaijan while their cities and their cultural and historical buildings were burnt to the ground.

Minister Gurban's secretary Mr Bakhtiar showed me a plot of land in Baku's Yasama area that could be used to construct a school for Azeri children. Work on the foundations had commenced and the minister probably needed assistance. I wrote a letter to the 'Cabinet of Ministers' indicating that I was indeed sorry to see the plight of over a million refugees in Azerbaijan but it was not possible for me to undertake another project in Baku. There were not that many volunteers at hand and many of them had done enough in the Balkans. Some like Shahid and Omar were married and in stable jobs. I was to continue receiving faxes from Wagit Amiraslanov, head of the education department. Our work was restricted to helping the school on Nizami Street for which we soon had enough funds to buy some computers and stationary.

On my next visit to Baku I could not get any rest in my broken down teacher's tiny flat, shared with seven Chechens who had escaped the massacre. The water supply was inadequate for us all and at times I could not even have a bucket bath. Such were the conditions in a land where oil was oozing out night and day! Thanks to the contacts obtained from Dr Al-Emin in London I met the Sudanese director of the Dan Fadio NGO. I requested if I could sleep in their offices which were far more comfortable. I was grateful for a quilt and the cushions of their office sofa. Hot water was also available for a shower. The NGO's staff members Iskender and Khoshal were also very considerate – Khoshal was in tears when the time came for farewells at the airport.

I survived on my own fruits and tea which I purchased. The Sudanese aid worker was married to a Muslim girl from Baku. With his help I was able to visit the local sights. Baku looked like a Turkish city in every aspect and the cuisine too was similar to Bosnian and Turkish meals. The coastline along the Caspian Sea was breathtaking. I visited the Turkish cemetery that was well-kept and peaceful but also a reminder of the cost of war and treachery. The sea below reflected an Ottoman mosque on the heights. For ages ships have traversed this route with fuel and other goods for Russia.

During my stay in Baku I made friends with a young teacher called Zarkan who had a boy of five years old. She invited me to her flat where five other members of her family lived in two rooms. She told me her story after coffee – I encountered the same hospitality as in the Balkans. She had only been recently married when the

Young Chechen refugees in Baku with teacher Zarkan (standing, middle) – 2003.

Russians bombed their village. Her husband then went to Moscow to find a job but was arrested the second day without charge and the Police also robbed him of his money and watch. Her son was now five years old and had never seen his father. I glanced at the little boy playing with the little toy car that I had brought for him and felt sorry. Zarkan visited her husband in prison every six months by taking a train ride of some twelve hours. She loved him and as she spoke, tears were rolling down her eyes. I then made a pledge that I would do my best to convey her tears to the outside world so people would learn the truth of the injustices committed by the Russian government.

* * *

I returned to London with a desire to go inside Chechnya to help the poor stranded people but it seemed impossible for someone with a Muslim name and particularly of Asian origin. I just had no way of getting in, without being kidnapped, arrested or charged for being a terrorist by the Putin-backed Chechen state's army and police. The pledge to help the Chechens kept me awake at night. Over the next few months in London, Hamid and I with other friends established a registered charity, the 'Save Chechnya Campaign', with the aim of letting the world know of Russian aggression and the plight of the Chechen people. I also made a pledge to expose the Armenian onslaught that was not given any prominence. Friends like Vanessa Redgrave and Lord Rea came forwards and stood up for the Chechens' cause. The Islamic Human Rights Commission (IHRC) provided us some office space and funds to employ a staff member, Hajra, who worked tirelessly and was an excellent organiser.

We commenced an annual commemoration at the Yalta memorial in South Kensington each year on the 23rd February, to mark the tragic events of 23rd February, 1944, when the Soviets undertook the mass deportation of Chechens and Ingush from their homelands. Lord Rea and other distinguished guests would make short speeches, a wreath laid in remembrance and a white balloon released as a symbol of peace. Photo exhibitions and films shows were also organized and on one occasion Dr Khassan Baiev spoke about his book 'The Oath: A Surgeon under Fire'. We also paid tribute to the fearless journalist Anna Politkovskaya, most likely murdered by the Russian secret service for her coverage of the genocide in Chechnya.

My granddaughter Ayesha was a committed activist and helped in organising a photographic exhibition of Stanley Greene's work on the Russian invasion of Chechnya as well as film festivals. She managed the 'Save Chechnya' stands at exhibitions together with other friends and relatives including Surayya Asim and her daughter Reefa. They distributed brochures and sold wrist bands and stood outdoors on cold and wet London Februaries to provide hot tea, coffee and biscuits to those attending the commemorations.

A Chechnya commemoration at Yalta Memorial, London – 2003.

The Golders Green branch of the HSBC bank stopped our transactions and closed our account without giving any specific reason, but we were able to open an account in another bank. The funds collected were dispensed by the organization 'Medical Aid & Relief for Children of Chechnya' for the purchase of school stationary and snow boots.

* * *

I remained in contact with CoM's relief work in Peshawar but friends in London chided me that perhaps the need in Pakistan was more than in the eastern European countries, particularly in the field of education. I was introduced to the work of the READ Foundation and met its chairman, Mr Mahmood Ahmed in Islamabad. I was invited to visit the network of schools it had established in parts of Kashmir. I grasped the link between illiteracy and poverty particularly in the remote areas of Pakistan and was also appalled to see the standard of teaching. The teachers lacked training in educational techniques while the text books were of equally poor standard. I noticed an absence of maps, diagrams or charts on the school walls. I visited a school situated near the Line of Control that had been bombed by India, leading to the death of a child. The Kashmiri children were beautiful and quite shy, though happy to be photographed. Their classes were sometimes taken out of doors in the sun because the class rooms were not heated. While touring the READ schools in Kashmir I was asked to give teachers' training to the three schools I visited. I tried to convey to the teachers that rote learning was not beneficial and that students should be prompted to understand what was being conveyed.

On returning to Islamabad, I entered into a contract with READ and we planned to open a school jointly in 2003 in a small village called Churian in Potha Sharif on the way to Kohala in the backwaters of Murree. I had mixed feelings while visiting these unfamiliar Himalayan hills. On the one hand the hill tops were overcast with grey clouds, but the fresh pine air was invigorating. If the vehicle slipped there was a drop of 500 metres – there were no protection barriers on the road sides. I had seen Murree in 1974 and remembered the forests and trees laden with apricots. Alas, as I approached Murree this time I could not recognise what I saw. The trees were gone and so were the apricots. It seemed that global warming was taking its toll on Kashmir's glaciers and logging too had contributed to the deforestation. The villagers could not afford gas cylinders and chopped down trees for fuel. The large hotels and houses of the past were replaced by dirty tin-roofed shops.

On the way to Churian I kept wondering whether the villagers would accept me. I did not dress like them and did not understand their language as they spoke only a mixture of Punjabi-Kashmiri. The last leg of the journey was on a *kucha* road. At times the vehicle would get stuck in the mud and the tyres would not move. We had to bring small rocks to place on either side of the tyres before restarting the engine. The people of the village gathered when they saw a Suzuki van coming on to the *kucha* road. News spread that a foreigner has come to Potha Sharif. A few looked at me with suspicious eyes. On arrival I noticed that the proposed school was just a two room half-built shabby structure, perched on top of the hill, without access to road. There were no windows and no doors. The young teacher Mazhar introduced me to the class he was taking. I saw a few children sitting on broken desks and benches. There was a small blackboard resting on a chair. In my mind I was comparing the scene to the schools of London and wondered where one could start.

The sun went down quickly and I had to stay somewhere. There were no hotels and only a few tin huts-cum-shops in Churian and Potha Sharif. The village itself had only recently been supplied with electricity. The women used to go up the hill to get clean drinking water as only few houses had water taps. The residents kept big drums which were filled by the rain water. There were no toilets with a flush system. The teacher Mazhar came forward and asked me to go with him and stay in his house. Tired and hungry, I accepted his invitation. I was greeted by his mother, whose name was Chaand, and father. They welcomed me and offered me their nicest bedroom. We had a meal of chapatti and vegetable curry. They had a lovely white goat that provided us the milk needed for a cup of tea. It was turning into a cold October. Their house was on top of a hill and the view of the huge Himalayan mountain range was breathtaking. In the distance was Bhurban with the shimmering lights of the Pearl Continental Hotel.

Over the next few days and weeks I set to work on the school construction. I tried to find a way of obtaining building materials since nothing was available in this little village except some eggs and vegetables. There was no road to bring in the cement, iron bars and cement blocks to the site and the supplies would be left two kilometres away on the main road going to Kohala. We hired a Suzuki van to transport materials down the road track. The men then carried them on their backs to the school. Meanwhile the classes continued in the two rooms because the children's learning time was precious to me. The village people were excited when they heard that a proper school would be built for their children. One old lady brought a bag of cement on her mule and shook hands with me saying that this was a gift for the school. Similarly one old man dragged a sack of old bricks for the school. Those gestures touched my heart and strengthened my resolve to get on with the work.

We would sometimes board a Suzuki taxi to take me the one and a half kilometres from Mazhar's house to the school. These so-called taxis had three benches and dirty cloth coverings stitched up on the sides and would be filled by a dozen passengers. I just could not sit with all those people staring at me, so I requested the taxi driver to take me as sole passenger for a fare of Rs.50. However at times even that service was not available and so Mazhar and I would walk the distance back to his house. In the beginning some people raised all kinds of gossip that I was a foreigner and aimed to corrupt the female teachers. There were mutterings that I did not observe *purdah*. In response, I decided to pray in the open and during the month of fasting, I recited Qur'an aloud.

I needed to go to Islamabad frequently to bring materials for the school such as white boards and stationary, and above all to raise funds to pay for the building work. I was fortunate that the daughter of my cousin Syed Mazhar Ali, a civil engineer, philanthropist and former senator was living there. Mona and her husband Masood would take good care of me in their spacious house by the Margalla Hills. It was my sanctuary when I needed to recharge my batteries. They helped me with fund raising for the school and took it upon themselves to sponsor orphan children who could not afford to pay a nominal fee or buy books. Many children did not even have proper shoes to wear during the winter months and walked in the snow in cheap rubber sandals. Like my practice with the Afghan refugee children in Peshawar, I bought jars of Vaseline as their skin became parched and dry in the sun and snow.

Award ceremony organised by the Pakistan Federation of Business and
Professional Women – 2003.

The first phase of building work on the CoM school was soon
completed with four rooms ready for use. Everyday more new
children kept coming in to enroll. I tried to teach the children in
the morning and the teachers in the afternoon. Mazhar and I would
sit after dinner till late at night reading small English story books
like Oliver Twist and preparing a lesson plan on computer which I
had bought for him.

My friend Mehmooda Bawani invited me to visit her in Karachi
to attend an event organized by the Federation of Business and
Professional Women. She may have mentioned the projects of
CoM to them, because I was happily surprised to receive a gold
medal at the Federation's Hazrat Khadijatul Kubra Conference
in December 2003 at the Marriot Hotel. I was also given a string
of expensive pearls along with a book by a Sindhi poet. President
Musharraf was due to give the prize but an assassination attempt

a fortnight earlier changed his plans. The Chief Guest instead was the Federal Minister for Information, Shaikh Rashid Ahmed. I was given the microphone and spoke a few words on the pressing need for educational institutes in the rural areas in a hall in which the ladies' diamonds and jewelry glittered in the hotel's chandeliers.

I returned back to Islamabad to get the Convoy of Mercy registered as a sister charity. I had to seek the help of a solicitor, Mr Azam, for submitting the papers. He kindly decided not to charge his fees after realizing that I was managing CoM's work single-handedly in Pakistan.

* * *

It was always a pleasure to come home to London but each time I found the garden was in disarray. New gardeners who were hired during my absence would uproot all that was planted the year before, not recognising the difference between gladioli plants and weeds. Gardening and planting trees has always been my passion. I noticed that gardening was quite therapeutic and that as I removed the weeds, all the hidden cobwebs inside me were also swept away and I emerged fresh and stimulated. My collection of poems and Urdu and English called *Kasak* was also published in Pakistan in 2004.

It had become my norm now to spend autumn and spring in Pakistan and the summer and winters in London. The school was shut in December since there were no heating arrangements and the *kucha* roads were snow bound. I would appeal for funds to friends and family which enabled us to buy shoes, school uniforms and books for the children. Asad Khan had started a new educational project in Gambia and I found myself alone. My commitments to CoM projects in Bosnia and Kosova continued as well as the Save Chechnya Campaign's annual functions. Many refugees from Chechnya had fled to Ossetia and Ukraine and were sending requests for help. I was kept constantly busy.

Assembly at Potha Sharif school being addressed by Dr Tariq Solaija – 2004.

I collected enough funds to commence the second phase of the Potha Sharif school comprising an office and a resident teacher's bedroom with attached bath – so I could stay on the premises. The building and facilities now looked like a proper school. There was a staff room for the teachers, a small library and PCs. Mazhar the principal had worked hard and managed to keep school accounts on computer. The student numbers grew and people got to know about the school as far as Murree and Islamabad.

My elder son and Dr Tariq Solaija also came to see the school and spoke to the students. They both were delighted and happy to see such a project. My old friend David Horsefield, who had helped me in the nursery school in Bosnia, also arrived at my request. Both the students and the teachers loved him. He too stayed in the beginning with Mazhar and we worked hard and trained and taught the teachers in the afternoon. Each class was assigned a flower bed to look after, and soon flowers started to blossom. Once a week they cleaned all the school grounds. We painted a notice 'Please Use

Me' on old oil and *ghee* drums in bright colours and placed them as dustbins on the school ground. The students' number reached three hundred and seventy two.

* * *

While I was in London in October 2005 a massive earthquake destroyed many cities on both sides of Himalayas. I went to see Mr Lukhte Hassanain, the chairperson of Muslim Hands in Nottingham. I had established links with this successful charity four years earlier during relief work in Peshawar in the Afghan refugee camps, particularly with their relief officer Rahimullah. Mr Hassanain received me cordially and we discussed the need for volunteers to help in the earthquake zones that had killed thousands and left millions homeless. I flew to Islamabad and from there boarded a bus to Abbottabad, where luckily Rahimullah met me at the bus stop. We went directly to his office cum residence in Abbottabad where I left my luggage there. I noticed that many of the Muslim Hands workers were living there. There were no

Pakistan earthquake scene – 2005.

proper bathrooms or kitchen, and a large tent in the grounds that served as sleeping quarters and a storage area. Rahimullah could sense that I was not keen to stay there. I was invited by my distant relative Khola Mustafa Shah, an educationalist, to stay with her in Abbotabad. She had established many schools and now was helping the earthquake victims. She opened a camp school in Angrahi, north of Balakot. My friend Shabbir Ahmed in London along with others raised a large sum of money which I passed on to her to help build a proper school in Angrahi. In any case I soon made my way to the Muslim Hands camp in Mandiar. I noticed that the World Health Organisation was providing a vaccination programme, immunising against measles, DPT and Polio. Medicins Sans Frontiers also came to the camp and distributed hygiene kits consisting of soap, washing powder, sanitary pads, shavers, towel, hair brushes and tooth paste.

I travelled daily via the devastated road and fallen rocks, inhaling the terrible stench of dead bodies buried in the rubble. I often thought of the tomb of my ancestor ShahWaliullah, who had written forty-four books on Islamic theology. His grandson Shah Ismail, and Shah Ahmed, were buried somewhere in Balakot. One day I was amazed to see a small mosque at the bank of the river, now dried up, where a few people were reciting Fateha. The ravaging hand of the earthquake had just stopped short by the mosque wall, saving the graves of Shah Ismail and Shah Ahmed. Their names were clearly marked on the grave stones. My mother had told me that they were called shaheed as they were killed while fighting for the freedom of India. I saw sad scenes like a woman's arm, still with bangles on it, sticking out from the rubble on the main road.

My granddaughter Dr Jamila arrived later to establish clinics at the Atar Shisha, Mandiar and Balakot camps. She described her experiences in a graphic way on the Salaam website's blog:

"The stretch of road from Mansehra to Balakot had taken days to clear after the earthquake on 8 October. Massive rocks and rubble had slid down and completely blocked the road. There were holes and craters in the road and the mountain slopes looked angry as slices of the mountains had been sheared away during the landslides. Twisted trees and electrical masts along the road prepared me for what awaited at the actual site. As we drove rows of white tents became visible in the valley below.

Balakot's 20,000 inhabitants are estimated to be dead. Almost every person I saw told me about a child, brother, sister, wife, husband or sometimes entire family dead. I have never seen destruction on such a massive scale. The three schools in Balakot became massive

My granddaughter Dr Jamila working in the tent clinics in the aftermath of the earthquake – 2005.

graveyards as the earthquake struck at 8.50 am, when the children were in classes.

The Muslims Hands Medical camp is situated next to the Pakistani army medical camps and one of the helipads. Two tents were allocated for providing basic healthcare for the sick and injured. It is well-stocked with medicines, dressings and bandages. There is no electricity and obviously there are no investigation facilities available. The tents were manned by me and an assistant who helped with the dressing of wounds. When I arrived the facility had been closed for 10 days as there had not been doctors available to run it. With the help of one of the Pakistani army doctors I organised the tents, arranging the medicines in order. In the immediate aftermath of the earthquake, Dr Yasmin Qureshi, an A&E consultant from the UK, and her husband Dr Zahid Nawaz had gone out and set up this facility with the help of the Pakistani army and Muslim Hands. I saw a beautiful 11 year old girl with right femur fracture injury. A rod had been inserted 4 weeks ago at the Ayub Medical complex in Abbotabad and she was brought to me because she was still unable to bear weight. Presumably due to the load of cases she had been sent back to Balakot with instructions to do daily exercises but without any further follow-up. Her mother's case was even more tragic. She had a previous neurological deficit and during the earthquake sustained terrible crush fracture of the tibula and fibula. Her leg was now held in an external fixator. Stuck in a bed in her tent, unable to manage her injury she was deteriorating daily, and transfer back to Abbottobad was arranged.....There were a lot of psycho-somatic illnesses such as headaches, aches all over the body, heart burn. Many people were just at their wit's end. They did not know what to do next. Old women who had lost their sons, young mothers who had lost their children, a father whose three teen-aged daughters lay in an Abbottobad hospital paralysed with spinal injuries. They cried in front of me, telling me they could not sleep at night. People were not hopeless or suicidal and retained a strong faith in God. I tried to provide whatever little comfort I

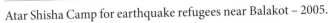

Atar Shisha Camp for earthquake refugees near Balakot – 2005.

could. I wish I had more time and better counseling skills to help these people. There is such a need for counselors in the area. On Monday 21 there was another earthquake in Balakot about 6 on the Richter scale that lasted for only approx 30 secs. The ground beneath my feet shook. The patient that I was seeing at the time became very panicky, frightened and described the sensation of palpations....In association with Convoy of Mercy a school has been set up in the camp which my grandmother, Saida Sherif is running. There are about 150 students. The school takes place in 2 large tents. My grandmother is training the teachers, providing teaching materials and uniforms and shoes to the children. The children are bright and eager to learn…"

Muslim Hands, Muslim Aid, Islamic Relief and other British-based charities provided much practical support to the displaced persons, though their work barely received a mention on British TV. Due to extreme cold some lit fires in their tents. One tent caught fire and a woman died with burns. I attended the funeral the next day. My poor school children were in a state of shock. I was myself in dire need of good tents for the classes.

One day while dropping Dr Jamila at Balakot, I could not help noticing the fragrance of freshly baked bread. It had been a long time since I had eaten freshly baked bread so following the aroma I arrived at a huge mobile bakery that was churning out five thousand loaves of bread daily for distribution in the camps. I recognized a young man named Bilal working there as someone I had met in Kosova. I was ushered inside the warm tent and accorded Turkish hospitality of hot bread and a coffee. Eyeing the marvelous Turkish tents I told him that I had come to see an army major as I needed waterproof ones for my Atar Shisha camp school. No one could beat the smart Turkish-built tents. I was told that their boss was due that afternoon and if I waited, I could see him and he surely would help me.

The sun was going down the snow-covered hills and an extreme chill was settling in but I was determined to see the head of the Turkish NGO, Mr Omer Güzelyazici of the International Brotherhood and Solidarity Association (IBS). A man with a large build finally appeared. When I mentioned Kosova and my encounter with Bilal he promised to deliver two blue rainproof Turkish tents and three gas heaters. I requested Bilal to help us erecting the tents because our Muslim Hands workers did not have the required skills. Years later I met him in Istanbul as I had not forgotten his kindness. Thanks to Dr Tariq Solaija's help a shelter room also arrived and I managed to obtain a desk and chair from the Human Resource Committee as well as a computer. With this help I managed to establish the Atar Shisha camp school and the classes continued for three months after Jamila's departure. Many Pakistanis visited the camps and distributed funds to the needy. The Government of Pakistan, then under General Musharraf, also provided Rs 75,000 to each family suffered in earthquake. I had the occasion to meet one Mr Miller H. Caldwell, a guest of Muslim Hands who had come for a short visit. Based on his experiences, he wrote a book later, and phoned me to say that I was mentioned in it. It should be noted that the Mandiar and other camps were managed by Mr Rahimullah who worked tirelessly and is an asset to Muslim Hands.

* * *

Matters were not proceeding smoothly with the Potha Sharif school project. On arrival in Islamabad in October 2006 I met Mazhar at the airport and we went directly to the school but it was closed being a Sunday. I spent the night in Mazhar's house and found his family as welcoming and hospitable as usual. Mazhar then told me that he resigned from the school. On visiting the premises the next day I was horrified to note that my locked residential room at the school had been broken into and was being used without my permission. The newly installed principal was one Mr Rashid, who was said to be of the Jamaat-e-Islami. I noticed that apart from two teachers, the rest of the staff was new. The principal's salary had been doubled and all other salaries also increased. The school fees for the students had also been raised high. The school did not have a maths or science teacher. The teachers in place possessed a BA degree in Urdu or Islamiat and did not know how to read or speak English. One teacher had no qualifications. A curtain had been placed in between the classrooms to segregate the girls and they had to cover their faces for seven hours daily inside the school. The educational standards were low – only *purdah* was high. There was no methodology in the teaching and the school had reversed to the old methods of rote learning. I could not bear it and decided not to interfere in the school. I could clearly see that READ, led by Jamaat-e-Islami, had taken over. I informed Mr Mahmood that I was most unhappy with the new arrangements and the manner in which READ had revoked our contract. However he was occupied with the earthquake's aftermaths in which he had lost relatives while READ's schools were also destroyed. I went to Wah and awaited an amicable resolution of the issues. Charity work sometimes brings happiness but at other times can be disheartening, so one should venture into this work with a sense of realism. My discussions with READ led to a promise that half of the cost of building the Potha Sharif School would be reimbursed to CoM, but alas this did not materialize. Mr Mahmood instead was very keen that I help the AFAQ (Association for Academic Quality) Foundation. He purchased my airline ticket to Lahore to visit their offices without disclosing his interest in AFAQ.

AFAQ needed help in improving the educational text books that it published and printed for schools. I was given a briefing of the Foundation's work and achievements which included not only authoring text books in all subjects but also later provided teacher training. I took on the task of making corrections to the text books, without seeking any payment, *fi sabeelillah*. The assignment turned out to be quite huge as I found many mistakes. This led to an increasing involvement with AFAQ, whose trustees I later came to know included Mr Mahmood.

I started work on AFAQ's social science books. I found it difficult to draw on their hospitality in terms of accommodation and food, yet also criticize the work of their young authors. Luckily they listened and did not mind. I had to rewrite much of their texts but they were content because the end product was better. I removed superfluous and out of place references to Islam. One or two did not like criticism and told me that because this was a Muslim country, they were obliged to insert Islam at every step. It was clear to me that such comments were being made by staff because they assumed this would please management. However the senior trustee Hasan Murad agreed with my approach. I had known his brother Farooq Murad from contacts with Muslim Aid in London and Sarajevo. It was always a pleasure to be in contact with them as I had remembered their father Khurram Murad, from whom they inherited a fine intellect, wisdom and above all kindness.

The atmosphere in Afaq was pleasant and I was happy to see the 'morning *tableegh*' in office, but the ladies were nowhere to be seen. Most of the ladies who worked there observed strict veil *purdah* and they were all cooped up in one room away from my office. Shahid Warsi, Afaq's director of training & research, was a chemical engineer by training while the chief benefactor, Mr Abrar Ahmad, owned chemical plants in the United States. At the time I tried hard to find educationalists among the young writers holding any key position in AFAQ.

Writing text books is not anybody's business. One needs to be an expert in a particular subject and possess a flair for writing to make the text interesting enough to capture the imagination of young minds. I found particularly offensive at the tendency of AFAQ's young writers to take material from other authors' works. I pointed out the law to the trustees and requested them to seek the various authors' permission. This and other suggestions were taken on board by the trustees which improved standards and book sales increased. Our previously casual acquaintance turned into a warm friendship when I was invited by Mr Abrar Ahmad and his wife to spend a weekend in their house and I felt less bitter of my experiences with READ over the Potha Sharif School and kept hoping that some of the funds would be returned according to the contract.

While I was in Lahore, my friend Surayya Saleem contacted me and picked me up from AFAQ's office for a visit to the Muhammad Pura village, previously known as Kot Bagicha Singh. It is about 40 miles from Lahore in tehsil Pattoki, Kasur district. The tarmac road had ended well before we arrived at a village in the midst of fields of sugarcane. There were bulls and cows visible from the car and women preparing fuel cakes from cow dung by pasting them on their mud houses' walls to dry. Surayya proudly showed me the school she had established.

The building gate and the boundary walls were impressive, but the construction and the layout of the school was poor. The school had ten rooms with small windows and no glass panes. There was a residential wing for the teachers or guests, and a doctor's surgery in the courtyard. I admired Surayya for all the hard work that she had put in, because it was a daunting task for a woman to single-handedly build a school in a village in Pakistan. Surayya begged me to stay on and take over the school. I thought about the distances and my age, but since she insisted, I agreed to do as much as I could. I reluctantly agreed to take Muhammad Pura School under the umbrella of Convoy of Mercy.

Surayya was not an educationalist and the principal she had appointed spoke pigeon English. He had been a factory worker in Huddersfield for four years before returning to Pakistan. Prior to this job he was head teacher of a government school. I began to understand why the educational standards in the state schools were what they were. I set to work organizing, preparing

Surayya Saleem and girls at Muhammad Pura School – 2006.

Girls' assembly, Muhammad Pura School taken by teacher Alamgir Khan – 2006.

teaching schemes and filing. I typed out the brochure of the school, admissions form and other donation forms for helping the poorer children and orphans. I also prepared the school timetable and staff job description, house rules and school assembly procedures, in the hope that all this would be implemented after I left. We soon had a rubber stamp and letterheaded paper, with a board on the school gate declaring 'Muhammad Pura English School – A project of COM'.

In the evenings I managed to edit AFAQ's social science text books. Surayya retired to bed very early and hence I had the time for this other work as well.

There are a number of problems one faces in the villages of Pakistan. There was shortage of electricity and no public transport. The nearest shops were often a distance away. I also faced a language problem as I did not know Punjabi and refused to learn it. The teachers understood Urdu, but not the children. I started to teach basic English language to the principal and staff and asked them to carry forward to the classrooms whatever they learnt. The village mosque's imam probably taught a few children and also bombarded the rest of the locality with loud sermons, which probably kept the villagers away rather than inviting them in. I did not get much sleep because of the noisy imam and tossed and turned till the early hours of mornings.

Reluctantly Surayya let me go with a promise that I should come back again. A taxi was hired, but it broke down within a short distance. The taxi driver tried to fix the problem while we waited for half an hour but without any results. It was getting late and dark. Luckily the principal was with me otherwise I would have been at a loss. There was no sign on the road and no public transport except the few taxis or the monstrous trucks and buses operated by Pathans. We hired another taxi and arrived finally at AFAQ's offices in Lahore late at night. The caretaker Yasin welcomed me and a typist was at hand. I had Mohammad Pura School's forms printed and photocopied which the principal then took back with him. I went to bed in AFAQ's office. The last of the editing of AFAQ's social studies books completed, the next day I packed my bags and happily left Lahore, travelling on the Davo bus for Islamabad, a journey of some five hours on a smooth highway with clean restaurants and mosques on the stops. This made the journey quite pleasant compared to the backwaters of Murree Hills or Chaman.

En route a lady passenger sat next to me and we started to speak. She asked me if I was a teacher. I told her what I did and she opened her purse and took out two thousand rupees. She placed this quietly in my hand saying, "please accept this humble contribution for your schools". She also mentioned that she was going to perform Hajj soon.

During various meetings and visiting many schools I raised my concerns about the deteriorating educational situation in Pakistan. I had arrived at the conclusion that one must teach the teachers starting from the nursery level so they could then implement learning effectively. The selection of the texts also needed to be scrutinized. It was now over sixty years that Pakistan had gained independence, but it seemed to me that proper textbooks had not yet been prepared to an acceptable literary standard. Schooling to matriculation level remained chaotic in government schools. Only those who could afford it placed their children in private schools. Though there is supposed to be a uniform curriculum for the country, in practice schools follow the textbooks that they decide to purchase. To my mind, the same textbooks should be implemented for the private sector as well as government schools and the learning should be comparable to international standards, incorporating the educational requirements of the country. I was amazed to find that some provinces had more than one examination board.

I felt that education should be made the top priority with an affordable standard fee for all schools. During my stay in Pakistan, with the exception of the three big cities, I met hundreds of graduates with degrees in Islamiat and in Urdu. These so-called graduate teachers were not even able to read the map of Pakistan, let alone the map of this world which is becoming smaller every day! They were not qualified, but nevertheless teaching in the villages' schools. There is an immense shortage of maths and science teachers throughout the country. Many of the science laboratories at government schools remain closed and do not function in most rural areas. There is a shortage of technical and vocational training as well. There is a huge demand within the country and abroad for qualified and skilled workers but unfortunately those Pakistanis are not accepted who do not hold a certificate. Education, alas, like buying and selling property, has unfortunately become a business in Pakistan whereas it should have been made a public service. The Government, I am told, has a very meagre budget for education whereas it should have been top priority! Our Prophet, peace be on him, made it a point that any captive who could educate or teach another person would be honoured and set free. We Muslims were once the pioneers of education. Universities such as those of Al-Azhar, Cordoba and Al-Karaouine were among the first of their kind. In Baghdad we had a 'House of Wisdom' and centres of learning in Mashad, Qom and Fez were famous. In contrast today we are begging to be educated by others. The poorer citizens remain unemployed and unemployable because of lack of proper education.

I visited palatial homes in Pakistan and sat in lavishly decorated drawing rooms, eyeing the frivolous display of stupid little crystal animals while sipping coffee with well-groomed ladies and saw no books. In my childhood days, some seventy years ago, there used to be 'One Paisa Library' in each street. Rich or poor, we could all read books of our choice in three languages – Urdu, English and Hindi – by giving one paisa, the smallest unit of currency. I did not see this facility in any street anywhere in Pakistan today.

What I am trying to convey is that considering our rich heritage, we ought somehow to improve ourselves. No outsider can change our condition unless we do so ourselves. This can be done through educating ourselves and then transferring the acquired knowledge to others. It will mean some sacrifice, but one cannot achieve anything without sacrificing self-interest. It is a shame

Accepting the Muslim News Award – 2007.

that Pakistan is considered one of the most illiterate in the world. May God help us!

* * *

The London-based Muslim community newspaper *Muslim News*, edited by Ahmed Versi, plays an important role in informing Muslims of current affairs in Britain as well as national and international events. I was happily surprised when I was invited to its prestigious Awards function in February 2007, at the luxurious Grosvenor House Hotel in Park Lane.

The banquet hall was elegantly decorated with fresh flowers. Each seat was reserved with a name display for approximately a thousand invitees in the packed hall. The guests included MPs, senior civil servants, business men, professionals and NGO representatives. We heard messages of support and congratulations from the Chancellor of the Exchequer of the time, Gordon Brown, and other leading political leaders. The prize-giving ceremony started towards the end of our meal. Suddenly my name was called and I was caught totally unaware that I would be honoured and given an award of excellence. It was a brass astrolabe in a red velvet case with the inscription of *Iman we amal*. I was quite embarrassed and drowned in emotions. I was then handed the microphone and asked to say something about my involvement in humanitarian activities. It was my memories of Bosnia that first came to mind and my encounter with the young man in Jablinica Hospital who had lost his hands. It brought tears to my eyes and to many in the audience as well. I expressed my regrets that I had not started such charity work earlier in life.

Amongst caring Muslims

Ihad always referred to London as my home. However, since around 2007, I could sense a growing anti-Muslim feeling emerging in Britain. Islamophobia was mounting and Muslims' political views, personal appearances and mosques were now under close scrutiny, suspicion and attack for an imagined association with terrorism. I had been in contact with Turkish NGOs in various trouble spots and their approach and professionalism impressed me. I met many young and polite Turkish students from the *Turkyar* hostel near my home who were here to learn English and they also attended the regular Sunday Qur'anic *tafseer* study circle in my home led by Saleem Kayani Sahib. I was frightened to see the growing hostility for Muslims in Britain and in Europe and the idea of finding a place to live in Turkey that could be of use to my family began to appeal to me.

I came to know Ahmet Kot, a publisher and literary personality of Istanbul, and his wife Hatije. When I decided to purchase a property, they very kindly gave me many days of their precious time and together we visited various locations. We came to the small town of Sapanca where a cottage by the lake in Iske Evler was up for sale. The scenery was breathtaking and I decided to make an offer. It was purchased in Ahmet's name as there were restrictions at the time for foreigners to purchase property. The fact that the property was not in my name later caused me some anxiety but I happen to be the sort of person who trusted others easily.

Outside my house by Lake Sapanca with Nudrat Muslu and Ameena Halil
Ibrahim and their children – 2007.

Luckily my *Turkyar* student Talha and Sajit also had their homes in
Sapanca. Sajit invited me to meet his parents and other members of
the family, who were originally from Georgia and lived in a palatial
house situated near a gate of the ancient Silk Route. It was a pleasure
to be with them, particularly their grandmother – *nur* seemed to
radiate from her face and no one could tell she was ninety years
old. All her children would come to see her daily, even if it was for
ten minutes. I admired their strong family ties and care towards
the elderly and was equally touched by Sajıt's kindness and care
towards me. Later in Istanbul his mother invited me for dinner and
I was presented a gift of a *janamaz, tasbeeh* and a beautiful scarf.
I was reminded of Bosnian practices that must have originated
from such Turkish Ottoman traditions. Sajit also introduced me to
his uncle Dr Fevzi Yilmaz, a professor and head of the Metallurgy
Department in the nearby Sakarya University.

While still in Istanbul I was taken ill with a cold and this, combined with lack of sleep, worsened my condition. The next day I was invited by Hatije to a *maulud* and was offered a seat in the front row. Various scenes from the Prophet's life were enacted on the stage and *nasheeds* and *illihiye* songs were sung. The participants were dressed alike in black embroidered dresses and matching silk scarves. At the end of the ceremony, a bottle containing a hair of the Prophet was brought to the stage and everyone came forward to kiss it. The Qur'an was recited by an elderly *hafiza* and a long *dua* followed. I was touched by this ceremony and later had an opportunity to express some words of appreciation. Dr Yilmaz was driving to Sapanca and I was grateful to be given a lift as this would save Hatije from much inconvenience.

Once in the car we had a nice long chat in between my bouts of coughing. Dr Yilmaz asked me if I would be interested in teaching English at Sakarya University to which I responded in the positive. He suggested that he would take me first to my cottage in Sapanca. The nearby hills were covered with snow and the closed cottage was chillingly cold. I will not forget Dr Yilmaz's kindness and care because he would not let me stay in the cottage in those conditions. He took me to a chemist to purchase some medicines. Everyone seemed to know him. The lady at the chemist's asked us if we would like a cup of tea. I could not believe my ears – would I be offered a cup of tea at my chemist in London? I was introduced to the University's Vice-Rector (later Rector) Dr Muzaffer Elmas, who gladly accepted me as a guest teacher. I could stay at the campus hotel till I felt better and a car was made available so I could visit my home in nearby Sapanca whenever I wished.

The campus was situated on a height overlooking the lake and the view from the campus hotel room was beyond description, as if from a picture postcard: the green rolling hills bowing down to Sapanca's waters, shimmering in the sun shine. My teaching assignments included providing lessons in English daily to Vice-Rector Professor Elmas and other senior members of faculty at campus. The kind and caring Vice-Rector gave me his personal telephone number and said I could contact him if I needed anything.

For the first time in days I slept well and the antibiotics helped. I woke up the next day the sun was ascending. It was a Friday. I noticed an elaborate display of olives and cheeses, boiled eggs, fresh tomatoes and cucumber and many homemade fruit jams – you name it and it was there for breakfast. Language was of course a barrier but there was always body language and the common Islamic culture and etiquette prevailed. My teaching program started immediately. These are some excerpts from letters I sent to my daughter Jasmine:

26th April 2007

Today the lesson started in the conference hall of Campus hotel, equipped with a projector, a white board and markers all ready for me. My keen students had already assembled five to ten minutes before the class's beginning. They are all professors and assistant professors and smartly dressed for the class, so I too have to keep my appearance fairly presentable. The atmosphere in the class is pleasant as Dr Cemaluddin Kubat and Gul Tekin from the Engineering Department have a terrific sense of humour. Home work is given and checked daily. So my time is spent in preparing interesting lesson plans, checking homework and watching TV mainly to keep my English intact. I must admit that when teaching foreigners I am prone to picking up their accent.

Back in my bedroom, I watched Aljazeera news on TV about 120,000 mercenaries hired by the Americans and the 'coalition' forces to fight in Iraq. Unfortunately it is these mercenaries who are responsible for the killings which are reported as sectarian violence. During the English-language news on the Turkish media I noticed that the Muslims selected to debate topics such as the head scarf issue were not the most eloquent.

I looked out of my bedroom window and noticed the midday sun shining on the silvery dome of the campus's mosque inviting me to go there. So I came down to the reception lobby and indicated my wish to pray the Friday prayer in the mosque. The hotel staff was not keen but when they saw my desire they took me with a prayer carpet to the mosque by car. There were at least two to three hundred students who prayed on hard ground covered with rubble and building material, even though the mosque was half built. But the carpet was spread there for me. I realised then the reason for their hesitance....

28th April 2007

I enjoy living in the pleasant surroundings of Sakarya campus. Tears came to my eyes as I prayed and thanked Allah for His mercy and the Turkish people's consideration and affection towards me. The hotel manager often brought freshly baked pastries and pitta and would send them to my table.

I have been teaching for four hours every day and am enjoying it immensely. I was told not to wear a scarf in the university campus but I noticed a hidden Islamic current and this morning the Islamic faculty – called the *Ilahiya* faculty – invited me, perhaps because they had seen me, the only woman, attending the *Juma* prayer in the partially built mosque.

Many ask me what is it about Turkey that appeals to me and led me to purchase property in their country. It is because Turkey is a beautiful country with lakes and mountains. There is abundance of fruit and people's diet is healthy, natural and rich. Turkish people are clean, sophisticated and very polite. Above all the mosques call out the *adhan* most beautifully.

The more I mixed with Vice-Rector Professor Muzaffer Elmas, his wife Nadera and his staff the more I realised their finer qualities and my esteem for Turkish people enhanced…

4th May 2007

Vice-Rector Elmas requested Dr Ramazan Muslu, the assistant dean at the *Ilahiya* or Theology faculty to drive me to Sapanca on the weekend. It was a brilliant sunny day and we stopped at Seredeven's open market to buy some groceries. Ramazan was delighted to see my house with its lake-side view and suggested that, if I agreed, he would bring his wife and children for a barbecue. I was happy to receive guests because at the time I did not have many friends in Sapanca. Ramazan filled my freezer with beef steaks and chicken and refused to accept money from me in spite of my insistence. One of his daughters was named Yusra like my granddaughter. His wife Nudhrat helped me hang the washed curtains and cleaned the kitchen.

With staff and students of the *Ilahiya* Faculty of Sakarya University – 2008.

I strolled in the evening outside the house and noticed three young girls and so we had a nice chat in their broken English. They were excited to learn that their professor, Dr Ayden, was one of my students. The girls were staying in a *pension* next door to Iske Evler. I offered them Turkish tea without milk and with sugar cubes. They then asked me to join them in their walk and showed me their rooms from the outside. The owner of the *pension*, Musherefia, knew German and was very welcoming. Here I was trying to learn a few Turkish language phrases from the young Turkish girls but ended up speaking broken German. In the end Musherefia could not resist and wanted to come to see my little house.

8th May 2007

The Spring Festival is on. There are displays of fresh flowers everywhere. The whole of the campus is resounding with jazz music and dance. Another of Ataturk's trends, I am told by my students. The cafeteria is moved outside to make space in the big hall for evening concerts. This is the other side of Turkey but nevertheless the Turks do have very Islamic traits. For example they will not visit a home if there are no men inside. They will not sit alone with a woman in the car. They don't speak loudly like the Italians or Asians – their voices are low in the restaurant. But the majority of them smoke and unfortunately my throat does not take to smoke at all. However there is no smoking in my class and my associate professors and lecturers try to hide from me even if one of them does need to smoke.

I get tired easily nowadays as I am teaching daily for six hours. There is homework checking and lesson preparation for two different levels daily and it takes quite a bit of time as I want to introduce new topics and new techniques to make the lessons interesting. But somehow we always end up discussing current affairs. In the afternoons I teach some of the hotel staff and one of them is Hakan. The youth unfortunately here have no role models so they are quite confused and are also brainwashed by the Turkish media. However I think I am breaking the ice and slowly hoping to influence a change in his thinking…..

10th May 2007

Dr Abdul Semmed the brightest student has returned from Istanbul and was back in the class today. I told the class that I would be teaching from the Campus hotel till the 28th May but could continue during the summer holidays from my house. They were happy with this arrangement. They wanted me to come back in July to continue. I said that I would if invited by the Rector.

Dr Ramazan Muslu is planning to come with me to London for a fortnight. Then there is Dr Ayden who lives in Sapanca and whose wife helped me painting the drawing room. He is coming to London on the 26th June. I am writing all this and smiling, remembering my Jasmine's words "Mum you and your social life! Don't you ever get tired?" It is so true – indeed I am an extrovert and love human beings. I get their warmth and affection in return, which keeps me going.

In fact the men here are so polite and so very clean! There is no comparison between Pakistani men and the Turks. The ordinary people all use tons of *eau de cologne* as a habit or rose water in summer. It is common practice here that on entering an office, you are offered *eau de cologne* or rose water to freshen up. There is an abundance of cultivated and wild flowers that are used for producing perfumes. I am told that *eau de cologne* is an original invention of Turkey and not of the German valley of Cologne. Similarly tulips were found naturally all over the hills in Turkey but now one is made to believe that these flowers are a speciality of Holland….

4th June 2007

Ramazan dropped me at Ahmet Kot's flat in Istanbul. Hatije's house is a store of all kinds of natural foods and herbs. She has many talents. She is petite but works ten to twelve hours daily publishing books, looking after her family and those in need, as well as being heavily involved in promoting a regime based on fasting and avoidance of foods with chemicals. She is calm and patient and does not impose her opinions on others. She is a true *Muslima* and loves Prophet Muhammad. I have not come across many women like her.

5th June 2007

Dear Sajit came and picked me up from Ahmet's flat. It was a lovely day and we walked through the old buildings of Aksaray to his law campus close to Suleymaniye. As we passed through the *sabils* and the old gates I was reminded of Cordoba. Suleymaniye Mosque's metal dome shone in the sun and below was the blue sea. In the streets below red and black cherries and apricots were being sold on the barrows. Turkey could be called a fruit and vegetable basket as there is an abundance of very tasty fresh fruits.

Our next appointment was with Ensar Foundation, an NGO that organises youth programmes and promotes European cultural activities by liaising with other foreign universities and higher educational institutions. In Ensar office's lobby I came across a Lebanese visitor, Joseph Nur. He had a friendly and engaging manner and we started talking. However when I expressed my sadness for Israel's attacks on his country, he became defensive and referred to his people by saying "it was their fault". I immediately sensed that he was not genuine and probably a spy. I was later told that he had been asking all kinds of questions. Under every stone we notice an enemy waiting to sting us! May Allah help us. I managed to have a quiet talk with Mr Mehmood of Ensar and told him about the good work of the Islamic Foundation in Leicester.

Jasmine, her daughter-in-law Shaheen and my two great-grandsons Yusuf and Yunus visited me in Sapanca. They loved the swimming pool. Ajmal, his wife and his three daughters also came twice and enjoyed their stay.

* * *

Shabbir and Shazia of the CoM Nursery School in Bosnia invited me to give away the prizes at the end of the term. Bosnia remains eternally beautiful and its ugly war of fifteen years ago is now hopefully behind it. New buildings were now to be seen everywhere and many foreigners had chosen to buy houses in this very special city.

I was invited to present a paper at the 4th International Conference on "Education for a culture of Peace" organized by Sabiha Hadzimuratović and funded by some European embassies. In my presentation I said that what I had witnessed was a culture of hate and not peace and that model citizens can become monsters when fed with prejudices over many years. I quoted Karen Armstrong: "in our polarized world we cannot afford to cultivate inaccurate perceptions that fly in the face of the facts and alienate people from themselves and from one another".

The genocide inflicted on Bosnians, the destruction of mosques and the concentration camps were not just a sudden flight of fancy inspired by Radovan Karadzic and General Ratko Mladić. It was the outcome of decades of books and poems of Serbian academics, writers and poets planting the idea of Greater Serbia and a pure race. I also referred to the book entitled 'The New Crusade, Constructing the Muslim Enemy', and the essay by Norman Ciger "The nationalist Serbian intellectuals and Islam – defining and eliminating a Muslim community". My paper made the point that a culture of hate takes roots after people have lived through years of distortion, misinformation and inaccurate perception. For example in my view the shooting of Palestinian children by Israeli Defense Force or the construction of the fifty-foot high Wall was not due to a sudden hatred. The seeds were planted decades earlier. It was in 1982 that Israel's Prime Minister Menachim Begin, in his speech to the Knesset, said "Palestinians are beasts walking on two legs." Similarly Putin's regime is following the footsteps of Stalin in the way Chechens have been brutalized and treated. Putin even accused them of blowing up apartments in Moscow in 1999 which killed 246 people, but later it was learnt that this was a scheme that involved the Russian Security Forces. Similarly the torture camps in Cuba and in Abu Ghraib and the animal-like behaviour of the American troops can only be explained in terms of years of exposure to cartoons, movies and TV in which Arabs and Muslims are treated as objects of contempt. The creation of a culture of peace to my mind requires both the truth and reconciliation. One cannot blank out history and expect peace and reconciliation. Those who were or are guilty must acknowledge and apologise for their crimes. Only years of serious efforts can bring a culture of peace and it has to be supported by all sections of society – the media, the political elites, the educationalists, the academics, the cultural and religious leaders and not forgetting the power of music which brings us together in common appreciation of something beautiful and worthy, reminding us that we all are part of one human family.

* * *

I returned to Sapanca the following year and resumed my English class, now located in the *Ilahiya* Faculty. Rector Muzaffer Elmas also was in contact with me. Dr Ayden invited me to accompany him and his wife on a holiday, together with about 120 students from the faculty. I was delighted at the offer as I had to pay a nominal charge for travel and hotel. We were housed in the luxury of Club Tortas on the Mediterranean Sea. There were a number of Russian students also staying there and I noticed that they appeared more composed and desisted from loitering late at night, unlike their Turkish counterparts.

Over the next five days we visited the Damlatas Caves and also a Seljuk fort built in 1126 on the heights of the Alanya hills. The huge fort wall surrounded the city. I wandered among the ruins and admired the solid structure still partly standing after nine hundred years. En route we visited the Manavgat waterfalls that reminded me of the Niagara Falls but these were of course on a much smaller scale, but more gentle and picturesque. Smoking restrictions were being implemented in Turkey but the professors and the students lit their cigarettes even in the moving bus. I reminded them of the rule and they desisted.

Very close to the cottage in Sapanca across the railway tracks was a mosque where I would go in the evenings for the *maghrib* prayer. One evening I met a tall gentleman also walking towards the mosque and he may have noticed that I was a foreigner. After the prayers I was introduced to Mr Sadetin Tantan who asked me in good English if I would like to come to his house for coffee, which I gladly accepted. While walking alongside I asked him what he did, to which he replied humbly, "I am a farmer". However the gates were opened by a police guard and we entered a huge lake-side house. Seeing this style of life I did not believe for a second that he was a farmer. He asked his wife Fatma to come out as we sat in a conservatory overlooking the lake. I was invited to have dinner with them. I politely refused but upon their insistence I accepted. I was happy to speak English as I did miss speaking the language. He showed me his garden with fruit trees while Fatma pointed out the dancing peacocks and pheasants roaming in the grounds. I later came to know that he had started his career as a commissioner in the Police, and later, after having been elected to Parliament, also served as Minister of Interior. The nearby mosque was built by his father. It became my routine to drop by Mr Tantan and his wife, where I was always welcomed. Fatma was very talented and had decorated the house with good taste. She had raised six children and kept an immaculate home. She also sewed dresses and I always had a slice of her delicious, home-baked cakes ready on my visits.

* * *

During my next teaching assignment at Sakarya in 2009 I received a call and an email from one of my former students, Dr Naki, urging me to conduct a language course at the Yüzüncü Yıl University in Van, a town in Eastern Anatolia. I told him that I was booked to go home but he insisted and said all my expenses would be paid and that I should proceed immediately. It took me almost a week to make up my mind because it was not easy to change the programme. My teachers in Bosnia were expecting me for the ceremony awarding annual leaving certificates, while Cemaluddin Kubat and Engineering staff at Sakarya as well as the *Ilahiya* faculty wanted me to continue teaching. I never knew that I would be as busy and in demand in my later years of life as when I was young.

Van was about a thousand miles from Sakarya. I was received at its airport by Dr Naki and taken to the town of Edremit. I compared the place with Istanbul and Sakarya and felt rather depressed at the absence of greenery. There was lot of dust and plastic bags full of rubbish were strewn beside the road and on the hills. It reminded me of Pakistan and its poor sanitary conditions. Blocks of flats had been constructed on the barren hills while below lay Lake Van, the largest lake in the whole of Turkey. I was gradually captivated by the region's own beauty. Dr Naki's flat was situated on a hill with a view from its balcony of snowcapped mountains and the blue waters of the lake of Van. I wondered why the eastern part of Turkey was not as developed as the rest of the country. I was determined to find out the reasons from my University's professors.

The Yüzüncü Yıl University was established in 1982. Dr Naki was a head of department and also taught elementary school trainee teachers on the methodology of teaching Physics. Mr Shenau, the head of the Fisheries department, lived in Edremit not far from Dr Naki and drove us every morning to the University. My English classes started in the large office of the head of the Faculty of Agriculture, Dr Kenan Gullu. He was in charge of four departments: food crops, soil fertilization, fish-farming and breeding, its

Standing by Lake Van – 2009.

processing and marketing. In one corner of his office, behind a board, there was a prayer area used by the professors. I could not be housed in the campus hotel as it was being renovated so I was given a flat adjacent to Dr Naki's flat and had my evening meals with his family. Each day I had to negotiate four flights of stairs to the flat and four flights of stairs to the big office-cum-hall for English lessons at the university. I realized that I was getting short of breath. It was cool enough in the mornings to require a warm coat and gloves but by midday the sun shone quite strongly. As soon as the sun set over the mountains it became cold and windy.

I soon began to understand some of the technical vocabulary used by my professor-students, for example the complexities of fish farming and the maximum weight of rainbow trouts! When I was taken round the laboratories they explained to me the research on fresh water and sea water fish. I missed my son Ajmal who had once worked as a fish farmer in Kent. I enquired about the comparative backwardness of this part of Turkey even though it had such scenic beauty and was given various explanations from the reluctance of professionals to give up the clubbing lifestyles to be found in the big cities like Istanbul and Izmir, to the struggle of the Kurdish population for greater autonomy. I was told that various outside interests were instigating enmity between the Anatolian Turks and Kurds. A further factor was the effect of drug trafficking across the mountains via Van which offered some a quick route to earn money without hard work.

I was taken to many historic locations and scenic spots by my student professors of the English communication skills course. I visited the Aghtamar Island in Lake Van that takes its name from a tragic story of a fisherman who fell in love with a princess named Tamara held captive in a tower on the island. According to legend, he would come to the island discreetly in his boat and she would

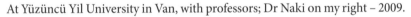

At Yüzüncü Yil University in Van, with professors; Dr Naki on my right – 2009.

call out to him and they searched for a way for her to escape. One night the young man's boat leaked and while drowning he called out 'Ah Tamara!' and hence the island took its name. I visited the old city of Van, where the Ottomans established themselves in 1548. During World War I the armed rebellion by the Armenians in 1915 led to much destruction and loss of life and property. There is tremendous propaganda by Armenia that the Turks killed them, while in fact in Van it is the Armenians who had long-prepared for the revolt and committed massacres. Van was taken over by the Armenians with Russian support and the historical Muslim part burnt to the ground. It was only in 1918 that Muslims returned to the liberated city. These cruelties were repeated in the late 1980s when Armenia ethnically cleansed its Azeri population and also expelled a million Muslims from Nagorny-Karabakh. These were the refugees I had seen in Baku some years earlier and tried to help.

Dr Naki and his wife were deeply religious and involved in *dawa* work. Dr Naki planted many trees near the blocks of flats where he lived. The absence of trees on the hills had reduced the beauty of Van and he wished to restore its greenery. His wife Zainab was the head of Muslim Women Association and I was asked by her to speak at a girls' hostel. I could not refrain from mentioning the importance of hygiene and the pollution of the environment in the way plastic bags were used and discarded. I also visited some private schools that charged exorbitant fees just because their medium of instruction was said to be English. Dr Naki was interested in opening a private English school and we discussed such a possibility.

* * *

I spent three weeks in Canada and was glad to be with my brother Misbah and his children and grandchildren. His grandson Ata was a medical student and interested in my charity work. He decided to raise some funds for my poor children's schools in Pakistan. It was nice feeling to see the shared commitment for humanitarian work within the family.

I flew back to London from Toronto and the next morning on 1st November caught the plane for Pakistan!

I embarked with mixed feelings. Age was catching up on me and my hands were not as agile as before. Now reaching 78, maybe I should cut down on my activities and attend to some of my health problems? I seemed to be out of the country a lot and missed my hospital appointments. While in London I met Robeena who had provided half the funds to Surayya for purchasing the land for the school at Muhammad Pura and also helped in its construction. I wondered why Surayya had not mentioned Robeena's name to me before. God Almighty had His own plans and Surayya requested me to proceed to Muhammad Pura straight away as she was unwell.

I was delighted to see my old friends from Bosnia, Afzal Cheema and his wife Nusrat, waiting to receive me at Lahore airport. I am always impressed by the hospitality and kindness of the Pakistani people. After my arrival at the village school I felt very frustrated because the teachers I had trained to teach for the last two years had left. The new principal Usman was good and honest but his promise to speak in English seemed long forgotten. The schools' accounts were in shambles. It was also freezing cold in the school. The chemistry lab and computers donated by my friends at Muslim Aid stood idle because there were no qualified teachers to utilise them. The main problem was that qualified teachers did not want to work in the villages as they could earn good salaries in the cities, where they could also supplement their income with private tuition. The life in the village was simple with limited leisure or shopping facilities, dirt roads or no roads at all. Gone were the days when highly qualified teachers at the Jamia Milia in Delhi were prepared to teach for low salaries because they believed in the cause. Alas there seems less of a sense of public duty in the younger generation since everyone is out to make money. Who is to strive to educate and uplift the poor masses?

However I do not give up easily. For the next three months I was occupied in management and teaching tasks at the Muhammad Pura School – the training of new teachers, administration and supervision started from seven thirty in the morning till late in the evening. I called Alamgir from Peshawar to help as we needed one more Maths teacher. Our small team worked hard and it was rewarding to see the young students flocking to the school. Their keenness to learn and attitude of respect towards teachers encouraged us to strive further for them.

Back in Lahore I managed to obtain class room furniture from Ms Margo of the Choueifat International School and also purchased stationary. I literally lived on cheese and spaghetti with tomato sauce and soup packets, though fresh fruits and vegetables were always available. The peace and quiet and the scene of miles of green fields took away all my fatigue. As always, there were opportunities to rest and recover at the comfortable homes of Mona and Masood, now in Karachi, and Dr Tariq Solaija in Wah. Even though occupied organizing the wedding of his daughter Javariah, he took special care of me. He lodged his own relatives in hired accommodation, keeping me in his own home in the double bedroom I was familiar with. His affection has made me realize that those with true greatness also possess humility. This highly intelligent pious individual always called me 'Ammijan' or 'Ma'am' and treated me almost like his own mother. All his children were highly educated, well-mannered, deeply religious and respectful of the elderly. They showed me the same great affection that I received from their parents, Tariq and Zareena. How could I not love them!

* * *

I next attended to the other CoM educational projects in Pakistan. The second new school in Murree in Aliot was nearing completion. Dr Tariq Solaija very kindly visited the school and later his friend Ziad, an architect, also offered advice. It had five rooms but the problem of access remained. The local *nazims* have been promising a road for the past six years – such is the plight of this well-resourced but neglected country. I could see pretty children in open rubber sandals in the extreme cold looking after their goats.

I proceeded to Peshawar where the school's building work in the Isa Khel village was slow due to the political situation and the Americans' drone attacks that only brought loss of life, suffering and greater resentment as refugees kept flooding in. I realised that the headmaster, Alamgir, needed a lot more cash for completion than was anticipated. Alamgir's house was some forty kilometres away and situated among fields of strawberries and corn. His parents only spoke Pushto and went out of their way to accommodate me by turning their drawing room into a bedroom. The nights were extremely cold in the winter months in Peshawar. Their courtyard had many fruit trees and flowers, but the house itself was without cemented floors. Alamgir's sister cooked food on a burner fueled by chopped wood. Luckily the bathroom was spotlessly clean and fitted with a hot water geyser. After spending one night with them I returned back to the school premises where I stayed most of the time in a damp and half-built school in extreme cold. I marveled at the resilience of the Pathans but my heart was saddened seeing children wearing only a shirt and with torn rubber slippers walking in the mud to their classes.

I had bronchitis when I returned from Peshawar to Tariq's house in Wah, which had become my second home. I commuted from Wah to Islamabad daily with Tariq or with his son Naveed, a mechanical engineer and senior manager of an oil and gas company. It was the norm of both father and son to read five suras of the Qur'an during the drive. At times I used to stay in AFAQ's office in Islamabad and managed to check the final proofs of the 'Children's Encyclopaedia' project that I had edited. I also kept in touch with Muslim Aid because the head office in London had asked me to visit some of their projects and report back.

* * *

My return to London was via Doha, where I stayed with my niece Jasmeen Ul-Haque, a commercial and marketing director. I had last been in Qatar five years ago and the airport seemed to have trebled in size. There were pine trees, water canals and flowers on the corniche. From Jasmeen's flat on the fifteenth floor of the glass-fronted 'Zig Zag' towers overlooking the lagoon I could see oil wealth had lit up the land, but it was also sad that energy was being wasted on huge illuminations and extravagances. We attended a play in English and visited an old *souk*. Muslims who read the Qur'an know that Allah does not like the wastage. I wondered in which directions we Muslims are going – luxury, frivolity and wastage of God-given bounties have become our norm.

* * *

My next visit to Turkey was during Ramadan 2010. My son Jimmy's dear friend Professor Sabri Tekir invited us to Izmir. In the 1980s he had been a student in London and would attend the Qur'anic tafsir classes led by our teacher Saleem Kayani. Now, thirty years later, his warmth and friendliness remained unchanged. During our stay we were taken on a long drive by him and his wife Perizad to the famous ruins that were supposed to be the cave of the 'Companions of the Cave' or *Ashab al-Kahf* mentioned in the Qur'an. We stopped by the Isabey mosque dating from 1375. The caretaker of this Seljuk mosque told us an interesting story: he once had to give a guided tour to some army officers from Pakistan attending a course nearby. As it was time for prayer, they all joined the *jamaat*, but not their Turkish colleagues. Such was Ataturk's lasting influence, fortunately now on the decrease.

The highlight however was our visit to the ancient Greek city of Ephesus. The sun had begun to shine in full fury and though we were fasting we walked through the cobbled streets between standing columns and remnants of the city's library and amphitheatre. Alexander the Great was said to have arrived there in 334 BC. Sabri must have read my mind because he hired a *tonga* to drive us around – the first time I had sat on one since my childhood in Delhi.

* * *

Eid was spent in Toronto with my brother Misbah and his family. I returned to Pakistan with my friend, the very capable Robeena Tahseen who had taken annual leave from her job in London. Our first destination was the school in Murree where construction work had stopped due to lack of water and funds. One classroom wall had collapsed due to the earthquake soon after *Eid*. The wall had to be rebuilt and firmer foundations put in place with proper iron rods. Classes were proceeding with four teachers and over forty children. I found that it was difficult for me to climb the hilly road or descend easily from Mazhar's house to the school below. There was a keenness for learning I felt missing in British children, who were more interested in Nintendo games and TV cartoons. After school hours there were English lessons for the teachers. We remained in Murree to the end of the school term that was also the end of the academic year. Parents were invited to the school for a programme of children's speeches and drama tableau. The function was attended by one hundred and fifty guests including the local elites of the district of Aliot.

Next we headed to Peshawar on the comfortable Davo's bus and made our way to the CoM school in Isa Khel. On the way I briefed Robeena about the problems of various schools and how one could solve them with her help. As a social services worker she was a good listener and I respected her suggestions. The school headmaster Alamgir arrived in a taxi and took us to Isa Khel village. Since my last visit he had managed to build an office with an attached bath, hot water geyser and modern toilet and hand basin. There was a TV, electric kettle and a gas cylinder to keep the room warm and for cooking. We were happily surprised to see that he had also managed to install two proper beds with mattresses and bedding linen. Robeena and I had not expected such facilities in a half-built school in such a short time. We realised the walls of our room and the floor were still wet as the cement had not dried up. The Isa Khel School provided education to seventy children with just two tutors. The classrooms had thatched roofs and uncemented floors. Fortunately there was enough land where children could spread their mats and sit outdoors for lessons and gain some warmth from the sun. Alamgir Khan's hard work and dedication encouraged us to help him fulfill his dream of establishing a fully functional school. I knew that he was managing with great difficulty but what I liked about him was that with true Pathan dignity he never asked for money. Robeena and I both started teaching the children and in the evenings, under the gas fires, we provided English classes for the teachers and Alamgir. A new computer was bought and money donated towards immediate expenses.

I wished Robeena to see all the schools and so we headed towards Lahore to the Township school project which thanks to Allah was now without deficit. Robeena's month-long stay was over and we returned to Islamabad for her flight back to London

Surayya was in Muhammad Pura and kept on ringing me to find out when I was coming to help the school. I spent a month teaching there. I was lucky to come across Mr Farrukh Hassan, my son's colleague at the Muslim Council of Britain, who was in Lahore on holiday. He not only brought my medications from London to Muhammad Pura School but also invited Surayya and me, along with our principal Mr Usman, for dinner at his family home where we spent the night. Surayya as usual went to bed early but being a night bird I stayed up late with the family. I felt as if I had known them for a long time, such was their friendliness and care. Much like my own family, they were both religious as well as keen on poetry and classical music. They asked me how the schools could be helped and I told them of the immediate need for school furniture in Murree. Farrukh's brother Brigadier Tariq Hassan fulfilled his promise and desks and benches were delivered.

* * *

With Sakarya University's Rector Professor Muzaffer Elmas – 2011.

In the spring of 2011 I was in Sapanca in the company of Jasmine and Robeena. Luckily I did not have to start taking my English class immediately because the faculty staff were busy with the student exams. I was happy to learn that Dr Muzaffer Elmas was the newly-appointed Rector of the University. With some free time at hand, I met up with Rachid Benaïssa who had purchased a flat in Istanbul. He kindly helped me rediscover the grandeur of this great city. I enjoyed eating freshly grilled fish at Sultan Ahmet and drinking loads of freshly pressed orange juice.

When teaching did commence, my students included the Vice-Rectors Professors Drs. Fatih Üstel and Musa Eken and also Secretary General Metin Kucuk. Professor Fatih was also in charge of the Metallurgy Department and he asked me to run a course for seven of his associate professors in the afternoons. As usual I absorbed information from my students about their technical specialties. At the time Turkey was also preparing for its general elections and there were huge posters everywhere as well as vans playing music and publicising their parties. Based on its record of growth in the economy and improved standards of life, the Justice and Development Party (AKP) won by a majority vote on 12th June 2011. Towards the end of my stay, news was arriving of the suffering in Somalia from famine. I encouraged the campus students to start a fund raising campaign – it was a new experience for them because in the past such initiatives were left to government or NGOs. Then with a bang the turmoils in many parts of the Middle East, particularly Syria, worsened. Nearly ten thousand refugees fled from Syria to Turkey and I again witnessed the hospitality and caring element not only of its leaders but also among the public.

* * *

I visited the school in Buća Potok in Bosnia in 2012. I was delighted to see the progress of the nursery but had mixed feeling on other developments. Sarajevo has now new buildings though the scars of war are still felt in a few places. On the whole people are carrying on with their lives and on the surface all looks well, but deep down there are problems. The youth is most frustrated because of lack of employment. Most factories still remain shut and instead one can see beauty parlours and expensive shopping arcades. The young girls are attracted to the glitter and fashion but cannot afford to buy the expensive items on display. Young people sit in coffee shops and smoke and loiter around. I felt sad to see them waste their life away. The money comes mainly from those who were lucky to go abroad and earn and send remittances to their relatives. The rest I suppose is paid by IMF. Deep down frustration is boiling inside them. Many can still not return to their own homes even after almost twenty years. Bosnians are still not given a visa easily to visit England like the Serbs, Croats and Montenegrins. They see food items coming from Slovenia, Croatia, Germany and other countries and notice non-productivity at home. I hope that they learn to strive and stand on their own feet and not become lazy. Cigarettes, alcohol and drugs are not the answer to despair but *iman* and strong faith in Allah is needed which can make a person work honestly and work hard. I hope I am right and tried to convey this message at each visit.

ca *Chapter 11*

Jerusalem

I had the opportunity to visit the three most sacred mosques in February 2013, thanks to the kindness of my young friend, Shabbir. On arrival in Mecca I recalled my last visit to *Baitullah* during my teaching period in Jeddah, some 32 years ago. There were now towering blocks of hotels and expensive shopping arcades. I also noticed rows of healthy-looking trees planted by the roadside, not there before. The roads were wide with hundreds of cars and crowds of people, all walking towards the Kaaba to pray in the mosque built by Prophet Ibrahim, peace be on him, some five thousand years ago.

Joining the crowd of thousands of men and women, spellbound and grateful to Allah, I could pray in the holy precincts of Kaaba. Each one of us was busy remembering our follies and sins and seeking His pardon oblivious of the material world we live in daily. I noticed that almost at each prayer time there were burial prayers – *salaat al-janaza* – for one or more pilgrims who had passed away. Not surprisingly, it is the wish of many to die and be buried in the *haramain*. One feels close to God Almighty's presence during the prostrations. Shabbir, his uncle Laal Hussain and I tried to perform as many prayers in *Haram* as we could.

There were many veiled women vendors outside the holy precincts selling all kinds of souvenirs, jewelry and perfumes. Food stalls and restaurants served a variety of food for all tastes and nationalities. Women do not cover their face in the precincts of Kaaba and I was surprised to see that some did not follow this rule. I was also shocked to learn that even in the vicinity of Mecca there was a US base for directing drone attacks.

Peace and tranquility prevailed in Medina where we spent seven days, offering our prayers in the vast Prophet's mosque where I met many Malaysian, Indonesian, Turkish, Pakistani and Indian Muslims. According to our hotel manager there were more than a million people performing prayers. Medina has also become a huge city and the Prophet's mosque was unrecognisable since my last visit.

From Medina we boarded a flight to Amman in Jordan for a journey to Jerusalem. I had been longing to see Palestine since 1967 when the Israeli forces grabbed even more Palestinian land; I remembered my friend Zahra, sitting in the Baker Street mosque and telling me how her house was bulldozed and she escaped to London.

We spent one night in Amman in a grand hotel, where a Palestinian marriage ceremony was taking place. We were too tired to appreciate their dance or music. In the early hours of the next morning we set off on the taxi journey towards Jerusalem. The driver pointed out features of Jordan's landscape and the surrounding high mountains. We passed old Roman amphitheatres and had a lovely lunch in Ajloun among the fig and cypress trees in a newly built restaurant on Jordanian territory. We also visited the *Ashab al-Kahf* near a beautiful old mosque – it is not just Ephesus that lays claim to the Companions of the Cave!

As we drove towards our destination we saw the Dead Sea, quite barren. We then passed near the Jordan River and the fertile valley. The driver happened to be a Palestinian and with a sad tone he told us the history of migration, emphasising the fact that the West Bank, Gaza, and the Golan Heights had been annexed by Israel as well as lands from Jordan, Syria and Egypt, whereas Palestine had shrunk to nothing.

We arrived at the Jordan River terminal and had to purchase a ticket to proceed. It was printed in Hebrew and English. There were more check points and a few kilometres of no man's land and then finally the Israeli post. We were twice checked at security points. Our passports were scrutinised page by page and then photocopied while we stood by the closed counter. A young officer asked me all sorts of questions including the purpose of my visit. I told him that it was to see and pray in the land of peace, *al-balad al-ameen*. Shabbir's uncle and I passed through the security and passport checks quite quickly, presumably because of our old age. There were many Canadians, Americans and Germans who were also processed without delay. I began to feel anxious for Shabbir who was held back for questioning. Our taxi was waiting and we were wearing warm clothes because it had been cold in Amman, while here it was very hot. Finally after 35 minutes Shabbir emerged and I sighed with relief. He came out looking exhausted.

We then headed towards our first *qibla, Baitul Maqdis* in the holy city of Jerusalem, but there were many hurdles ahead. We passed through more check points and vast areas were no-entry zones. Our taxi reached a point where it could proceed no further. We then had to board a bus for a short distance and then take another taxi with a yellow number plate that could drive in Israeli territory. We traversed the region that had once been in Jordan and was now under occupation. The water from River Jordan, the fertile land of Palestine and part of the Dead Sea had been taken by Israel. We could see the borders marked by fences and road signs either in Hebrew or Hebrew and Arabic.

There were hundreds of agricultural fields and fruit gardens along the 150 kilometre route to *Baitul Maqdis*. We could see the shanty dwellings where Palestinians worked and lived, hidden behind the date and fruit tree groves. Many poor Palestinians were bussed to work in the fields. The Arab driver of our yellow taxi still called it Palestinian land and he told us how villages had been bulldozed and fruit groves taken away.

At the Dome of the Rock with Laal Hussain – 2013.

We arrived in al-Quds after a whole day of travel and stayed at the Vista View Hotel. We were disappointed to see this poor and shabby hotel but were impressed by the owner's hospitality, a Palestinian, who was lame and walked with crutches. His hospitality and warmth and that of his staff dissuaded us from moving to another hotel, though I spent an hour having my room cleaned and dusted. The hotel charges included a breakfast and dinner with generous portions. There were many Russian Orthodox Christians amongst the guests.

From my bedroom window, I could see glimpses of the the the *Haram al-Sharif*, the Noble Sanctuary, with the golden Dome of the Rock glistening in the sunlight. Our next few days were spent in the Noble Sanctuary and its surrounds. I was unable to walk long distances so each day we hired a taxi at a cost of 30 shekels – about £5 –to be dropped by the Lion's Gate, *Bab al-Asad*. It was manned by gun-toting police who checked passports though being British we could enter easily.

Apart from *Bab al-Asad* there are numerous other gates in the walls surrounding the *Haram al-Sharif* with names such as *Bab al-Sakina*, *Bab al-Silsilah* and *Bab al-Mutahara*. The swaying coniferous and olive trees seemed to greet us with a gentle *salam*, the message of peace and tranquillity. Towards one end of the 35-acre sacred compound stands the Masjid al-Aqsa with its silver coloured dome while at the centre is the magnificent Dome of the Rock. Five thousand years of history are preserved in these walls of stone and marble as well as in the archives, witness to miracles and acts of both great piety and cruelty. This is where Prophet Zakariya, peace be on him, worshiped and prayed for a son, and Maryam and Jesus, peace be on them, lived. This is where our Prophet, peace be on him, was miraculously brought from Mecca and then raised to the highest Heaven. I thought of the many prophets who had prayed here – Ibrahim, Ishaq, Dawood, Solomon, Moses, Yahya, Jesus...

I remembered the exact words of Alistair Duncan, author of 'The Noble Sanctuary', that he said to me so many years ago: "I am afraid what all I have documented in my book may not be there tomorrow". As a result of Israeli incursions the whole area has shrunk to a tenth of its original size. I could see Arabic inscriptions and Qur'anic verses missing from many of the domes and gateways surrounding Al-Quds but renovations were not permitted.

After climbing many more steps we finally reached the higher grounds towards the Dome of the Rock. The walls were covered with blue and green ceramic tiles and Qur'anic verses embedded amongst the tapestry of flowers. I could not believe that I had finally reached our destination. I was almost in a trance with tears flowing freely, remembering my God Almighty and grateful for the opportunity to pray under this grand dome where our Prophet ascended to the Heavens and beyond! The rock on which the dome was built was said to have fallen from the sky thousands of years ago and another piece believed to be in the second *qibla* in Mecca.

There was a hushed silence inside the Dome and many people were busy praying. The rock was surrounded by a wall. We descended down the steps and prayed underground at the same place where our Holy Prophet had prayed. Shabbir pointed out to me the impression of Prophet's foot. On our way up we saw the massive white rock from where our Prophet embarked on the *miraj*. Silence prevailed everywhere and one could feel the divine presence inside the Dome. There were religious books and many copies of the Qur'an, and I noticed versions in Braille as well. These were all neatly placed in glass cabinets in the worshipping places. There was a striking contrast when we emerged from the mosque: the precinct was surrounded by tall Israeli buildings on the hills yet the Dome maintained its position quietly and splendidly at the centre.

* * *

Our daily routine was to have breakfast, take a taxi and rush to the *Haram al-Sharif*. After the *dhuhr* prayers we would explore the area around precinct. There were children playing in the courtyards after school was over. One day we ventured into the Jewish praying area, passing through a security checkpoint. Armed police and the security officers were on patrol everywhere. We made our way to the original *al-Buraq* wall but now better known as the Wailing or Western Wall. There were notices welcoming visitors and reminders to dress modestly and respect the place, though many of the young tourists did not respect the dress code. A separate section on the right side was allocated for Jewish women and I noticed some of them trying to push folded pieces of paper between the bricks of the huge stone wall. I walked to this section and held my hand on to the wall and prayed with them. I prayed to Allah the Almighty to bring peace and harmony to this *al-balad al-ameen*, land of peace, and for the deliverance of its suffering people.

I noticed an underground tunnel that was being excavated as part of the Jewish search for Solomon's Temple. Nothing has yet been found but there is an area now called the Western Wall Plaza with models, sculptures and illuminations and a 'Generation Centre', all to reinforce Israel's claims on Jerusalem. I fear that the excavations would weaken the foundations of masjid al-Aqsa. There was an iron gantry leading up to the mosque which could offer the elderly like Hussain bhai and myself a more convenient route, but we were barred from entry.

Exhausted by the hot sun, I sat under the shade of a tree and surveyed the rabbis in their robes and hats pacing up and down with lowered gaze. Groups of police and army cadets and batches of school children were coming and going, most likely brainwashed into a version of history that teaches hatred of Palestinians. In a nearby alley way we saw a Jewish museum being prepared to display the old artefacts that were being dug up. This was not far from a bulldozer at work excavating what seemed like another underpass.

I entered a synagogue that was along our path. It was clean and peaceful and I liked the atmosphere. There were benches and tables for the religious books. A lady with her hair covered was sitting and reading the Torah quietly. Seeing me she looked up and I went forward to shake hands and we exchanged smiles. I also sat on a bench and recited *Sura Fatiha*. As in the case of the Wailing Wall, the men and women prayed in different sections. There were many Canadians and Americans strolling outside but not many went in to pray in the synagogue. We also visited the Gate of the Prophet Dawud that was near a church.

I would walk in the grounds of the *Haram al-Sharif* daily, though the pebbled pathways were difficult for someone like me with painful feet. The serenity of the place had won my heart and whenever I reached the main mosque a kind of closeness to Allah *Jalla-Shanuhu* became dominant, for which I was grateful. I could pray sincerely with devotion and concentration seeking His pardon and His forgiveness. This feeling does not come to me easily.

* * *

One day after prayers at al-Aqsa I met a young medical student named Aliyah, who had kindly brought me a chair to sit on, perhaps realizing my age. It was easy to converse since she spoke very good English. She had also spent some time in Oxford for her elective. She recited a long surah in the Qur'an, *al-Ahzab* to me in a melodious voice which moved my heart; I could not help myself and kissed her. She came there every day after her college in order to memorise the Qur'an. I only had a butterfly brooch in my bag and that was the only thing I could offer her as a gift. Aliyah told me that it took her an hour and a half to travel from her small flat in Genin to her college. Without the apartheid Israeli wall, it would take her ten minutes. She lived in Genin with her three other sisters and three brothers, all younger than her. Aliyah told me that she felt happy to see some Muslim visitors from abroad and hoped that Muslims would not forget Palestinians.

Aliyah told us about a recent incident at the *Haram al-Sharif* which highlighted the volatile situation. A few days earlier Israeli soldiers had attacked two Palestinian girls for being too close to the Wailing Wall. The *mushaf* carried by one of them fell to the ground which was then kicked by a soldier. There was an immediate wave of resentment and some young teenagers began throwing stones at the soldiers. The Israelis then retaliated in force with chemicals leading to burns on the youngsters' faces.

Later I also met a young French lady working on a thesis on Jerusalem who had also witnessed the Israeli soldiers trampling on the Qur'an and was horrified. She told me that if the Muslim boys and girls chant "*Allah Akbar*" out loud, the Israeli police note down their ID details and they are prohibited from entering the mosque. There were special discriminatory laws that only apply to Arab Israelis.

On a separate occasion I was offered a chair by a Palestinian caretaker at the *Haram al-Sharif*. We were joined by two of his colleagues and I noticed that the older generation spoke good English compared to the young ones. The men described their poverty and meagre salary. Their only way of earning a little bit of money was by serving as guides and they wished for more Muslim tourists. They told me how all the gates of the al-Aqsa mosque were controlled by Israeli armed guards, while they themselves had nothing to protect the worshippers. They told me about the Nakba of 1948 and the atrocities in 1967: "the world has forgotten us; now the whole of Palestine including the holy city of Jerusalem is controlled by Israel." I did not have much to give them except fifty riyals, having lost my money in Saudi Arabia. The oldest man passed the note on to another saying, "he is younger and is needier than I am".

I could see that the occupation has taken its toll. A generation has grown who know little of their history and have to learn Hebrew. I found the situation not dissimilar to the situation in Bosnia, where there were plenty of TVs and mobile telephones, but few institutions providing a good standard of education. However a few do achieve success like Aliyah, because of their love for Islam which moulds their character and leads them to study and work hard.

* * *

Our stay allowed us to perform a Friday Prayer at the *Haram*. There were no taxis available that day and while walking we noticed that many roads were blocked and new check points everywhere. There was extra police surveillance and even more severe intimidation of Muslims as a result of the earlier disturbances. We were able to pass through the check points because of our British passports but not many Palestinians. Some argued that at the preceding Friday it was announced that people above the age of forty years could enter the holy mosque to say their prayers and that they had travelled a long way for this reason. The Police response was, "No negotiations. Today only people above fifty can go". All ID cards were checked.

After *Juma* we met a resident of Jerusalem, Isaq. He led us away from the armed police and showed us his mother's grave in the dilapidated cemetery near *Bab al-Asad*. He told me that all the adjacent land was now taken over by the Israelis and Muslims were not allowed to put up even a brick to maintain the small part of the Muslim cemetery. He had twice planted three olive trees but the next day they were pulled out and thrown away. He also showed us the mausoleum of the great Indian Khilafat Movement leader from my home town Delhi, Muhammad Ali Jauhar. After attending the Round Table Conference in London in 1931 while seriously ill to negotiate independence for his homeland, Jauhar had famously declared that he did not wish to be buried in a land that was still unfree, and requested to be buried in Jerusalem.

Later that day we visited *Masjid al Buraq*, located in one corner on the other side of the Wailing Wall. This was the place where the Prophet, peace be on him, had tethered Buraq and then prayed two *raka* before the ascension. There I met some Palestinian ladies who had only been able to get a pass to enter the mosque after a lot of struggle and difficulty. They told me that many had travelled from Genin, Ramallah and Nablus just to pray in the Noble Sanctuary. They had brought their own food for the journey which they ate outside the mosque. I was kindly offered some. Dates and biscuits also were distributed by some elderly ladies inside the mosque. Time passed quickly and we performed our *'Asr* and *Maghrib* prayers there. For our return journey we walked back to *Bab al-Asad* for a taxi, but only to find out that it was shut.

We then walked to another gate further away. On arrival we noticed that there were other people too waiting to leave. The Muslim caretakers had temporarily closed this gate to avoid a confrontation with a group of Israelis who were singing songs declaring their ownership of Jerusalem. The caretakers did not wish any more young Palestinians to confront them and so end up in Israeli prisons. When we were allowed out it was to an unfamiliar part of Jerusalem. We passed through narrow alley ways with large dustbins. Luckily a young man who lived near our hotel guided us. There was no taxi in sight and we were exhausted when we arrived at ten o'clock at night. Though it was past dinner time, the kind hotel manager made it a point to ensure we were served with warm food. What an eventful day it was!

* * *

The next day Isaq's son, Barak, took us in his car on a tour of Jerusalem or whatever was inside the 26 foot high 'Separation Wall'. We saw the Al-Quds University and also the rich residential areas going all the way to Mount Scopus. It was as if the new settlements and hotels on all the surrounding hills were laying siege to the holy city below. In the evening we went to see the famous church and the mosque of Caliph Umar who had personally visited Jerusalem in 637 AD. We read his Proclamation granting Christians the safety of "their persons, their goods, churches, crosses – be they in good or bad condition – and their worship in general." The marble slab is still placed on the wall but unfortunately not translated in English. My mind went back to the actions of the bishop of the Serbian Orthodox Church in Srebrenica who gave orders for a church to be built on the land of my friend Fata.

Barak also welcomed us on the week-end to his home for breakfast where we were welcomed by his wife and family as well as his father. As we sat under the shade of the fig and olive trees, they pointed out to us their fifteen kilometres long plot of land on Mount Scopus confiscated by Israel. The few Muslim families on the Mount live in conditions of fear and intimidation, not knowing what might befall them the next day. They are not allowed to build on their own land and have to do so surreptitiously at night. I came to know that two months previously, a neighbour who owned a large hotel on Mount Scopus was forced at gun point to abandon his investment and no compensation had yet been offered. The elderly ladies sat and chatted with us. Everyone from the neighbourhood came to greet us and convey their pleasure at having Muslim tourists coming to Jerusalem.

I was introduced to an eighty-eight year old aunt who once lived in Lifta, a Palestinian village that was ethnically cleansed in 1948. The village was not far from Mount Scopus. She told us that the Israelis, at gun point, took possession of her three-story house, and land. She then went with her husband to the town of Ramallah and later they built a new house in East Jerusalem in 1965. However, after the 1967 war, they lost this too. They were unable to return to Jerusalem and so settled in Amman, where her husband died, sighing and weeping to the end for his Palestinian home. She remained in Jordan. Her two sons now lived in Mount Scopus, but she cannot spend her last days with her near and dear. After much difficulty she was given a visa to visit them for only two weeks. She was not only pleased to see her sons but also a nephew, who had been imprisoned at the age of seventeen without charge and held for twenty seven years till his recent release. She had friends in similar circumstances who died without being able to see their children. It is Israel policy not to allow refugees to return to their land. On the other hand settlers from Poland, Germany and Russia keep coming in. Similarly Barak's wife is prevented by Israeli law to visit her mother in Genin, where she was born: "No negotiation".

I was glad that I had come to meet these families and see for myself their perseverance and bravery. They did not meet many outsiders and wished the world would not forget them. All this was said while fresh fruits and warm food kept coming from inside the kitchen. That was the hospitality we received throughout our stay in Jerusalem. It was not possible for us to travel beyond the Wall separating Palestinians from each other in their own homeland. They have to live in a small, congested area, lacking all facilities as if in a cage.

We fail to realise that we are all travellers in this world and we all will reach the final destination one day when we will be accountable as to how we lived and behaved in this world.

Reflections

My friends and relatives are now telling me that I should realise my age and take it easy. I am in two minds. I look at my half-finished book staring at me with a 'finish it quickly' expression. I look at the amount of clothes that my wardrobe has acquired over the years. I decided to start disposing off my *saris* that I had ceased to wear since a long time and the Kashmiri shawls. I was not able to part with as many items as I might have wished! However I made a firm promise to myself not to take on any new responsibilities and concentrate on the work at hand.

There seems to be no end to the calamities affecting the Muslim world. Corrupt leaders are shooting at their own civilians instead of stepping down or solving the situation through dialogue. I fail to understand why Muslims are not adhering to Islamic teachings and solving problems by *masalehat*, regardless of foreign intervention or not. I am in anguish to see Muslims in conflict and the bloodshed. We have been beset by our own naiveté and ignorance of religion. The world laughs at our follies and internal quarrels.

I am also in dismay that here at home in Britain, the English Defence League is organizing demonstrations and campaigns against mosques and causing mischief. I note that organizations such as 'United against Fascism' and 'Hope not Hate' are confronting the EDL and seeking public support for it to be banned. Whenever there are tense situations I cannot seem to detach myself and feel unconcerned.

Britain had a tradition of respecting public opinion and taking public demonstrations and protests into account. Yet Britain succumbed to US pressure and embarked on an unjust war in Iraq lasting eleven years and leading to the loss of life of hundreds of thousands under the false pretences of eliminating weapons of mass destruction. I was astonished that Tony Blair was chosen as a Middle East peace envoy. Double standards prevail: Israel's nuclear arsenal and weaponry is justified along with its high wall, imprisoning and subjugating Palestinians, but Iran is not even allowed to produce electricity from its nuclear plants while babies and patients are dying because of strict sanctions.

What lessons are we giving to our younger generation? To my mind the objectives of education should be to inculcate values of honesty and fairness and develop the sense to treat others the way we would like to be treated ourselves, regardless of religion, nationality, colour or race.

I began to reflect on the outcomes of the various educational projects that I had been involved with in many parts of the world. I pray that after I am no longer here, these should not be abandoned or discontinued. I have found an able friend and volunteer helper in Robeena Tahseen and our travels together offered me an opportunity to acquaint her with the realities of the projects. My daughter Jasmine assured me that after her retirement, the two would supervise and train the teachers for a month each year in the various schools in Pakistan and also help the Sarajevo Nursery school. Mr Farrukh Hassan, Dr and Mrs Anwar and Rubina Azam Qureshi, the new trustees of Convoy of Mercy in Pakistan, have also promised to continue their support for Isa Khel and Aliot schools. This reassured me and so I proceeded to complete the final account of my life's story.

I remain in touch with Asad Khan and cherish his beaming smile. He is now busy with educational projects in Gambia and his creativity also finds expression in poetry. *Alhamdu lillah* the centre we initiated in Kosova is running efficiently under Mohiuddin's guidance. Shazia is responsible for the nursery project in Sarajevo because Shabbir is spending more time in building a large school in Duska village in Sialkot, which I visited and provided some help.

It was a pleasure to receive a cutting recently from the Oslobodjenja newspaper, sent by my dear friend Mela Mlivo from Sarajevo, describing the success of the academic year and included pictures of children's activities. My last visit gave me immense delight seeing the little darlings and the efficient teaching staff under the guidance of Shazia who speaks perfect Bosanski now and the nursery is thriving in Buća Potok, Sarajevo. I was equally happy to learn Vasvija had become a medical doctor. Harun Imamović and his wife have an art studio and he also teaches. Halima Hadziamacović is no longer a mayoress but is working as an economist in a bank. Unfortunately her husband passed away after an heart attack. He had suffered emotionally during the war. Mela and the Centre for Islamic Architecture's office have now shifted to an office block in a posh mosque built by the Indonesians. Mustafa Ceric has retired. Amir Hodzić is still with MINA and Ibrahim Ahmetagiĉ, jolly as ever, has become a granddad and is still with *Riasat*. Ajsa Hasimbegović, the brave Bosnian war helper, has recovered from throat cancer.

I received a letter from Annie Bates, the daughter of Bill Croker, who was a great friend and helper of CoM in Croatia and Bosnia. She informed me of her father's death. When Annie was going through his papers and photographs, she saw my name on a post card so she wrote to me. Seeing her address and phone number, I could not resist calling her and she came to meet me though she lived quite a distance away. An embrace with Annie was almost like embracing Bill. I remembered our times in Solin with Bill and the period when he was being hunted by the Croatian military police for providing aid to the besieged Muslims. He had always felt so much at home with us.

My talented and pretty friend from Omiš, Jasmina Cosic, has become a well known writer with three books to her credit. She has a nice little flat in Titova Ulica and in spite of all the sadness and strife has climbed up the ladder of success. I also receive news from my 'little friend of Ostrožac' – Idriz – who is now a young father and lives in the United States. It is always a pleasure to see old friends in Sarajevo and in my heart I wish that one day the poor Palestinians also see the end to their misery. It is a good feeling that those students I have taught in various places have progressed and are doing well. They are sending money home to improve the living conditions of the less fortunate.

Even now the burial procedure in Srebrenica is proceeding each 11 July as the bodies or the remains are continually identified and black bags are labeled with their names and distributed to next of kin for burial. The Čhetniks, that is the Serbs, remain openly hostile to Bosnians when they return to their own homes even as I write today. Fata is one brave woman who returned to Srebrenica in spite of the fact that she has been beaten up many times by them. She still lives alone in her house, but what is worse is that the Serbs have built a huge church on her land. Not only that, another church is also being built exactly where the massacre took place, right next to Potoçari's massive graveyard. The irony is that there are hardly any churchgoers in the area. It is this type of provocation that is brewing all the time and making Bosnians feel unsafe and humiliated.

The annual functions of the 'Save Chechnya campaign' at Yalta memorial are no longer continuing and instead we send funds to Satanay Dorken of MARCCH (Medical Aid & Relief for Children of Chechnya) for poor children's snow boots and school bags. With heavy heart I sold my lovely little bungalow which was situated on Lake Sapanca. Realising my age, I found it hard to maintain two properties. However the Vice-Rectors at Sakarya University have asked me to come and teach again.

I feel that here in London, and most other places where I have worked and visited, the youth lack an ideal to follow and indulge in frivolities. Children are not taught the basic rules of good behaviour, austerity and avoidance of extravagance. The global consumer culture to my mind is destroying our beautiful world's harmony. We seem to be living only to earn and spend and create heaps of rubbish thus spoiling the environment. How my heart longs for the peace and security for all mankind, only God Almighty knows. Why cannot we love and tolerate one another? I still feel that I do not have a nationality but can be at home anywhere. When asked my nationality, I usually fumble for words. I say that I am the citizen of the world. What I have learnt is to accept and take the good from each society and try and leave what is not beneficial. Maybe this is the reason I have generally experienced kindness and love from people and this is a real blessing from God Almighty.

When I hear my teacher Saleem Kayani Sahib describing man's accountability on the Day of Judgment I am in anguish. I fear for having failed as I have not thanked Almighty God enough for all the blessings He bestowed upon me in spite of my failings. I firmly believe that the love of God makes us humans love and care for one another. I have learnt many things during the changing seasons of my life and that is to live simply, love generously, care deeply, speak kindly and leave the rest to God Almighty. Although happiness keeps us glowing, only God keeps us going. Do I have miles to go before I sleep? But the passion for learning does not die and so I continue. The sparks are still aglow.

September 2013
Willesden Green, London

Index

Abdul Jalil, Datuk Seri
Shahrizat, 261

Abidi, Agha Hasan, 124

Aga Khan (Senior), 62, 67

Aga Khan, Karim, 64

Ahmad, Abrar, 284-285

Ahmad, Shahida, 122

Ahmed, Mahmood, 270,
283-284

Ahmed, Syed Mubin, 97

Ahmed, Munzir, 95-100

Ahmed, Shaikh Rashid,
275

Ahmed, Maulvi Syed
Saeed, 18-20

Ahmed, Kausar & Shabbir,
123, 277, 319-324

Ahmedi Begum, 21

Ahmetagić, Ibrahim, 221,
335

Akhtar Jahan Begum, 15,
23, 51

Aksami, Leila, 224

Al-Abidin, Zainal, 129

Al-Emin, Dr Muhammad
Osman, 267

Alamgir Khan
(headmaster), 286,
310-311, 313-314

Ali, Ashraf & Nisa, 116

Ali, Lynne, 136

Ali, Muriel, 45

Ali, Naheed, 103

Ali, Syed Afsar, 31-32

Ali, Dr Syed Akbar, 31,
36,103, 143

Ali, Dr Syed Akhtar, 31,
44, 134

Ali, Syed Arif, 143

Ali, Syed Asghar , 20, 45,
103

Ali, Syed Athar, 45, 92,
96-97, 123

Ali, Syed Mazhar, 103, 273

Ali, Syed Parvez, 31

Ali, Syed Safdar , 20, 31,
44, 47

Ali, Syed Tahir, 46

Ally, Dr Nazir JP &
Zubeda, 112, 114

Al-Shawi, Dr Tawfik, 127-
128, 131

Al-Shawi, Dr Zarina, 131

Aly, Nazli, 116-117

Amiralanov, Wajit, 267

Amtul Shakoor Begum, 17

Ansari, Ata, 308

Ansari, Ayesha, 132, 221,
226, 269

Ansari, Misbah ul Haq, 23,
26, 41-42, 48, 51-52,
62, 65-67, 74, 79, 89,
98, 103, 117-118,
125, 129-130, 137,
230, 313

Ansari, Nusrat Begum, 77,
79, 89, 117

Ansari, Omar, 118

Ansari, Saba, 133, 226

Ansari, Salam ul Haq, 46,
48, 96, 98, 117-118,
125, 133, 136

Ansari, Shaheen, 302

Ansari, Yunus, 302

Ansari, Yusuf, 302

Ansari, Dr Zafar, 129

Ante, 150

Anwar, Ismet & Dr
Muhammad, 334

Arafat, Mr , 106

Arif, Iftikhar, 124

Asifa Begum, 25, 32, 34-35,
45-47, 50, 54, 62-63

Asim, Reefa & Surayya, 269

Asmodi, Dr Fatma & Dr
Yusuf, 255, 258, 260

Ayden, Dr, 299-300, 303

Aziz (CoM helper), 199-200

Azra (friend), 49

Azra Begum, 22

Babić, Mirsad, 225

Baiev, Dr Khassan, 269

Baksh, Nabi, 247-248

Balfour, Lord, 113

Balmer, Ian, 149

Baluch, Aziz, 113-114

Bates, Annie, 335

Bawani, Mehmooda, 274

Beg, Ishaq, 130-131

Begović, Rizwan, 222-223

Begum Daultana, 106

Begum Shaista Ikramullah, 54

Begum Jan, 116

Benaïssa, Rachid, 115-116, 174, 184, 187, 315

Benn, Tony, 184

Bilge (friend), 211

Bismillah Begum, 17

Block, Robert, 213

Brohi, A.K., 70, 113

Bronkhurst, Danny, 193, 206, 210, 210, 217, 222

Brown, Jean, 100, 103

Brown, Marjorie, 97

Bugaighis, Fatima, 109

Burney, Hasan, 124

Butt, Rashidah, 157

Caldwell, Miller H., 282

Caldwell, Mr, 112

Carrol, G.A., 23, 42

Castle, Douglas, 173

Cemila (aid worker), 190-192

Cerić, Mufti Mustafa, 217-218, 220, 335

Chai, Dr Ang Swee, 137

Chalmer, 149

Chammi ki Amma, 24, 50

Cheema, Afzal & Nusrat, 214, 224, 309

Conrad, Mrs. Max, 72, 74

Cosić, Jasmina, 166-168, 335-336

Cox, John, 178

Croker, Bill, 153-154, 159, 335

Cutting, Dr Pauline, 137

Davies, Mrs, 132

Dragica, 163

Duncan, Alistair, 112, 319, 323

Duncan, Colonel, 146-147

Eken, Dr Musa, 315

El-Droubie, Leila, 116

Elmas, Dr Muzaffer & Nadera, 295, 298, 303, 315

Emira, Dr, 157-158, 163-164, 166

Faiz, Faiz Ahmed, 123

Faraz, Ahmed, 123

Farhana (CoM volunteer), 242

Farooqi, Samina Hasan & Sultan, 116

Faruqi, Hashir, 105

Fata, 329, 336

Fatima Sultan Begum, 85

Fletcher, Clare, 137

Gatrad, Dr Anis & Nusrat, 187

Gellman, Derek & Sylvie, 98, 106, 108

Ghaus Pasha, 87, 110-111

Glazebrook, Rev., 80

Golithy, Neil (Shaheed Ibrahim), 155, 166-167, 174-177, 179, 182, 195-196

Grist, Ryan, 166

Gullu, Dr Kenan, 305

Guy (CoM volunteer), 179

Güzelyazici, Omer, 282

Habiba, Inam, 115

Hadziamacović, Halima, 224, 335

Hadzimuratović, Sabiha, 302

Hafeez Begum, 42-43

Hajra Qureshi, 269

Halilović, Amina, 221

Halimović, Nizam, 187

Hamdo, Murveta & Sefer, 180-181, 190-191, 196

Hamid, AbdulWahid, 105

Haq, Ameen ul, 48, 51-52, 90, 92, 103, 115-116, 132-134, 136, 211

Haq, Bushra, 253

Haq, Imad ul, 79

Haq, Inam ul, 16, 20, 25-27, 32, 41-43, 46, 49-50, 52-53, 62, 79, 86, 117, 134-135, 230

Haq, Islam ul, 16, 39, 41, 45, 47-48, 51-52, 82, 84-86, 101

Haq, Misbah ul, see Ansari, Misbah

Haq, Nayar ul, 24-26, 41, 48, 51-52, 74-75, 77, 79-80, 82-83, 85-86, 89-90, 92, 101, 114, 117, 125, 253

Haq, Riaz ul, 21, 44

Haq, Saud ul (Baba), 22, 82

Haq, Shams ul (father), 15-18, 21-27, 30, 38-39, 42, 48, 89, 97-98

Haq, Uzma, 114

Harun, Imam Abdullah, 108

Harun, Shamila, 108

Hasan, Syed Bashir, 21, 32

Hasan, Mahdi & Shameem, 137

Hasimbegović, Ajsa, 190, 335

Hassan, Farrukh, 314, 334

Hassan, Mrs Fatima, 116, 156, 187

Hassan, Mehdi, 128

Hassan, Brigadier Tariq, 314

Hassanain, Lakhte, 277

Herbert, Peter, 214

Hodžić, Amir, 218-219, 223, 335

Holyman, Miss, 118

Hoosen, Dr Abdullah & Ruqaya, 187, 208

Horsefield, David, 226-228, 276

Husnara Begum (Apa Misya), 22

Hussain, Laal, 319, 321-322, 325

Hussain, Safia, 29

Hussain, Dr Zakir, 28-30, 50

Ibrahim, Ameena Halil, 294

Idris (CoM volunteer), 157-161

Idriz (young Bosnian), 200-201, 205, 336

Imamović, Harun, 183, 335

Inam, Habiba, 115

Inam, Nafisa, 48

Inam, Tayyaba, 120-121, 123, 133-136

Iqbal, Sir Muhammad, 20

Islam, Qamar ul, 51

Islam, Hakim Shams ul, 43, 51

Islam, Siraj ul, 91

Islam, Yusuf, 134, 185, 187, 217, 224

Israel, Catherine, 98, 103, 108

Izetbegović, Alija, 216, 224

Jackson, Ms, 112, 114

Jaffer, Firoza, 122

Jagajnić, Dr Azra, 224-225

Jilani, Mohsina, 122-123

Jinnah, Muhammad Ali, 52, 64

Jinnah, Fatima, 52

Jujo, Adis, 214

Julage, 165

Kafader, Mu'amer, 263

Kantharia, Mahboob, 262

Kapić, Ediba (Deeba), 155-156

Kapitanović, Amira, 223

Katme, Dr Majid, 208

Kaul, Kishen, 76

Kay, Ms, 68, 112

Kayani, Saleem, 293, 312, 337

Kazmi, Dr Quddusi, 122

Keith (CoM volunteer), 178-179

Khalid, Anwar, 122

Khayal, Akber, 83-84

Khan, Asad, 138-139, 143-144, 148-150, 157, 161-162, 164, 166, 169-171, 173, 182, 184-185, 204, 210, 222-223, 225-226, 236-237, 241, 253, 256, 275, 334

    Convoy of Mercy (CoM), 139, 153, 169-170, 175-176, 189, 195, 199, 203, 207, 230-232, 236

    Mahmooda Apa (mother), 174, 191

Khan, Hakim Ajmal, 28

Khan, Laiq Ali, 52

Khan, Dr Ehsanullah, 88

Khan, Hameedullah, 36

Khan, Dr Inayatullah, 35-36

Khan, Nasra, 138, 222

Khan, Samiullah, 36, 96, 114

Khan, Sir Zafarullah, 61

Kidd, Bertie & Bettie, 121-122

Kot, Ahmet, 293, 301

Kot, Hatije, 293, 295, 301

Kubat, Dr Cemaluddin, 296, 305

Kucuk, Dr Metin, 315

Kulsum Begum, 45, 136

Kulsum (CoM volunteer), 196-197

Laycock, Dr Elaine, 207-208

Laycock, Richard, 207-208

Lepara, Mr, 184

Mahjouba, 244

Maidman, Marietta, 95

Maidman, Mr & Mrs, 92, 95

Malik, Irfan, 205, 208

Marasović, Nada, 148

Margo, Ms, 310

Maseeti Begum, 18, 20-21, 27

Masood Tabish, 21

Matloob, 45

Mazhar (headteacher), 272-274, 276, 282, 313

Memisević, Fadila, 158

Mersuddin (Bosnian boy), 205

Mike, (CoM volunteer), 148

Mills, Mr, 105

Mirza, Babar Beg (Bobby), 226-227

Mirza, Farida, 35-36, 114

Mirza, Parveen, 32

Mirza, Parveen (Barg-e-Gul), 122

Mlivo, Mela, 219, 223, 335

Mohiuddin, Imam, 236-237, 242, 252, 234

Mohiuddin, Qazi Sahib, 253

Moillen, Mademoiselle, 71-74, 109

Morse, David, 76

Mountbatten, Lord, 41-52

Mughals

    Mumdo Begum, 40

    Pacho Begum, 40

    Shah Zafar, 39-40

Muhammad, Ebrahimsa, 105

Muhammadi Begum, 77, 82, 90, 117

Mulić, Amir & Majida, 262

Mumtaz Begum, 17, 34-35

Munevera (nurse), 158

Murad, Farooq, 262, 284

Murad, Hasan, 284

Murad, Khurram, 284

Musherefia, 299

Mushtaq Mamu, 42-43

Muslu, Nudhrat & Dr
     Ramazan, 294, 298,
     300-301

Mustehsan, 22

Najjar, Dr Zaghloul, 129

Naki, Dr Erdimir &
     Zainab, 305-308

Nana Bhutta, 19, 46

Naseef, Abdullah, 131

Naseef, Fatma, 129

Naseef, Rabia, 100, 129

Nasiruddin, Choudhury,
     76

Nawaz, Dr Zahid, 279

Nazir ud Din, 98

Nichols, Mr & Mrs, 78

Nizam of Hyderabad, 15,
     30, 51

Nona, 60-61, 76

Nurak, Amrudin, 217

Oly, Major, 208

Palcic, Jure, 157-161-164

Palmer, Ruth & Woody,
     61-62

Parker, Jack, 83

Pat (friend), 69

Peduto, Kristine, 214

Pervaiz, Amjad and Safia,
     247-248, 257

Peter (CoM volunteer),
     148

Philip (CoM volunteer),
     206

Pico, Basil, 232

Politkovskaya, Anna, 269

Puri, Mr, 82

Puskin, Amela, 226

Qadri, Ahmed Hassan,
     117

Qaisar Jahan Begum,
     20, 27

Quddusi, Irshad, 48, 79,
     82

Qudsia Begum, (Baigma),
     103, 143

Qureshi, Rubina Azam,
     334

Qureshi, Dr Yasmin, 279

Rahat Begum, 20-21

Rahimullah, 277, 282

Raisuddin Sahib, 77

Razia Begum (mother),
     11, 17-19, 22-27, 34,
     38-39, 42, 44-46, 48,
     51-53, 58, 60, 65, 80,
     82, 85-86, 98-100,
     111, 121, 124, 134,
     136

Razik, Hanifa, 105

Rea, Lord, 269

Redgrave, Vanessa, 269

Richards, Tony, 196

Sabri Cochi, Mufti Hafiz,
     232-235

Sabina (CoM volunteer),
     147

Sacranie, Sir Iqbal, 262

Sadakat (CoM volunteer),
     169

Sadigov, Gurban, 265-266

Sadiq, Maulvi, 15

Sajit, 294, 301

Saleem Bhai, 42-43

Saleem, Shahed, 224

Saleem, Surayya, 242, 285-
     287, 309, 314

Salihi, Shaikh Zymer,
     231-232

Salima Begum, 43, 46, 51

Sardar, Ziauddin, 106

Sarwar Jahan Begum, 35

Sefo, Alma, 172-173

Seiler, Ingrid, 93, 115

Seiller, Juta, 93, 115

Semmed, Dr Abdul, 300

Shabana (CoM volunteer),
     157

Shabbir Sahi, 226, 252, 302,
     334-335

Shah, Syed Jamaat Ali, 27

Shah, Khola Mustafa, 277

Shah Waliullah, 17-18, 278

Shakir, Parveen, 123

Shamima Begum, 42, 124

Shamsuddin (CoM worker),
     237-238, 242

Shaukat Ara Begum, 22, 82

Shayan, Dr, 205, 208, 215,
     217

Shazia, Naureen Sahi, 226-
     227, 252, 302, 334-335

Shenau, Mr, 305

Sherif, Ajmal, 83-84, 87-89,
     93, 96-99, 102, 105-
     106, 113, 115, 120-121,
     132-134, 138, 302, 306

Sherif, Ansaruddin, 46,
     53-65, 68-71, 74-78,
     83, 85-88, 100-102,
     106-111

Sherif, Jamila, 123, 134, 221,
     226, 278-282

Sherif, Jasmine Fatima, 75-
     76, 78, 80-82, 88-89,
     91, 97-100, 105-106,
     108-109, 116-118, 125,
     132-133, 135-136, 138,
     185, 202, 204-205, 211,
     242-245, 300, 302, 315

Sherif, Jimmy, 65, 76-77,
     80-81, 84, 88, 91-92,
     95-95, 99, 105, 107,
     109-110, 113, 115,
     118-120, 123, 134-137,
     185, 312

Sherif, Saida

     All-India Radio, 32-33

     Awards, 290-291, 274

Barg-e-Gul, 122-123

Convoy of Mercy
    Albania , 232-236
    Balkans, 141-230
    Kosova, 237-242
    Pakistan, 247-257,
        270-275, 280-
        282, 285-287,
        310

Employment
    Air France,
        Karachi, 82-83
    Air Lebon,
        London, 99
    American School,
        Karachi, 87
    Aylestone School,
        London, 125
    Bank of England,
        London, 99-
        103, 109-110,
        112-114, 116,
        118-120, 125
    BBC, London, 66-
        67, 96, 118
    Greenhill College,
        London, 132,
        136, 150
    Hammersmith
        & North
        Kensington
        Community
        School,
        London, 125
    Harrow Council,
        London, 132,
        141, 150
    Holborn
        Polytechnic,
        London, 118
    Islamia School,
        Karachi, 90-91
    Manarat School,
        Jeddah, 127-130
    Olympic Airways,
        London, 99
    PATLO, London,
        96-97

Selfridges,
    London, 65-66
Hajj, Umra, 129-131,
    319-320
Places
    Abbottabad, 277
    Aliot, 310, 313, 334
    Amman, 320
    Anyar, 258-260
    Baku, 263-268
    Balakot, 278, 280-
        282
    Buća Potok, 221-
        222
    Butrovic Polije,
        191-192
    Chaman, 253-256
    Ciglana, 182-183,
        186
    Cordoba, 243
    Delhi, 11-51
    Ephesus, 312, 320
    Ernsthausen, 92
    Farnham, 111
    Fez, 243
    Geneva, 57-77
    Gibralter, 65, 244
    Grenada, 243
    Isa Khel, 311, 313-
        314, 334
    Islamabad, 270-
        271, 273, 277,
        282, 287, 311,
        314
    Istanbul, 294-295
    Izmir, 312
    Jablanica, 169-197
    Jakarta, 258
    Jeddah, 126-129,
        131
    Jerusalem, 319-331
    Kandahar, 255-256
    Karachi, 51-54, 77,
        79-92

Kingston, 101-102
Khetri, 14, 16-17,
    22-23, 42
Kuala Lumpur, 257-
    258, 260-261
Les Diablerets, 71-
    74, 109
Lahore, 283-285,
    287, 309, 314
London, 54-55,
    65-67, 95-126,
    132-139, 168, 184,
    187, 197, 231,
    245, 252, 263,
    268, 277, 299, 314
Mandiar, 277
Montreal, 101
Muhammad Pura,
    285-287, 309-310,
    314
Murree, 117, 271,
    276, 288, 310,
    313-314
Mussoorie Hills, 44
Nemira, 150, 152,
    155-161
New York, 100-101,
    103
Omiš, 162-166
Ostožac, 199-215,
    220, 222, 225-226
Peshawar, 247-257,
    311, 313
Port Said, 70-71
Potha Sharif, 271-
    274, 276-277,
    282-283, 285
Pristina, 236, 242
Prizren, 236-241
Rabat, 243
Risalpur, 82
Rhoda, 115
Rohri, 89
Saharanpur, 44

Sakarya Campus, 295-300, 305, 315-316

Sapanca, 293-295, 298-304, 315

Sarajevo, 215-219, 222-230, 252, 262-263, 302, 316

Spin Boldak, 254-255

Split, 141-147

Srebrenica, 214, 329, 336

Tangier, 243

Toronto, 308-309, 312

Van, 305-308

Wah, 283, 311

Kasak, 275

Save Chechnya Campaign, 268-270

Sherif, Shamila, 133-134

Sherif, Tayeb, 123, 134, 221

Shuko, Dr, 188, 190, 192, 194, 205, 208

Siddiqui, Ayesha & Rashid Ahmed, 111

Siddiqui, Dr Ismet, 22

Siddiqui, Dr Kalim, 263

Siddiqui, Hamda, 22

Siddiqui, Mahmood ul Haq, 22

Siddiqui, Masood & Mona, 273, 310

Siddiqui, Saad, 132

Siddiqui, Safia, 122

Siddiqui, Saud, see Haq, Saud ul

Sinatra, Frank, 65

Sittai, Mr, 87-88

Solaija, Javariah, 310

Solaija, Naveed, 311

Solaija, Dr Tariq Jamal & Zareena, 105, 248, 276, 282, 310-311

Sooliman, Dr, 147

Spence, Mr, 113, 119

Stewart, Col. Bob, 146

Stride, David, 96

Subhani, Dr Zubeda, 83

Suleman, (Sulio), 159-160

Sultan Jahan Begum, 35-36

Surbland, Dr, 255

Swaleha Begum, 42-43

Tahseen, Robeena, 309, 313-315

Tajuddin, 83

Talha, 294

Tammanai, Mujeeb Ahmad, 17, 21

Tantan, Fatma & Sadetin, 304

Taylor, J.H., 12

Tekin, Gul, 296

Tekir, Perizad & Dr Sabri, 312

Teresa (friend), 69

Thanvi, Maulana Ihtishamul Haq, 51, 81

Thompson, Jean, 88

Tijani (teacher), 106

Tirmidhi, Dr Nasima, 36, 122

Tono (young Bosnian), 200-201

Ul-Haque, Ameen see Haq, Ameen ul

Ul-Haque, Idris, 134

Ul-Haque, Jasmeen, 312

Ul-Haque, (Mechthild) Peggy, 90, 93, 103, 115, 136

Ul-Haque, Salima, 136

Üstel, Dr Fatih, 315

Vasvija (Bosnian student), 219-220, 335

Velić, Imam Senad, 170-172, 184, 194-195

Versi, Ahmed, 290

Von Halem, 124

Wadi, Amma Ratna, 124, 133-134

Wayne, John, 74

Wolsley, Major, 146

Wright, Eddie, 153-154

Yilmaz, Dr Fevzi & Nadera, 294-295

Yusufzai, Dr Bakhter Amin, 247, 249, 257

Zabadne, Omar, 224

Zaidi, Feroz Hasan, 25, 42

Zaidi, Dr Manzoor, 75

Zaidi, Muzaffar & Nasreen, 103, 124

Zakaeva, Kheva, 265

Zarkan (teacher), 267-268

Zuka, Zulfika, 183

Zukić, Kemal, 218-219

Zulekha Bibi, 112